The War That Used Up Words

The War That Used Up Words

American Writers and the First World War

Hazel Hutchison

Yale

UNIVERSITY PRESS

New Haven & London

89061456

Published with assistance from the Mary Cady Tew Memorial Fund.

Yale University Press books may be purchased in quantity for educational, business,
or promotional use. For information, please e-mail sales.press@yale.edu (U.S. office)
or sales@yaleup.co.uk (U.K. office).

Set in Bulmer type by Westchester Book Group, Danbury, Connecticut.
Printed in the United States of America.

Library of Congress Cataloging-in-Publication Data

Hutchison, Hazel.
The war that used up words : American writers and the first world war / Hazel
Hutchison.
    pages cm
Includes bibliographical references and index.
ISBN 978-0-300-19502-6 (hardback)
1. American literature—20th century—History and criticism. 2. World War,
1914–1918—United States—Literature and the war. I. Title.
PS228.W37H88 2015
810.9'358—dc23

2014032474

A catalogue record for this book is available from the British Library.

This paper meets the requirements of ANSI/NISO Z39.48-1992 (Permanence of Paper).

10 9 8 7 6 5 4 3 2 1

In memory of my grandfather
William Craig Eadie
1892–1982
who served in the
Royal Army Medical Corps, 1914–1919

Contents

Acknowledgments

In 2001, as a raw, new teaching fellow at the University of Aberdeen, I was given the task of writing a lecture on First World War poetry for a course on writing and gender. I was already having an absurdly busy year, and I knew almost nothing about war poetry. I remember thinking that this could turn out to be a lot of work. How right I was. A dozen years on, however, I am very grateful to Jeannette King and Flora Alexander for conspiring to set me to work on this subject. Without the groundwork done for that lecture, and the discovery of poems by Mary Borden and Grace Fallow Norton, which instantly caught my imagination, this book would never have happened.

Since then, I have read and traveled widely, and have incurred many debts to individuals and institutions that have facilitated access to print and manuscript sources. I would like to thank: the Beinecke Library, Yale University; Boston Public Library; Cambridge University Library; the Carnegie Trust; the Center for Henry James Studies at Creighton University, especially Katie Sommer and Greg Zacharias; Churchill College Archives, University of Cambridge, especially Sophie Bridges; Jane Conway; Duff Hart-Davis; the Houghton Library, Harvard University, especially Susan Halpert; the Howard Gotleib Archival Research Center, Boston University; the James Graham Leyburn Library, Washington and Lee University, especially Vaughn Stanley; King's College Archives, University of Cambridge; the National Library of Scotland; the Special Collections Centre, University of Aberdeen; the United States National Archives and Records Administration; University of Chicago Archives. Ellen Weiss is due special thanks for her hospitality and generous sharing of unpublished family papers.

Many friends and contacts offered wisdom and encouragement, corrected stray facts, or pointed me in the direction of new material: Mairi Brunning, Pat Carter, Santanu Das, Alison Fell, Tamara Follini, Christine Hallett, Margaret Higonnet, Philip Horne, Tim Kendall, Tim Lustig,

Angela K. Smith, Mark Van Wienen, and Mark Whalan. Eric Brandt at Yale University Press offered excellent advice. Christine Hallett, David Hutchison, Jeannette King, and Mhairi Pooler all read sections of the manuscript and gave very useful feedback. I am grateful to all.

Finally, and most importantly, thanks to my family—David, Carrie, Jamie, and Fraser—who kept their patience with this project, even when I occasionally lost mine.

Certain passages of this book are also published elsewhere, though in very different form, and appear here by permission. Such passages can be found in: "The Art of Living Inward: Henry James on Rupert Brooke," *Henry James Review* 29, no. 2 (2008): 132–43; "A Period in Limbo: Placing People and Punctuation in E. E. Cummings' *The Enormous Room,*" in *War and Displacement,* edited by Sandra Barkhof and Angela K. Smith (London: Routledge, 2014), 134–48; "The Theatre of Pain: Observing Mary Borden in *The Forbidden Zone,*" in *First World War Nursing: New Perspectives,* edited by Alison Fell and Christine Hallett (London: Routledge, 2013), 139–55.

The poems and photograph of Grace Fallow Norton appear by permission of Ellen Weiss. Correspondence between Grace Fallow Norton and Ferris Greenslet at Houghton Mifflin appears by permission of the Houghton Library. The photograph of Henry James appears by permission of Smith College Archives. Quotations from the poems of Mary Borden appear by permission of Patrick Aylmer.

brutal and yet compelling. It is stripped of all natural solace, and yet remains strangely beautiful. It is crowded with marching armies and roaring machines, and yet is lonely and silent. This is a world in which speech is redundant, and yet the writer bears witness to it in words. Borden's language operates through paradox and contrast: the animal is juxtaposed with the human, the organic with the mechanical, the monstrous with the gorgeous. These conflicting elements, however, should come as no surprise. From its opening weeks, the First World War was a war of contradictions. Fought in defense of idealism and civilization, it quickly became the most incoherent and inhumane war in history. Supposedly about freedom, it was sustained by mass conscription and the suppression of free speech. These incompatibilities surface in the literature of the war, which is in itself something of a contradiction—the superb made out of the monstrous. There are also deep inconsistencies in our consumption of such texts. Generations of readers have approached the literature of the First World War through a series of illogicalities. We assert the futility of mass violence, but we sense that we are touching something profoundly human when we read about it. We refute militarism, but we privilege the combatant's point of view. We hanker after immediacy and authenticity in accounts of the war, but we gravitate toward texts composed with hindsight, free from the ideological confusion and personal indecision of wartime. We insist on the centrality of the war as a defining historical event, but we dismiss those texts which engage too closely with politics as propaganda. We validate artistry, style, and a dispassionate command of form, but we want to be told the truth. Its seems that writing, or even reading, about the First World War is (pardon the expression) something of a minefield.

This book is about a group of American authors who observed the war in Europe between 1914 and 1918, and who wrote about what they saw. American writing from the First World War is not read as often as that from Britain or the other nations involved in the conflict, perhaps because it defies many established cultural preferences and misconceptions about war literature. The most significant texts are by those who did not fight, who openly voiced their political agendas across a range of positions, who believed in the power and the right of literature to sway public perspectives, but who also felt that observing was not enough of a response to the demands of war: one should also act. American cultural memory of the war tends to be focused through the work of "lost generation" writers such as Hemingway, Faulkner, and Fitzgerald, who actually had minimal exposure to frontline activities—Hemingway was an ambulance driver for only three weeks, while Faulkner and Fitzgerald never even got to Europe—and who did not write about it until the mid-1920s. Alternatively, readers often embrace the work of writers such as T. S. Eliot, H.D., or Ezra Pound, who were personally remote from the war, though alert to its effects, and who wrote about it obliquely. These writers are credited with inventing many of the literary techniques and stating the emotional positions which would come to be seen as central to the aesthetic agendas of twentieth-century writing. Cultural observers usually agree that the First World War was a catalyst for dramatic changes in the theory and practice of literature, painting, dance, music, and architecture. But if this is the case, then the mid-1920s seems somewhat late to be looking for the origins of traits which emerged so distinctly from the conflict: detachment, disillusionment, disparate perspectives, montage, irony, the renegotiation of gender, the disruption of time, the inadequacy of language. As this book argues, the really creative moment, the ignition spark of innovation, happened *during* the war through the work of writers such as Mary Borden and Henry James, Edith Wharton, Ellen La Motte, Grace Fallow Norton, E. E. Cummings, and John Dos Passos. America's neutral status in the early stages of the war allowed its authors and journalists an experimental and polemical freedom that was not available to British writers, whose publishing activities were curtailed by censorship from August 1914. It also quickened their sense of the war as a cultural rather than a sociopolitical event. American observer-participants of the war, unlike those of warring nations, could be intimately involved in its progress and yet remain detached from many of its urgencies. As this book shows, these wartime writers made many of the stylistic choices and innovations for which others would later be celebrated. However, those early texts which were produced in the context of political uncertainty and a climate of propaganda and censorship can be ideologically demanding for present-day readers, and often pose uncomfortable questions about the relationship between literature and politics. They do not, therefore, always sit easily within "modernist" agendas, which tend to value formal and stylistic concerns over issues of history and politics.

Modernism, like many other cultural labels, turns out to be somewhat evasive when put under any kind of scrutiny. As a marker for a particular movement in literature between 1910 and 1930, concerned with self-expression, form, fragmentation, and with the self-consciously new, it was not in common usage until the 1960s, when it was, ironically, projected onto what was by then already old.[2] In disciplines such as architecture or music, the term covers different characteristics including functionality or atonality; in some, such as anthropology, it is more often connected to period than to style or an existential perspective. Wherever it appears, it is difficult to gloss. As Susan Stanford Friedman notes, any cultural movement that finds its mainspring of identity in a rebellion against the past is always going to struggle to define itself independently of that past: "Modernity's grand narratives institute their own radical dismantling. The lifeblood of modernity's chaos is its order. The impulse to order is the product of chaos. Modernism requires tradition to 'make it new.' Tradition comes into being only as it is rebelled against."[3] However, even this critical passage harks back to an earlier expressive tradition. With its aphoristic syntax and its paradoxical reasoning, it sounds almost like something Oscar Wilde might have written in the 1890s—which is not inappropriate. For all its self-vaunted newness, there are many, many elements in "modernist" literature that have their roots firmly in the aestheticism of the late Victorian period, and in the burgeoning fascination of writers, thinkers, and scientists of that era with questions of subjectivity, perspective, artistic value, and the unreliability of language. Human events never take place in a vacuum. So, while the First World War can certainly be seen as some sort of cultural watershed, the attitudes and techniques that are often ascribed to it do not appear without context or precedent. For now, suffice to say that modernism is a deeply problematic term, and one that is increasingly unhelpful as a means of identifying or evaluating certain literary traits, or of understanding history. While many concepts and devices which have been grouped under that heading are discussed at length in this book, the term itself is used sparingly and usually appears in quotation marks.

So, whether writing, reading, or analyzing, it seems that one cannot approach the literature of the First World War except through a forest of contradictions. This book also will, no doubt, contain some of these contradictions. Nevertheless, the contradictions built into the process of writing about war are worth thinking about because they raise questions that lie at the heart of all literature. How can words summon up that which is long absent? How does one create out of loss—and why? How should one read the lives of the past, real or imagined? These questions are especially hard to ignore in the context of war writing, because however highly one values aesthetic experience or self-expression, the story of how individual lives and social groups are torn apart by violence, and of how humanity persists even in such extremes, demands our attention. In the same way that war strips humanity down to its basic constituents, war writing calls the reader's attention to the fundamental function of literature, which is to tell us something we need to know. How we read the texts of war will define the ways in which we read all other texts. The writers who are the focus of this book and their works, therefore, are not just interesting as some sort of missing link in the development of literary taste and style—though that is certainly a part of it. They are important because they narrate a powerful human story, and because they continue to insist that the writer can do so much more than simply stand back and watch.

In April 1917, America readied itself for war. For two and a half years, the nation had warily observed the conflict that was engulfing Europe and the Middle East, apparently determined to remain detached. President Woodrow Wilson declared that America should offer the example of peace. There was such a thing, he said, as being "too proud to fight."[4] There were also compelling reasons, political and economic, for keeping on good terms with all the warring nations, and avoiding the upheaval and expense of intervention. Right up until the early weeks of 1917, Wilson had hoped that his administration might broker a negotiated end to the bloodshed.

War did not come naturally to this thoughtful and idealistic man; he believed passionately in international arbitration. Yet America's neutral
stance was dramatically abandoned on 2 April when Wilson addressed a
joint session of Congress to call for a declaration of war against Germany.
"It is a fearful thing," he told a hushed chamber, "to lead this great peaceful people into war, into the most terrible and disastrous of all wars, civilization itself seeming to be in the balance." U-boat harassment of Atlantic
shipping, and an incipient threat to America's own borders in the shape of
German efforts to forge an alliance with Mexico, had driven Wilson to the
conclusion that he had no other option. He wrapped political inevitability
in the language of moral crusade: "The day has come when America is
privileged to spend her blood and her might for the principles that gave
her birth and happiness and the peace which she has treasured. God helping her, she can do no other."[5]

Ostensibly, Wilson spoke for America, a nation united in support of
justice and democracy. In reality, he spoke to a deeply divided society—
and he knew it. In the days following his speech, the Senate and the House
of Representatives overwhelmingly backed military action, leading to a
formal declaration of war on 6 April. Yet public opinion was starkly polarized, ranging from the pacifism of left-wing labor movements, such as the
International Workers of the World (IWW), to powerful manufacturing
and financial interests, who saw in the war an opportunity to assert the
dominance of the American economy. Sympathy for the plight of occupied Belgium was high in some quarters, especially among the East Coast
middle classes. Many college-educated Americans with cultural affinities
and family ties with Britain, France, or Italy campaigned long and hard
for financial and military aid for the Allies. Some had already volunteered
for military service with British, French, or Canadian forces, or for humanitarian roles with varsity-sponsored ambulance units or as nursing staff.
In 1914, however, 9 million American citizens considered German their
first language, and a further 15 million were of German descent.[6] With a
national population approaching 100 million, these numbers meant that
nearly one in four American residents saw themselves, to a greater or lesser
degree, as German. Some of them, perhaps, noticed the irony that seemed

to escape Wilson's audience in Washington, that the climax of his speech borrowed its authority from the words of the great Protestant Reformer Martin Luther in 1521, "Here I stand. I can do no other"—words originally spoken by a German in Germany.[7] Many German-Americans, like their Irish and eastern-European neighbors, had very different ideas from Wilson about where the moral high ground lay. Thousands of them, perhaps as many as half a million, crossed the Atlantic in the early stages of the war to serve with the Central Powers: Germany, Austria-Hungary, the Ottoman Empire, and Bulgaria. America's massive influx of immigrant labor since the 1870s may have been a key factor in the astonishing industrial and economic growth the nation had witnessed in recent decades. But this same diversity also made the political consent required for war difficult to manufacture.

So, for many months before America officially entered the First World War in April 1917, it had been engaged in a war of words. It was not just political parties or ethnic groups who took sides in this tussle. The nation's neutrality had been a key topic of debate in the press and among the academic and literary classes since the war began in August 1914. On the one hand, respected cultural figures such as the educationalist John Dewey and the journalist Walter Lippman writing in the pages of the *New Republic* magazine laid out their Progressive hopes that the war would create an opportunity to reshape not just American society, but the whole world, for the better. Like many others, they believed the war would sweep away old political structures and hierarchies, clearing the way for "the prospect of a world organisation and the beginnings of a public control which crosses national boundaries and interests," as Dewey expressed it.[8] On the other hand, writers such as H. L. Mencken (another American with a German surname) and the cultural critic Randolph Bourne voiced dismay at the apparent appetite for violence among so many of America's intellectuals. In the radical magazine the *Seven Arts* in June 1917, Bourne expressed outrage that "college professors, publicists, new-republicans, practitioners of literature" should play such an active role in justifying military intervention: "A war made deliberately by the intellectuals! . . . An intellectual class, gently guiding a nation through sheer force of ideas into what other nations entered only through predatory craft or popular hysteria or militarist madness!" Others, he wrote, would find it hard "to understand this willingness of the American intellect to open the sluices and flood us with the sewage of the war spirit."[9]

Bourne's inclusion of "practitioners of literature" in his list of warmongers was not just for rhetorical effect. Fiction, poetry, and song, along with film and the visual arts, played prominent roles on both sides of the cultural debate about the war. From pacifist lyrics, such as those of Alfred Bryan and Al Piantadosi's popular song "I Didn't Raise My Boy to Be a Soldier," which sold 650,000 copies in 1915, to Alan Seeger's wistful anticipation of his own death at the front in his poem "Rendezvous," and Grace Fallow Norton's powerful evocations of mobilization in rural France, verse was one of the key vehicles of emotional and ideological response to the war. Ninety anthologies of war poetry were published in America between 1914 and 1919, many sold in aid of war-related charities.[10] Newspapers also carried poems engaging with the war, from the pro-interventionist *Boston Globe* to the skeptical *New York Call,* as did mainstream periodicals such as the *Atlantic Monthly,* the *Ladies' Home Journal,* and the more radical, small-circulation magazines such as the *Seven Arts* or the *Masses.* In a climate of political uncertainty, poetry had many virtues, not least that it was quick to write, cheap to publish, and attracted less stringent censure than other genres. As Mark Van Wienen observes in his work on American popular poetry of the war, many magazines and newspapers continued to publish a mix of "patriotic" verse with poems calling for peace or questioning government policy, even after April 1917. Such poetry was often presented in the formally conventional style of "genteel" verse, which many critics now perceive as unrepresentative and remote from the urgent, modern energies of the second decade of the twentieth century. Yet, it remained a powerful vehicle for partisan debate and political dissent in an increasingly restrictive publishing environment.

Writers of fiction and prose also found that the conflict in Europe threatened to engulf their personal and imaginative lives. Over the four years of the war, books by writers as diverse as Owen Wister, Sherwood

Anderson, Sinclair Lewis, and Dorothy Canfield were full of the themes of war: adventure and heroism in France; social unrest and the fear of German spies at home; the thrill of romance in a time of death.[11] There were more politically inflammatory works too, such as *The Conquest of America* (1916), by Cleveland Langston Moffett, who wove real-life diplomatic figures, including Wilson and his cabinet, into a grisly and alarmist counterfactual account of an invasion of the eastern seaboard. The plot was designed to demonstrate the need for military preparedness and to celebrate America's technological ingenuity. One military encounter leads to 113,000 German soldiers being trapped in ditches, doused in American petroleum, and burned to a crisp on the outskirts of Baltimore; the final decisive battle, fought at sea, is won after Thomas Edison invents a mechanism for an airborne guided missile.[12] At the other end of the literary spectrum, James—the ageing, exiled novelist, who usually remained aloof from political debate—wrote a series of reflective yet passionate essays on the conflict, the echoing guns of which he could hear at his home across the English Channel in Rye. James visited wounded soldiers and became a fund-raiser for the American Volunteer Motor-Ambulance Corps in France—the same corps in which many young intellectuals and artists including Cummings and Dos Passos would enroll later in the war. In the end, James was so frustrated by Wilson's reluctance to join the war that in 1915 he renounced his American citizenship and became a British subject.

For American writers who chose life in France the war was more than an abstract principle: it was a daily reality, and a number threw themselves into war-related activities. Wharton, now permanently settled in Paris, used her diplomatic and society connections to arrange visits to the front, which she wrote up for an American public eager for firsthand information from the battle scene and for pitiful accounts (some genuine, some less so) of suffering by Belgian refugees. She also persuaded her distinguished set of literary and artistic contacts to contribute to *The Book of the Homeless* (1916), a luxury-edition volume of poems, pictures, and fragments of writing and music on the theme of the war, sold in aid of her own refugee charity. Borden, the beautiful and sophisticated Chicago heiress and romantic novelist, left her home in London's Mayfair to run her field hospital, an experience which would prompt her haunting book *The Forbidden Zone* (1929). In 1916, Gertrude Stein, whose home was the hub of American intellectual life in Paris, bought a Ford automobile so that she could deliver medical supplies to hospitals; later she would take a number of American "doughboys" under her wing. Staying in France somehow made Stein feel more, rather than less, American. She would write afterward that "the war was so much better than just going to America. Here you were with America in a kind of way that if you only went to America you could not possibly be."[13] Meanwhile, Stein's friend the drama critic Mildred Aldrich shot from obscurity to fame with *A Hilltop on the Marne* (1915). In this memoir, narrated as a series of letters, Aldrich and her aged French housekeeper live at the front during the First Battle of the Marne in 1914, overlooking the war zone from a rented farmhouse, charting the impact of the conflict on the lives of those around them. One day, Aldrich encounters a troop of German cavalry in the lane outside her house. A few days later, the British arrive, and her home with its panoramic view of operations is briefly transformed into a military command center. Another friend of Stein's, the nurse Ellen La Motte, offered the reading public less palatable impressions of the war. La Motte's book, *The Backwash of War* (1916), an eyewitness account of several months spent working in Mary Borden's hospital, offered few political opinions, but unflinchingly presented the traumatic human cost of the conflict in all its pathetic absurdity: dehumanizing injuries, military complacency, gangrene, and shell shock. The book was later withdrawn by its publisher under government pressure. "Truth, it appears, has no place in war," La Motte remarked grimly.[14]

The U.S. government's determination to control cultural production was a strong indicator of the power of literature to influence public opinion in time of war—or it indicated, at least, the government's fear of that power. Just a week after declaring war on Germany, Wilson established the Committee on Public Information, a formidable operation costing 5 million dollars, which at its height employed 150,000 workers, to market what its flamboyant front man George Creel called "the American

idea," an image of national identity that equated patriotic loyalty with support for the government's military objectives.[15] Promoting this image was
not just a matter of massaging the facts in newspaper reports, or even of
suppressing material which, like La Motte's *Backwash,* was "damaging to
the morale."[16] The CPI also generated artistic and journalistic content,
making innovative use of the new media of cinema and radio. It sponsored
art exhibitions, such as the nationwide tour of Louis Raemaeker's vividly
anti-German war cartoons in 1917 to venues including the Art Institute of
Chicago, the Corcoran Gallery in Washington, DC, and the Cleveland
Museum of Art. It liaised with Hollywood about the production of films
with anti-German plotlines. It organized the distribution of war posters
and xenophobic pamphlets. It crammed donated newspaper advertising
space with calls for the public to preserve food supplies and to buy Liberty Bonds to help fund the Allied war effort.[17] A group of 328 writers and
artists, including Vachel Lindsey, Amy Lowell, Edgar Lee Masters, and
Hamlin Garland, formed a syndicate known as the Vigilantes, pledging to
support the work of the CPI by producing patriotic work to order during
the course of the war. As Harold Lasswell would point out in his 1927
study of First World War propaganda, age-old methods of whipping up
tribal feeling may have been replaced in this war by more subtle and apparently more civilized means. But the objective of awakening a deep and
irrational hatred and fear of the enemy remained as primitive as ever: "In
the Great Society it is no longer possible to fuse the waywardness of individuals in the furnace of the war dance. . . . Talk must take the place of
drill; print must supplant the dance. War dance lives in literature and at
the fringes of the modern earth; war propaganda breathes and fumes
in the capitals and provinces of the world."[18]

The "furnace of the war dance" would reshape America. The First
World War brought profound and far-reaching change to its military and
political machinery and to its social and economic structures. In June
1916, the American army numbered 107,642 men, ranked seventeenth in
the world, with a Marine Corps of 15,500 men and a National Guard of
132,000.[19] The United States considered itself a peaceful nation with little
need for a large standing army. However, by the time of the Armistice in

November 1918, 24 million Americans had registered for the draft, 4 million were in uniform, and over 2 million had traveled to France, including two hundred thousand African-Americans and thirty thousand women. Around 1.4 million of these saw action at the front. Of these, 205,000 returned home maimed or wounded, 50,280 were killed in battle, and a further 27,618 died in the accidents, suicides, and epidemics that the war brought in its wake.[20] Thousands also died of Spanish flu in army camps and troopships without ever reaching France.

This swift and widespread mobilization of the general public was matched by an expansion of government bureaucracy into new areas of private and corporate life. The massive hike in the federal budget from $0.75 billion in 1916 to $19 billion in 1919 was not just the result of soaring military expenses, but also of new war-related government agencies, such as the U.S. Food Administration, which promoted food conservation, and the Bureau of Investigation, which carried out surveillance of foreign nationals and disruptive labor agitators whose activities threatened (or were alleged to threaten) the supply of food and weapons.[21] However, the biggest social change brought by the war was the acceleration of industrial growth. The gross national product, which had hovered around $36 billion between 1910 and 1914, shot up year after year to $91 billion by 1920. And it was not just the amount of manufacturing that was changing; it was also the style. Although time and motion studies such as Frederick Winslow Taylor's *Principles of Scientific Management* (1911) had already embedded the idea of assembly-line production in certain areas of industry, including Henry Ford's automobile empire, the war would make such methods increasingly widespread as the practices of the battlefield and the factory overlapped.[22] Small repetitive tasks assigned to each worker, carried out with discipline toward a greater collaborative end: these were the signs of the militarization of civilian life, which Wilson and many others like him had feared. On the eve of his historic speech on 2 April, he had told his friend Frank Irving Cobb, editor of the *New York World:* "Once lead this people into war, and they'll forget there ever was such a thing as tolerance. To fight you must be brutal and ruthless, and the spirit of ruthless brutality will enter into the very fiber of our national life, infecting Congress, the courts, the policeman on the beat, the man in the street."[23]

The changes which war brought to American national life were pervasive and enduring. The wave of Progressive optimism with which the war began quickly gave way to despair as the reality of the conflict and the frustration of its aftermath took hold. The war shifted the balance of power from state to federal government, and swept away a set of social conventions that had lingered on since the end of the previous century. It altered attitudes to immigrants, to women, and to race relations—not always for the better. It inflated wages and prices, and curtailed civil freedoms. For those who served in the forces or aid agencies, it provided a defining personal experience, physically and emotionally devastating for some but empowering for others—especially those who might never otherwise have left their hometowns, including many African-Americans and low-paid white workers. It also brought long-term hardship to the hundreds of thousands of soldiers who came home to find that their jobs were gone and the government had nothing to give them.

Perhaps most importantly, by the end of the war, Americans *felt* differently about themselves and others. With Europe exhausted emotionally and financially, America was suddenly the world's strongest economy and main creditor, but the changes were about more than money. Wilson's stated purpose of going to war to make the world "safe for democracy" had also given the nation a new sense of itself as a diplomatic player, a powerful arbitrating presence on the international stage, a role that it would relish and expand in decades to come.[24] The CPI's marketing of "the American idea" had imposed a new model of national identity on the many racial and ethnic groups within the country. Increasingly, the establishment called for Theodore Roosevelt's ideal of "100 percent Americanism"—total assimilation in the melting pot society. "We insist upon one flag, one language, one undivided loyalty to this nation and to the ideals of this nation. . . . We accept no substitute for Americanism. We insist that all our people must be Americans and only Americans," he wrote in 1918.[25] But this rhetoric simply masked a deep cultural confusion about the ethnic, social, and sexual changes which the war had fueled. It is no coincidence that the titles of several studies of the impact of the war characterize this historical moment as a loss of innocence.[26] After 1918, this was a nation less willing to identify with the virginal "Christy Girls" and hopeful young men of wartime recruiting posters, and more likely to be drawn to the overtly sexualized glamor of Hollywood, the New York flapper girls of F. Scott Fitzgerald's jazz world, or the rugged, cynical, outdoor masculinity of Ernest Hemingway's novels. Historians of the period argue about whether these changes signaled a sudden rupture with the past or were simply an acceleration and intensification of social trends that had been operating long before the war began. But these same historians do not dispute that the First World War left the nation transformed— although hardly in the shiny, positive ways that the Progressive intellectuals had envisioned in the spring of 1917. By the end of the war, America was a modern, urban, materialistic society and a powerful player on the international stage, but its social divisions were deeper than ever. It was not long before many were looking back to the prewar years with nostalgia as a golden era of American life.

And yet, despite the intensity of the changes it brought, the First World War rarely figures in contemporary American culture. Unlike the Civil War (still within living memory in 1914), or the other major conflicts of the twentieth century, including the Second World War and the Vietnam War, America's role in the 1917–18 conflict occupies a rather obscure corner of the collective memory. Even though there have been a number of fine historical studies of the subject, it has never quite captured the public imagination. We rarely encounter the American experience of the First World War in fiction or film. Many Americans don't know what happened, or why, and are not especially interested to find out. "Well, you know, it wasn't really *our* war," an American friend said when I told him I was writing this book. To an extent this is true. Compared to the casualties of the European nations, America's losses were minor. Britain lost nine hundred thousand troops, France lost 1.3 million, Germany 1.6 million and Russia 1.7 million. In the face of such numbers, words do not express much. Nor was the emotional investment of most American citizens as extensive as the government liked to believe. Although the CPI and the they have deteriorated like motor car tires; . . . and we are now confronted with a depreciation of all our terms, or, otherwise speaking, with a loss of expression through increase of limpness, that may well make us wonder what ghosts will be left to walk."[29] Hemingway's novel about a young volunteer ambulance driver in northern Italy in 1918 is still the best-known American book about the First World War. Its sharp, metallic style and forthright exploration of violence, sexuality, and disillusionment in the war zone made Hemingway a celebrity, and his novel a classic—although it has to be said that not everyone these days appreciates his handling of politics and personal relationships. Michael Reynolds, Hemingway's biographer, suggests that James's words were originally intended as an epigraph to the novel. If this is the case, they would have suited very well. Reflecting on his experiences, Hemingway's hero Frederic Henry muses on the pointlessness of trying to speak about the war in the terms handed down by previous generations: "I was always embarrassed by the words sacred, glorious, and sacrifice and the expression in vain. . . . There were many words that you could not stand to hear and finally only the names of places had dignity. Certain numbers were the same way and certain dates and these with the names of the places were all that you could say and have them mean anything. Abstract words such as glory, honor, courage, or hallow were obscene beside the concrete names of villages, the numbers of roads, the names of rivers, the numbers of regiments and the dates."[30] Hemingway was not always very enthusiastic, or even very polite, about James and his novels. Indeed, the stylistic and tonal differences between the two appear at first glance to demonstrate the changes that the First World War brought to literary culture: on the one hand, James, elegant, interiorized, digressive, wordy; on the other, Hemingway, bitter, terse, particular, raw. This new cynical voice is often understood as a rupture with the values of the past caused by the conflict of 1914–1918, as the rebellion of the impatient, war-weary young against the banal idealism of their elders. So, it is something of a surprise to find Hemingway looking back to James in 1915 for an articulation of the ways in which the war devalued language and determined the need for new ways of thinking and writing about reality. It is impossible to know if Hemingway came across James's newspaper interview casually in the late 1920s, while he was writing the book, or if he read the article in 1915 and through it was inspired to sign up as an ambulance driver as soon as he was old enough.[31] Either way, it is curious to see the ways in which James's words haunt Hemingway's novel like the ghosts of language which the passage calls up.

Hemingway, of course, could write about the war with the benefit of hindsight. His novel is an answer to James's question about what it will be possible to say when the tide of war recedes—but it is not the only one. Most of the major writers of the 1920s and 1930s on both sides of the Atlantic—and many, many more forgotten ones—found something to say about the conflict. Those who had observed it recorded it in a remarkable range of genres: poetry, fiction, memoirs, biographies, histories, letters, spy-thrillers, romantic potboilers, hair-raising tales of battle and survival. Not all of these were as bold or as brutal as *A Farewell to Arms*. Others—such as Robert Graves's *Goodbye to All That* (1929) and Erich Maria Remarque's *All Quiet on the Western Front* (1929)—were more so. The language and the imagery of the war, the pity and futility, the absurdity, the physicality, the incompetence, and mechanized destruction, found their way into the imaginative fabric of the modernist era, and thence into patterns of culture and consciousness that have shaped our own. In 1967, Stanley Cooperman could write: "In a very real sense we are all creatures of World War I, both in aesthetic and political terms. The great authoritarian movements of our century; the experiments in art and literature against all forms of rhetoric; the triumph of technological civilization—these things were then new, and they were the raw material for art."[32] It could be argued that this holds as good today is it did a half-century past—though other ways of locating significance in the literature of the First World War have surfaced in the decades since Cooperman was writing. The question of how closely we can really identify with works written about events a hundred years ago will, naturally, come up in later chapters. For now, suffice to say that the war and the texts which emerged from it are often seen to have a seminal place in the cultural consciousness of the Western world.

This book is about how the war first imprinted itself onto the patterns of American writing. It has become a commonplace to assert that the

innovative forms and devices of postwar writing evolved in response to
the despair and disillusionment engendered by the war. However, as Vincent Sherry notes, such statements are often little more than "a sort of ritual invocation," and it can be hard to find any detailed inquiry or "rational
elaboration" about the channels through which these unfamiliar patterns
of thought and language were embedded so enduringly into literary culture.[33] One of the reasons for this paucity, especially in an American context, is that very few people start looking early enough. Sherry's own work
focuses on the emergence of these traits in the work of T. S. Eliot, Virginia
Woolf, and Ezra Pound in the 1920s. However, these writers had no direct
experience of the war, and could only absorb its most vivid themes and
motifs through the words and pictures of others. For example, Eliot's letters suggest that his "rats' alley / Where the dead men lost their bones," in
The Waste Land (1922), originated in the horror and fascination he felt
at his brother-in-law Maurice Haigh-Wood's descriptions of life at the
front.[34] Meanwhile, *A Farewell to Arms,* hailed as so unconventional—
which it certainly was in terms of tone and moral daring—also repeated
and mimicked forms of war writing which had become almost hackneyed
by the late 1920s, especially eyewitness memoirs by ambulance drivers
and nurses which had emerged in the hundreds during and after the
war. So, yes, the images and vocabulary of the war were in the air in the
years after the war, but they had not simply drifted across the cultural
landscape—like a poison gas, perhaps—without means of transmission.
Hemingway, clearly, was shrewd enough to look back to Henry James in
1915 in search of a point at which something new in literature was born out
of the hurt of war; but few critics have done likewise.

   If we are to take seriously the idea that literature, and ways of reading that literature, are shaped by real, historical events, such as those of
the First World War, then it seems important to locate key moments and
writers in that sequence. As Paul Fussell reminds us, the literary scene in
English of 1914 is almost impossible for present-day readers to imagine:
"There was no *Waste Land.* . . . There was no *Ulysses,* no *Mauberley,* no
Cantos, no Kafka, no Proust, no Waugh, no Auden, no Huxley, no Cummings, no *Women in Love* or *Lady Chatterley's Lover.*" One read the great

Edwardian novelists, such as Hardy, Kipling, and Conrad, and "fre-quented worlds of traditional moral action delineated in traditional moral language."[35] In writing this book, one of my aims has been to look far enough back into that prewar literary world to rediscover the shock and the thrill of watching it transform into something much more like that of our own time. It is easy to forget how quickly this happened: there are only a few months between the death of Henry James in the spring of 1916 and the publication of La Motte's *The Backwash of War* in the fall. Con-ceptually, it seems much longer. Nevertheless, this transition was not clear-cut, and there are many lines of continuity that run through the nar-rative of change. James, for example, was profoundly aware that the liter-ary world would be irrevocably altered by the war, and was open to the possibility of new ideas and techniques emerging from it. Stein was radi-cal and inventive before the war; Wharton maintained her measured prose after it. Nevertheless, this book aims to map that shift of balance from the old to the new, as it was experienced and expressed by American writers close to the war in Europe in the years 1914 to 1918. It goes in search of early glimpses of disillusionment, irony, and fragmentation, so enthusias-tically taken up by later writers as valid responses to the war, but it also seeks to understand the sense of social and political responsibility that led many writers to use their work or their reputations for purposes that seem with hindsight to be beyond the remit of the artist, or to hark back to Victo-rian standards of public duty. It explores how the work of these writers was received in the volatile publishing context of the war, and it asks, not only what literature gained by this sudden shift of priorities, but also what it lost.

There could have been, no doubt, other ways of approaching these issues; there is certainly no shortage of material to work through. When I began to take a serious interest in American writing of the First World War, over a decade ago, I was continually assured by more experienced researchers (and by one much-decorated novelist) that there wasn't any. How wrong they were. In the end, the difficulty was not finding enough texts worth reading, but finding sensible ways to focus attention on a small enough group of writers and texts to give any sense of depth and progres-sion.[36] As I read, however, the group of writers at the heart of this study emerged distinctly from their surroundings, for reasons which appeared at first unsettling and have over time become positively disruptive. The most surprising thing about this group was that it did not contain any frontline combatants. "First World War literature" was for so long equated with the output of the soldier-poets from the trenches of the Western Front, that any other definition of the genre seemed almost disrespectful. Over recent decades, however, other perspectives on the writing of the war have evolved; approaches concerned with gender, class, and race; with the impact of the war on women, civilians, and colonized nations; with the role in the war of noncombatants, especially medical personnel; and with the home-front literature of the war, written as popular entertainment or powerful political comment. As I discuss below, many of these studies have offered illuminating glimpses of how the war reached far beyond the theaters of combat to affect the lives of millions. In so doing they also opened up the category of war literature to bewilderingly wide criteria. Nevertheless, the soldier's account is often perceived to have an authenticity, and often a deep note of pity, that other viewpoints cannot match. American soldiers who saw action on the Western Front wrote some powerful, brilliant books about the war: Thomas Boyd's *Through the Wheat* (1923), John W. Thomason's *Fix Bayonets* (1925), and William March's *Company K* (1933)—to name but a few. Nevertheless, the dates of these novels tell their own story. America was not prepared for war when it entered the conflict on the Allied side in April 1917, and it was not until May 1918 that the American Expeditionary Force was playing an effective role at the front. By early November, the war was over. During that time, American troops were involved in key engagements and took heavy losses along the front line. Those close enough to the action to be gathering powerful impressions had little time for writing until after the war. Even if they had had the chance to write up their experiences, they would not have been allowed to use them; between January and October of 1918, U.S. military personnel were legally forbidden from publishing any kind of literary or journalistic output, and the content of wartime publications was heavily censored. In the postwar reactions of relief and distaste, these same writers also had difficulties finding publishers until the mid-

1920s. For a project concerned with the intersection of experience and language in the earliest phases of American writing about the war, it became apparent early on that the soldier's perspective would be of only limited help.

There were, however, many Americans who watched and participated in the war without rifle and pack between 1914 and 1918, and who did not wait until it was over to speak out. They worked through a complex range of responses in that period, from euphoria to abject desolation, and their stories of how optimism gave way to disgust and resignation, but also to a newfound respect for individual points of view, can be seen to encapsulate the story of the war itself. While a large number of writers and publishers appear in the chapters that follow, the central focus of this book is on seven selected authors who saw the war in Europe at close quarters, and on the texts which they wrote, or had at least partly drafted, before the Armistice in November 1918. These writers were all self-conscious literary artists, who had published in other arenas before observing the war, and who responded to it by going in search of new forms of expression and new expressions of form, in which to catch the vividness of their experience. These experiences *were* vivid. As I am interested in finding out how literature and history speak to each other, I have concentrated on writers who were much more than observers. All seven felt that words were not enough for this war, and that artistic response had to be matched by action, though that action took many different forms: James, the fund-raiser and hospital visitor; Wharton, the aid-relief worker; Norton, the tentative political activist; Borden and La Motte, the nurses; Cummings, the reluctant volunteer and political prisoner; and Dos Passos, the ambulance driver and then enlisted soldier. This grouping may seem strange. I hope so—because it cuts across a number of the familiar categories and binary opposites within which writing of the war is more usually understood: modernist, conservative, pacifist, interventionist, male, female, young, old, canonical, obscure. However, I also hope that as the book unfolds, this selection will come to make sense. These writers overlapped and intersected in curiously entangled ways; several of them knew each other and worked together or shared publishers. The most

unlikely pairings also found common ground both politically and artisti-
cally, suggesting that these familiar critical categories have not proved
adequate for defining the American writing of the war—which may be one
of the reasons why it is so often marginalized. If there is a single unifying
characteristic linking these seven writers, it is that all of them developed
a view of the artist in wartime as one who should not only observe, but as
one who can, perhaps even should, intervene in events, in ways that many
other contemporary writers, including the conscientious objectors of the
Bloomsbury set in London, staunchly refused to do. Postwar aesthetic
ideals, often defined by those writers who did not participate in the conflict, tended to valorize nonparticipation (in many different forms) as artistic integrity. Thus, the intensely personal and autobiographical nature
of many of the American texts generated by the war is, I suspect, one of
the reasons why these works have drawn comparatively little critical attention throughout a century which has often derided life-writing as mere
journalism.

American writing from the First World War has not, however, gone entirely under the radar—although certain writers, such as Grace Fallow
Norton, have come close. Just at the point that the public seemed to be
ready to read about the war again in the late 1920s, the Wall Street Crash
and the Great Depression which followed focused American attention on
struggles closer to home. As canons of twentieth-century writing began to
form in the midcentury, American war writing was increasingly sidelined.
Authors such as Thomason or Boyd, for whom the war was a central
theme, found themselves excluded from critical debates which focused
largely on questions of form and style. A number of writers with a stake in
the war, including Willa Cather, Archibald MacLeish, F. Scott Fitzgerald,
and William Faulkner, were admired primarily for their engagement with
other subjects closer to home. Certain texts from the First World War, especially those by Hemingway, Cummings, and Dos Passos, were acknowledged as important within the oeuvres of single writers, but often more as
formative experiences on the route to something more accomplished.
Comparative approaches to the work of two or more writers, or consider-

ations of American First World War writing as a distinctive body of literature have been extremely rare, although Patrick Quinn's *The Conning of
America: The Great War and Popular American Literature* (2001) and
Keith Gandal's *The Pen and the Gun* (2010) have both demonstrated in
recent years how fertile this field can be. For many decades, British and
Commonwealth critics and editors were more interested in their own rich
legacy of war writing, viewing American perspectives on the war (if at all)
through the eyes of the "London modernists," such as Eliot, Pound, or
H.D.[37] Ironically, perhaps, the book that still remains the most influential
critical study on either side of the Atlantic about the literature of the war
was written by the American scholar Paul Fussell. *The Great War and
Modern Memory* (1975) reread the war as a cultural and intellectual event,
asserting that its images, tropes, and core narratives provide the founding myths of the modern consciousness. For Fussell, "anxiety without
end, without purpose, without reward, and without meaning is woven
into the fabric of contemporary life," and all postwar literary production,
from T. S. Eliot's *The Waste Land* to Thomas Pynchon's *Gravity's Rain-
bow* (published in 1973, as Fussell was writing) is clouded by the shadow
of the parapet and the barbed-wire fence.[38] But, because Fussell made
little mention of any American literature that tackled the war directly, he
compounded the illusion that there wasn't any—or at least that there
wasn't any worth reading. This perception is now changing, as an increasing number of researchers, often with interests in women's writing,
popular fiction, or social history, explore the social impact of American
war narratives and make connections between different authors' treat-
ments of themes such as race, domesticity, and the labor movement.[39]
Studies in the history of nursing have also drawn attention to the powerful material written by medical personnel both during and after the war.[40]
Meanwhile, the years 1914–18 often figure vividly in specific chapters in
the literary biographies of individual authors, though such texts, naturally enough, take an episodic approach, and often have little space to
explore literary methods.

    Nevertheless, two such biographies are among the books that have
been indispensable in the writing of this book. Alan Price's painstakingly

researched study of Edith Wharton during the years of the war, *The End of the Age of Innocence,* details her extraordinary humanitarian efforts throughout the war, via an impressive paper trail of letters and diaries, without ever losing sight of her identity as a writer. Jane Conway's biography of Mary Borden, *A Woman of Two Wars,* which emerged midway through my own research, provided answers to a number of puzzling questions, and illuminated the life of this remarkable woman. Several other texts have rarely left my desk in recent years. Arlen Hansen's cultural history of the ambulance services, *Gentlemen Volunteers,* draws so widely and so carefully from the dozens of literary texts produced by ambulance drivers, both during and after the war, that it is in many ways also a work of literary analysis. Van Wienen's study of the political poetry of the American home front, *Partisans and Poets,* recovers a wealth of forgotten primary material, and demonstrates the interplay between poetry and public life during the war in ways that interrogate many aesthetic assumptions about the uses of literature. Finally, Mark Whalan's study *American Culture in the 1910s* offers a persuasive reading of the war as an integral part of America's social history, not a distant, disruptive event that was soon forgotten, but an integral element of public and creative life, which was evident not only in literature but also in the photography, music, popular entertainment, and business practices of the decade. My own book is very different from all of these studies, yet is a much richer thing for having rubbed shoulders with them. In truth, there is not, as yet, a single volume which provides a satisfactorily comprehensive study of the American literature of the war—and there may never be. As I will argue later on, the war itself could only be apprehended through a sequence of multiple perspectives, and its literary output may fall under the same rubric.

There are so many things to say in a book about the First World War, that the question of how to order them is not simple. This book is both biographical and analytical. I am serious enough about history to believe that what happens to writers makes a difference to what and how they write—which is not the same as saying that they are always writing about their own experiences, or that their work is completely determined by circumstance. I also believe that writers have the potential to shape the pattern of history, both as it unfolds and in retrospect, as we look back through their eyes, although this process is also subject to the actions of publishers, governments, critics, and public taste. This, however, is not a history book, although it does attempt to give enough context to make sense of the artistic response to events which is its main subject. This is a book about the relationship between words and actions, about the writer and how he or she experiences reality and transforms this into art, and about the means that the literary artist uses to coax the reader into a particular understanding of life. Consequently, this study moves forward through chapters which deal with the years of the war in sequence. Some dislike this sort of deference to Time; personally, I think there is no point arguing with him. Taking things roughly in order is by no means an avoidance of dealing with key themes and relationships. Indeed, many interesting patterns have come more sharply into focus by looking synchronically at several writers at different stages of the war. For example, the early cultural obsession with abstract values, especially "civilization," in 1914, and the humanitarian impulse of 1915 seem logical even laudable in their time, although in retrospect they can appear overidealistic or complicit with military objectives. Likewise, the freedom of American writers to express politically controversial and graphic descriptions of the war emerges as a powerfully distinctive element of American war literature, especially when set against the more heavily censored output of British and European writers. The sudden repression of such voices in America after April 1917 is also striking, as is the swift movement of American writers toward dislocated perspectives and points of view which negate the political and military discourse of war almost as soon as that discourse has been invented. The development of individuals diachronically is also notable. For example, James's and Wharton's writings about the war have often been dismissed as "propaganda," but viewed on a timeline, it quickly becomes clear that their opinions were developing rapidly in response to what was happening, that these writers were often more measured than others around them, and that their early belligerent and optimistic reactions should not be taken as their last words on the conflict. Both came to complex and unsettled positions on the war, and both did so when complex and

1914—Civilization

The future is very dark in Europe, and to me it looks as if we
were entering upon a period quite new in history. . . . Whether
our period of economical enterprise, unlimited competition,
and unrestrained individualism, is the highest stage of human
progress is to me very doubtful; and sometimes when I see the
existing conditions of European (to say nothing of American)
social order, bad as they are for the mass alike of upper and
lower classes, I wonder whether our civilization can maintain
itself against the forces which are banding together for the destruction of many of the institutions in which it is embodied,
or whether we are not to have another period of decline, fall,
and ruin and revival, like that of the first thirteen hundred
years of our era. It would not grieve me much to know that this
were to be the case. No man who knows what society at the
present day really is, but must agree that it is not worth preserving on its present basis.[1]

These were strong words—but they were not about the Europe of 1914.
Disillusionment, disgust and the anticipation of disaster lend a sharply
modern tone, but this was Charles Eliot Norton (1827–1908), editor, art
critic, and educator, writing home to America in 1869 as he toured Britain, Italy, Germany, and France. Over sixty years later, as Europe yet
again spiraled into unrest, T. S. Eliot would quote this passage in his lectures in honor of Norton at Harvard University in 1932. To Eliot, Norton stood for the viewpoint that culture was the mainstay of a decent

27

society. Without it, everything came to ruin. As Eliot put it, "the people which ceases to care for its literary inheritance becomes barbaric; the people which ceases to produce literature ceases to move in thought and sensibility."[2]

Henry James wrote to Edith Wharton in August 1914 that he felt "all but unbearably overdarkened by this crash of our civilization."[3] But this was a crash that had been a long time coming, and which would not prove to be final. Norton and Eliot's comments, straddling several decades either side of the First World War, demonstrate that a sense of impending disaster for humanity, and the hope that culture might avert it, were long-standing concerns. In his Harvard lectures of 1932–33, Eliot carefully distanced both himself and Norton from Matthew Arnold's mid-Victorian view of culture as a force for the propagation of good morals.[4] Although he shared Arnold's concern for "literary inheritance," Eliot would place the value of literature not in what it taught but what it showed. Culture was not the cause but the product of a balanced society, one rich in "thought and sensibility." Good writing was not a conduit for truths passed on from the old to the young, but an indicator of a healthy, individual curiosity about self and context. "We must write our poetry as we can," Eliot concluded, "and take it as we find it"—a sentiment very much in line with Ralph Waldo Emerson's delight in "*Man Thinking*" instead of parroting the traditions of the past.[5]

This habit of mental self-reliance, so prevalent in American literature from Emerson onward, was, and perhaps still is, counterbalanced by the potential consequences of its failure, the specter of the "barbaric" so vivid to Eliot in the 1930s.[6] From the mid-nineteenth century, ideas of evolutionary progress derived from the work of Charles Darwin and Herbert Spencer were projected into the swiftly changing scenery of Gilded Age America by social theorists such as William Graham Sumner and Adna Weber, for whom urban life was an endless and vicious round of competition for space, work, food, and time. Darwin and Spencer had promised improvement toward perfection, but Weber's generation projected bleaker outcomes. Failure in this daily battle for resources could lead to personal extinction in the greater cause of social refinement, or could result in the kind of degeneration forecast by Ray Lankester, and dramatized in the naturalistic fiction of Émile Zola and Theodore Dreiser, or in the dystopian romances of H. G. Wells.[7] Success in the struggle, as Thorstein Veblen argued, led merely to interclass conflict and, through "conspicuous consumption" and "conspicuous waste," to the atrophy of the leisure class— whose very existence was both the defining element of a "civilized" society and its most potent internal threat.[8] Although these ideas did not all originate in America, they resonated strongly in the imagination of many early twentieth-century citizens, who inherited, or self-consciously adopted, a powerful but confused legacy from the nation's Puritan past, in which the value of the individual, the power of the written word, a strong work ethic, the taint of materialism, the certainty of retributive judgment on society, and the hope of some ideal world beyond were haphazardly jumbled together. Even for those who rejected the religious framework which supported (and rationalized) such concepts, stubborn patterns of thought remained. The anticipation of destruction was perhaps the most enduring. James called it "the imagination of disaster."[9]

So, the idea of "a war that will end war" was nothing new in 1914.[10] Rumors of secret pacts and alliances between European nations from the beginning of the century had raised public expectations of conflict, which had been narrowly avoided in a series of diplomatic crises from 1908 onward.[11] When war came, it shocked the world, but simultaneously fulfilled an expectation of an epic conflict between the great nations of the world, which would ultimately purge and strengthen the civilized and virtuous races of humankind. Wharton wrote to the American scholar Gaillard Lapsley in December 1914, "The only consoling thought is that the beastly horror *had* to be gone through, for some mysterious cosmic reason of ripening and rotting, and the heads on whom that rotten German civilisation are falling are bound to get cracked."[12] For others, the progress brought by war was not so much a bitter consolation as a positive objective. Cleveland Moffett would write in 1916 that the American union "born of war" proved that conflict was essential for peace: "And why not ultimately the United States of Europe, the United States of Asia, the United States of Africa, all created by useful and progressive wars? . . . 'United we stand, divided we fall,' applies not merely to states, counties and townships, but to nations, to empires, to continents. Continents will be the last to join hands across the seas (having first waged vast inter-continental wars) and then, after the rise and fall of so many sovereignties, there will be established on earth the last great government, the United States of the World!"[13] From the sinking of the *Pequod* in *Moby Dick* (1851) to the freezing over of New York in *The Day after Tomorrow* (2004), the secular apocalyptic narrative is a powerful, recurring presence in American popular culture. Eliot's poem *The Waste Land* (1922) both drew on and helped to define the genre. To Henry James, schooled in his father's Swedenborgian conceptions of heaven and hell; to Edith Wharton, well-versed in the social theories of the early twentieth century; and to Grace Fallow Norton, raised in the evangelical fervor of small-town Minnesota, the apocalyptic habit of language and thought was a hard one to break.[14] Each of these writers in their own way carried a deep sense of the precariousness of human civilization. When the war began, it seemed to them, as to many others, that something decisive was finally at hand. Whether judgment and destruction would be meted out by a vengeful deity or an indifferent nature, whether the end would be swift or slow, everyone had a theory and a secret fear.

Henry James, Grace Fallow Norton, and Edith Wharton were among many American exiles for whom London and Paris were irresistible points of cultural attraction and production, centers of the very "civilization" which appeared to be threatened by the political and military maneuvers of the European nation-states. As John Dos Passos would note decades later, American international perspectives in the early twentieth century were characterized by "a nostalgic geography of civilized and cultured Europe where existence was conducted on a higher plane than the grubby materialism of American business." In the popular imagination, this was especially true of Paris, which seemed to many "the crossroads of civilization."[15] James, who had lived in Europe, mostly in England, for some forty years, was more shrewd than most people about the failings of European society. However, as the following pages show, the coming of war, and the threat which it offered to a social world which he had observed, admired, and mimicked for decades, forced a searching reappraisal of the value of that world, and raised sharp questions about how the writer should respond to conflict and distress: with actions or with words? Wharton, however, based permanently in Paris since the break up of her marriage in 1910, had quickly made herself at home in the elegant and exclusive circles of the Faubourg St. Germain, where the good conversation and sophisticated taste which she prized were recognized and maintained. As her friend Percy Lubbock noted in later years, "She had attained, and not without complacency she knew it, to a far closer intimacy with France than is often granted to an alien—with France of the French, the old and the traditional, which has never easily opened to a stranger's knock."[16] However, in 1914, this process of assimilation was in its early stages, and Wharton's passion for the integrity of France during the war had all the idealism and raw enthusiasm of the newcomer. At this stage, her attitude was not unlike that of the fictional American exiles in her postwar novel *A Son at the Front* (1923) who felt that, "If France went, western civilization went with her."[17] But, there was self-irony in this retrospective statement, and Wharton's idealism would be tested and overhauled during the next four years. Nevertheless, in the political and ideological tussle for American popular sympathy during the early years of the war, the trope of France as a symbol of civilization was a recurrent one. Both Wharton and James would exploit it for practical, if charitable, purposes. Grace Fallow Norton, too, would subscribe to the apocalyptic vision of the war as a threat to social, political, even to geological, stability. However, her conception of civilization was more concerned with the rights of the common citizen than with the preservation of an elitist culture—even while she participated in that culture. France, to Norton, represented the possibility of personal freedom, both in terms of democratic governance and moral tolerance. If her concerns were less commonly voiced among the literary classes of the day, they were perhaps more representative of the attitudes of less privileged, and also younger, Americans. Norton's views at the outbreak of the war certainly suggest that the later, more pronounced social perspectives of writers such as Cummings and Dos Passos were not kneejerk reactions to their experience of war, but rather extensions of deep-seated changes already in process in the fabric of American society. However, in August

1914, the most urgent question for each of these writers was how to define the boundary between the demands of artistic response with those of real life. Put more simply, if civilization was falling apart, what on earth were they supposed to do next?

This Grand Niagara

It began for Henry James as a nightmare from which there was "no waking save by sleep."[18] On 5 August, through the balmy summer weather, news of Britain's declaration of war in response to Germany's invasion of Belgium reached James's home in the little town of Rye, near the coast of Sussex on the English Channel. The change in James's mood was immediate and electrifying—captured with photographic clarity in a letter to his friend Howard Sturgis. The first half, written the previous day, before papers arrived in Rye bearing the dramatic news, is relaxed and expansive, full of chatter about friends; the second half, written in full knowledge of events, is a darker, yet strangely energized text, passionate in its dismay and its condemnation of the German and Austrian rulers: "The taper went out last night, and I am afraid I now kindle it again to a very feeble ray—for it's vain to talk as if one weren't living in a nightmare of the deepest dye. . . . The plunge of civilization into this abyss of blood and darkness by the wanton feat of those two infamous autocrats is a thing that so gives away the whole long age during which we have supposed the world to be, with whatever abatement, gradually bettering, that to have to take it all now for what the treacherous years were all the while really making for and *meaning* is too tragic for any words."[19] Nevertheless, words were what James turned to, over the following days, as a means of ordering his intense reactions. Always richly articulate and self-conscious, his letters now took on an unfamiliar sense of urgency and scope. Treachery, nightmare, murder, abyss: these words flowed again and again from James's pen as his powerful imagination struggled to accommodate the scale and the horror of the conflict. It was, he recognized at once, about much more than the immediate political objectives of the warring nations. James appeared to grasp instantly what many social commentators would take voices of Thomas Carlyle, John Ruskin, and Matthew Arnold.[23] James had to an extent distanced himself from this triptych by his decision to settle among the complex social systems of Europe, and there to refine his sharp sense of the subjectivity of all human judgment—although he was hardly going to escape the legacy of Carlyle, Ruskin, and Arnold by moving to England. However, like Charles Eliot Norton, who traveled with the young James in Europe, published his early work in the *North American Review,* and introduced him to Ruskin in person in 1869, James was ready to form his own opinions about European civilization and its relationship to culture, especially to literary production. For James, "civilization" denoted something rich and precious and old—but it was not always, for him, a concept above censure. In his biography of Hawthorne (1879), James noted the lack of "items of high civilization" in American life in the 1840s: "No sovereign, no court, no personal loyalty, no aristocracy, no church, no clergy, no army, no diplomatic service, no country gentlemen, no palaces, no castles, nor manors, nor old country-houses, nor parsonages, nor thatched cottages nor ivied ruins; no cathedrals, nor abbeys, nor little Norman churches; no great Universities nor public schools—no Oxford, nor Eton, nor Harrow; no literature, no novels, no museums, no pictures, no political society, no sporting class—no Epsom nor Ascot!"[24] It is a notorious list, but many of James's readers forget that he had his tongue firmly in his cheek when he made it. James's point was that Hawthorne did *not* need these things to write. No American author did: "The American knows that a good deal remains—that is his secret, his joke, as one might say."[25] It was a joke at Arnold's expense. For Arnold, "civilization" consisted of the physical infrastructure of a highly developed society: institutions, architecture, and amenities.[26] James admired Hawthorne's rejection of European institutions and tropes, and celebrated his ability to observe, to think for himself, and to draw his own conclusions about American society. Elsewhere, the young James took an even sharper view of "civilization," which seemed at times to signify little more than the fripperies and frivolities of Parisian life that he lampooned in his essays for the *New York Tribune* in 1875–76. Here, French civilization was characterized by consumption and display—extravagant clothes, light opera, and candy boxes. "The *bonbonnière*, in its elaborate and impertinent uselessness," he wrote, "is certainly the consummate flower of material luxury; it seems to bloom, with its petals of satin and its pistils of gold, upon the very apex of the tree of civilization."[27]

Forty years later, James had apparently changed his mind. Civilization seemed to him now to denote not just the trappings of a fair and cultured society, but also the abstract principles on which such a society was built. In his essay "France," published in *The Book of France*, a fundraising venture edited by Winifred Stephens to raise money to support war refugees, he would write ardently that "the idea of what France and the French mean to the educated spirit of man" would be the most "general ground in the world, on which an appeal might be made, in a civilised circle."[28] He was no longer thinking about chocolate wrappers, or even social niceties. Civilisation now encompassed the complex social, personal, and artistic relationships within a community or a nation, the "good deal that remains" when artefacts and systems break down—or as he phrased it in 1915 "the life of the mind and the life of the senses alike." Like so many of his countrymen, indeed like his own fictional characters, James had grown to see France as the place where these elements could be "taken together in the most irrepressible freedom of either."[29] Now it was under shell fire. After the initial disbelief and dismay, James reacted with fury, especially after the bombardment of Rheims Cathedral, which seemed to him "the most hideous crime ever perpetrated against the mind of man," a turn of phrase which emphasized how he perceived even the brutally physical effects of the war, in its early days, in intellectual and historical terms. "There it *was*," he wrote to Wharton, "and now all the tears of rage of all of the bereft millions and all the crowding curses of all the wondering ages will never bring a stone of it back!"[30] Unknown to James, Wharton's friend Alfred de Saint-André translated a long section of this passionate letter and read it to a session of the Académie Française on 9 October. It was also published in the *Journal des Débats* the following day. On receiving the news, James declared himself "honoured by such grand courtesy," but this incident must also have alerted him to the possibility that he could have a public role in the crisis.[31] This was, one suspects, an unfamiliar idea to this media-shy writer, who had found the reading public increasingly elusive over the past twenty years—unfamiliar, but not unwelcome.

In contrast, Wharton lost no time in stepping into the limelight. In July 1914, she had taken a three-week motoring trip to Spain with her intimate friend Walter Berry, the president of the American Chamber of Commerce. They had driven back to Paris, now thick with rumors and apprehension, at the month's close. Her original plan had been to leave at once for England, where she had taken a two-month lease on Stocks in Buckinghamshire, the country mansion owned by her fellow novelist Mary Ward. But Wharton found herself caught up in the chaos of national mobilization on 1 August, which rushed away men of fighting age to the front but also immobilized the civilian population. It was not just that it was impossible to travel, all trains having been commandeered for military purposes; there was also a sense of emotional heaviness and helplessness that fell on the city with the momentous events of the war. It seemed to her like a "monstrous landslide" which had "fallen across the path of an orderly laborious nation, disrupting its routine, annihilating its industries, rending families apart, and burying under a heap of senseless ruin the patiently and painfully wrought machinery of civilization."[32] Civilization—it was the word of the moment, but no one seemed to be able to agree exactly what it meant. For Wharton, who used the term more generously than James, it encompassed the architecture and government of a nation, its history, its tradition, its artistic culture, its cuisine, its daily, domestic way of life. Having just selected France as her permanent home, these things currently seemed to Wharton to be infinitely more superior there than anywhere else in America or Europe. France and civilization seemed indivisible, and Wharton was ready to defend both.

Within a fortnight of the mobilization, she had joined the executive committee of the American Ambulance, and had opened an *ouvroir* for twenty seamstresses, laid off from the couture houses, which had closed as soon as war was announced. This workroom, supported by donations from Wharton's wealthy friends, would quickly grow to accommodate ninety women, including refugees from Belgium and northern France, and would lead Wharton into a further series of charitable projects over the months and years ahead. As though to symbolize the two directions in which Wharton's life was being pulled, the workshop produced French army uniforms to be worn at the front, alongside fine lingerie and couture dresses to be worn in the glamorous townhouses of Washington and New York. However, no sooner had she set this project going than Wharton was on the move again. Through Berry's influence, she managed to secure a passage across the English Channel to Folkstone on 27 August, where James met her and took her back to Lamb House for the evening to hear the news from Paris, before she joined her servants at Stocks for her holiday as planned. Berry even pulled strings to allow Wharton's car to be shipped to England, a remarkable feat at a moment when most vehicles and their drivers were being requisitioned by the army. But Wharton couldn't relax. Restless and anxious for news, after only two weeks in the lush English countryside, she negotiated with the Wards for them to return to Stocks, while she moved up to stay at their London house in Grosvenor Square. In mid-September, James came up from Rye to visit her for four days, and found himself confronted with both the feverish atmosphere of the capital city and Wharton's growing resolve to return to Paris—which she did a week later. James watched her go with a mix of admiration and concern. Her impulse was, he told her, "a very gallant and magnificent and ideal one," but he also implored her, "for pity's sake—if there *be* any pity in the universe now!—'take care of yourself.' "[33]

When Wharton arrived back in Paris at the end of September, she found that she had missed momentous events, and that she had a tricky situation to resolve. While she had been away, the German army had advanced with breathtaking speed to within thirty miles of Paris, only to be halted by a combined French and British force at the First Battle of the Marne, a costly engagement on both sides in which nearly half a million men died. As the two great armies tried to outmaneuver each other along the line of the River Marne, the precarious balance of strength was tipped toward the Allies by General Maunoury's inventive move of rushing six thousand extra troops to the front in Parisian motor taxi cabs, thus creating what was later hailed as "the first internal combustion-engined army

in history."[34] After a week of vicious fighting, the Germans were driven
back to the River Aisne, and the long stalemate of the next four years began to take shape. During the crisis, thousands of civilians had been evac-
uated south of Paris, including the "philanthropic lady" in whose house
Wharton had established her workroom, and the manageress of the venture, who carried away all the operating funds, worth nearly two thousand dollars.[35] The Red Cross intervened and the money was returned,
but Wharton had to find the workshop a new home, which was eventually
secured in a building owned by the Petit St. Thomas, a few blocks from
her home at 53 Rue de Varenne, to assemble a new team of volunteers and
to restore the confidence of her workers. She was not sure where to start,
but two women who had heard about her difficulties came to her aid, and
would prove invaluable over the coming months: Renée Landormy, who
assumed responsibility for the workshop, and Elisina Tyler, the Italian
wife of Royall Tyler, an American art critic living in Paris. Elisina Tyler
would become Wharton's right-hand woman in all of her charitable projects. Tyler, formerly the Countess Palamidessi di Castelvecchio, was en-
ergetic and charming, a woman of "inexhaustible resourcefulness"; she
was not intimidated by committees, and knew how to soothe the impetu-
ous and occasionally high-handed Wharton.[36] Undoubtedly, Wharton's
wartime activities were an astonishing achievement, but she could not
have done half of what she did without Tyler's organizational flair and
diplomacy.

    In the autumn of 1914, Wharton formed a committee of her Ameri-
can, French and Belgian contacts to establish a new charity, the American
Hostels for Refugees. This organization worked in collaboration with the
Foyer Franco-Belge, which was founded in the opening weeks of the war
by a group of French intellectuals including the writer André Gide and
the critic Charles du Bos, but which was now overwhelmed by the numbers of refugees pouring into the capital after the fierce fighting around
Ypres, which decimated the civilian population and left over ten thousand
people homeless.[37] The American Hostels for Refugees was in many ways
a glamorous enterprise; it was based in a large, handsome building in the
Champs Elysées owned by the Comtesse de Béhague, and financially sup-

ported by a glittering list of American literati and socialites, including
Henry James, Wharton's publisher Charles Scribner, her sister-in-law
Mary Cadwaladar Jones, the new American ambassador to Paris William
Graves Sharp, and other recognizable names from the East Coast upper
classes: Adamses, Roosevelts, Chanlers, and Nortons. Hermione Lee
finds it ironic that the social world which Wharton had abandoned, and
which she satirized so ruthlessly in her fiction, was the main source of
support for her aid work—so much so that the list of contributors to her
charities "reads like the *New York Social Register*."[38] All the same, it worked.
As Wharton's biographer Shari Benstock notes, her fund-raising activities
were "on a scale that in our time only corporations could undertake."[39]
Her organization was committed to providing the basics of shelter and
cheap food for the displaced arriving in Paris, until they could find jobs
and homes of their own. The demand was daunting; in the first month
alone, the two organizations working together lodged and clothed 878
refugees, found work for 153 of these, and served 16,287 free meals.[40] But
the numbers would only increase, and by the end of the war, the *accueil*
(reception), as Wharton called it, was caring for five thousand refugees at
a time. Wharton wrote appeal after appeal in the American press, shame-
lessly exploiting the most emotive stories she could find. As she wrote to
Elisina Tyler: "I always get money by the 'tremolo' note, so I try to dwell
on it as much as possible."[41] The committee soon realized that to operate
effectively, they required support services such as cheap restaurants, coal
supplies, a pharmacy, a nursery, and a hospital. Most of the new arrivals
were hungry, exhausted, and ill. The small medical unit of thirty beds, for
which Wharton launched an appeal in January 1915, would grow into a
network of health services, a section of which developed as the Tubercu-
leux de la Guerre, a group of four large hospitals for civilian and military
victims of tuberculosis. One of these, La Tuyolle, was taken over by the
French government at the end of the war, and was still running when Wharton wrote her autobiography almost twenty years later.[42]

Just as this project was taking shape, in November 1914, Walter Berry
left Paris to travel as a neutral observer to Germany and Belgium. His
Chamber of Commerce position as the representative of a nation which

both the Allies and the Central Powers were hoping to win over allowed him to move freely across Europe as few others could in those months. Wharton complained on his return that "his imagination seems less sensitive than it used to be" and that he had little to tell her in the way of "illuminating incident."[43] She did not consider that he may have been reluctant to describe to her in vivid detail all that he had seen. But even the "solid facts" that he did pass on gave Wharton a fascinating and disturbing glimpse of the world behind the front. The German army was in good order, prisoners' camps were "fairly decent," and the German people seemed to believe they were fighting to defend themselves. There was no chance of an early end to hostilities. Belgium on the other hand had been ripped apart, orphaned children roamed in devastated villages, and the great medieval library at Louvain had been burned to the ground—although Berry suspected the Germans of having carried off its treasures to Berlin before they set it alight. Wharton's curiosity was fired, as was her sense that her own literary abilities would do more justice to the scene than Berry's stolid account.

As 1915 approached, Wharton began to organize a series of fashionable concerts to raise money for out-of-work musicians, another category of Parisian worker with little means of making money in the general austerity of war. But she soon tired of making arrangements for refreshments, and ordering up programs: "I vaguely thought one had only to 'throw open one's doors' as aristocratic hostesses do in fiction," she wrote to her friend Mary Berenson in Italy. "Oh my! I'd rather write a three volume novel than do it again."[44] It was a telling remark; Wharton would much rather have been writing than organizing. Her comment also suggests that her models for activity were as much drawn from the world of fiction as from reality. She was not alone in this; many others, including those fighting at the front, had equally little idea of how to approach the new challenges facing them. There was also in Wharton's deeply aristocratic mind a distaste for the crush and the crowd of such events and for throwing open one's doors. She passed on the project to her friend Alice Garrett after half a dozen events. Nevertheless, she would find a use for these experiences later, when she came to write her fiction about Paris during the war.

Wharton, however, was not the only American who felt the need to support the Allied war effort. Upper-class American exiles swiftly endorsed and supported it, but also at times exploited it. Indeed, some of Wharton's sharpest vitriol in her letters and fiction is reserved for the high-society volunteers who appeared to be enjoying themselves more than they were making any discernible contribution, for the large hotels which set aside some rooms as "hospitals" to be able to fly the Red Cross flag and thereby avoid shelling but without taking in patients, and for those bankers, businessmen, and their wives who seemed to regard the war as another curiosity of Europe. This charge could hardly be levied at Richard Norton, son of Charles Eliot Norton and former director of the American School of Classical Studies in Rome. Norton had been holidaying in England when war broke out, but traveled at once to Paris to see how he could help. At the American Hospital, hastily established at Neuilly in a new stone building intended as a boys' school, Norton was struck by the number of needless deaths caused by the hopelessly slow process of getting the wounded to the operating table—a combination of hand stretcher, horse-drawn cart and railway train, which often took days. He also heard that American motorists trying to drive to the front to catch a glimpse of the fighting were getting in the way.[45] He set to work to reverse this irony. A few days after leaving, he was back in London working with the British Red Cross to set up an independent ambulance unit, which would swiftly take shape as the American Volunteer Motor-Ambulance Corps. Later in the war, this would merge with the Morgan-Harjes unit to form a group that became known as the Norton-Harjes Section.[46] This unit remained distinct from the larger American Field Ambulance Service organized by A. Piatt Andrew, until both were disbanded and subsumed into the U.S. Army Ambulance Service in August 1917. Richard Norton, refined, highly educated, and sporting a monocle, was an unlikely but charismatic leader. As the war unfolded, he organized scores of young volunteers, mostly Ivy League students and graduates, to serve at the front, many of whom paid their own expenses and brought their own valuable automobiles. Dos Passos, who joined the corps in 1917, described Richard Norton as an "aesthete, indomitable archaeologist, the man who smuggled

Burgess Noakes, who had worked for him since 1901, enlisted and left for training. It was, as James complained to Wharton, "like the loss of an arm or a leg."[50]

James's emotional reactions to the first few weeks of the war were characterized by the contrasting economies of scale and time in which he attempted to locate them. On the one hand, the tragedy was of biblical proportions, the failure of the civilized world, the climax of history; it was also a deeply personal wound, a keenly felt and permanent loss. James's desire to identify with the pain and dismemberment of war is striking for many reasons—not least because of its similarity to his feelings about the American Civil War and the mysterious injury which prevented him from serving in the Northern Army. His two younger brothers Wilky and Robertson had enlisted, as did two of James's cousins, Gus Barker and Will Temple. Both cousins were killed in action, leaving James with a complex emotional legacy of regret and relief. In the second volume of his autobiography, *Notes of a Son and Brother,* published only a few months before the First World War began, James describes—with a tantalizing lack of detail—how while helping to work a fire pump at a blaze in a Newport stable in 1861 he had done himself "in face of a shabby conflagration, a horrid if an obscure hurt."[51] The nature of this injury has been hotly debated. Many scholars have interpreted it as some form of physical or psychological castration—through it may simply have been a back strain.[52] Whatever had actually happened to him, it seemed to James symbolic of the violence on the national battlefield: "One had the sense, I mean, of a huge comprehensive ache, and there were hours at which one could scarce have told whether it came most from one's own poor organism, still so young and so meant for better things, but which had suffered particular wrong, or from the enclosing social body, a body rent with a thousand wounds and that thus treated one to the honour of a sort of tragic fellowship."[53]

This incident and the language in which James describes it have been so heavily analyzed that it has become a critical commonplace to point out the sexual potency of the imagery; the fantasy of inclusion in the masculine community of military service; the artistic withdrawal to an observing rather than a participating role; and the eerie, generational repetition of the childhood accident in which his father, Henry James Senior, lost a leg after a fire in another stable.[54] When James said that Noakes's absence was "like the loss of an arm or a leg," he used an image charged with a deep, familial echo—an image that must have seemed doubly resonant when Noakes returned from the front the following spring, with his hearing impaired and a permanent limp from a shrapnel wound. Adeline Tintner interprets James's willingness to publish "propaganda" in order to "publicize the British war effort," as a belated reaction to the repressed guilt he experienced for his nonparticipation in the Civil War, a guilt which he had finally overcome by relating the event to his readers in *Notes of a Son and Brother*.[55] However, there are other ways of interpreting James's own personal discomfort.

James's sense of the interplay between the individual and the nation governs his response to war both in 1861 and in 1914. Physical pain is always a lonely experience—a fact thrown into sharp relief by the inability of scholars to fathom the nature of James's own isolating injury. Nevertheless, his image of the nation as a wounded body highlights his sense that in wartime the normal boundaries between self and society are realigned, and the pain of the individual, whether soldier or civilian, takes on a broader political significance than at other times, as do other kinds of sensation and action (or inaction). In James's description of his "obscure hurt," as is so often the case in his fiction and letters, suffering becomes an opportunity not to recoil into the self, but to make contact with others, to feel a part of a wider system of relationships—one sympathetic observer, a circle of friends, a community, a nation. It is the cry of the single, sobbing woman in the street that is "the voice of history," but only because she reenacts the experience of so many other grieving women down through the ages. That solitary cry and James's experience of it, disseminated through writing, take on a richer significance and become expressive of a collective experience both of anguish and of empathy. So, when he made a claim for the validity and commonality of his own experience within that of the American nation during the Civil War, James also determined how he would position himself in 1914—as a register of the feelings of society, and as a conduit of impressions across some liminal zone between reality and published text. As Thomas Otten points out, James's own pain during the Civil War allows him not to take sides, but to occupy "some place in between."[56] In 1914, this place was between participant and reader, between France and Britain, between Europe and America. In many ways this was, of course, exactly what he felt he had been doing for the last fifty years by observing and analyzing the experience of the individual, and aiming to communicate these to the reader. The role of the writer, as James defines it in "The Art of Fiction" (1884), is to move from the single to the general, or as he puts it "to guess the unseen from the seen, to trace the implication of things, to judge the whole piece by the pattern."[57]

Despite the basic optimism of this approach to the role of the writer in wartime, many of James's readers have found the extent of this desire to speak for others solipsistic or "self-aggrandizing."[58] However, these readings both exaggerate and underestimate the place of the Civil War in James's imagination. In casting the old conflict and the "obscure hurt" as suppressed events in his psyche, it is all too easy to overlook the fact that it is James himself who first articulates and analyzes these complex connections. In his essay about the early stages of the war, "Within the Rim," written in February 1915, James muses on the uncanny overlap of sensations with that earlier conflict. He felt that he knew "by experience" what the early excitement of war would bring: "The sudden new tang in the atmosphere, the flagrant difference, as one noted, in the look of everything, especially in that of people's faces, the expressions, the hushes, the clustered groups, the detached wonderers, and slow-paced public meditators, were so many impressions long before received and in which the stretch of more than half a century had still left a sharpness."[59] This sense of recognition, he felt, saved him from any illusions about what might happen in northern France. Anyone who had lived through that earlier conflict "had known, had tremendously learnt, what the awful business is when it is 'long,' when it remains for months and months bitter and arid, void even of any great honour." But he knew very well that the two wars were not the same, and the past is invoked in this essay not as a totem of security, but only to highlight the contrast with the present. All too swiftly, he felt, there was a moment "at which experience felt the ground give way and that one swung off into space, into history, into darkness, with every lamp extinguished and every abyss gaping."[60]

Nevertheless, James's own tendency to view the First World War through the lens of his experience of the Civil War does raise tricky questions about how he saw the balance between past and present and between the private and the public. It is tempting to trace a neat parallel between James's resurgence of memories about the Civil War in 1914 with his decision to abandon work on *The Ivory Tower*, and restart work on his time-travel novel *The Sense of the Past*, as though James like his protagonist Ralph Pendrel had experienced some strange warping of linear time. Yet James's ostensible jolt back to 1861 at the outbreak of the First World War is better understood as evidence of his continual sense of connection with the past. The Civil War was always with him. James had just spent two years reworking childhood recollections for his autobiography, patiently mapping out the mechanisms by which early experiences, including his impressions of that war, had formed his adult consciousness. There were also physical reminders of the old war. Every day in his study James worked to the rattle of the typewriter which bore the name of the Union Army's rifle maker, Remington. Burgess Noakes recalled that even James's trousers "were held up by an old belt from the American Civil War. His cuff-links were miniature cannons."[61] These unexpectedly military accessories were probably inherited from James's younger brother Wilky, who, serving as an officer in the Fifty-fourth Massachusetts, was critically wounded in the disastrous attack on Fort Wagner in 1863. Brought home to Newport by the father of a fallen fellow officer, Wilky, barely eighteen years old, hovered close to death for days, lying in the hallway of the family house on the stretcher which had carried him home. The doctor pronounced him too ill to be moved. He struggled back to action, but his health never fully recovered, and he died in 1883, in his late thirties. James had not forgotten. Like the severed limb, the image of the wounded body was a powerful one for him, not glibly employed.

As the glorious late summer of 1914 waned into October, Rye suddenly felt lonely, and James shifted camp to his flat in Chelsea, where he usually spent the winters. He found London "agitating but interesting," at

1. Henry James in the years before the war. Photograph by
Katherine McClellan, courtesy of Smith College.

times even "uplifting," but he was frustrated by the limited range of things
he could *do*. "To be old and doddering now," he wrote to Rhoda Broughton, "is for a male person not at all glorious."[62] He did a little writing, but
unusually James felt that the drama was outside these days, not in the
imagination, and he was finding it compelling to watch. He wrote to his
childhood friend Thomas Sargeant Perry that there was something "that
ministers to life and knowledge" in the "collective experience, for all its

big black streaks."[63] He found small but meaningful activities. He wrote anxiously to Noakes, sending chocolate and socks. He visited Belgian refugees at Crosby Hall, in Cheyne Walk where he lived. This grand, old, fifteenth-century building had been moved from its original site at Bishopsgate in 1910 to save it from demolition, and to James's mind there was a poetic symmetry in the way that this salvaged, dislocated construction should offer shelter to those in such a similar position. He was also empathetic enough to wonder what it must be like to find oneself in "some like exiled and huddled and charity-fed predicament."[64] He visited wounded soldiers at St. Bartholomew's Hospital—at first the Belgians, to whom he could speak French, but increasingly the wounded British, whom he found "even more interesting." They struck him as "quite ideal and natural soldier stuff of the easy, the bright and instinctive, and above all the, in this country, probably quite inexhaustible kind."[65] But even this immediate confrontation with the consequences of the modern conflict raised ghosts from the Civil War. He remembered how with Perry he had visited a vast, tented hospital in Portsmouth Grove, Rhode Island, and had mused then, as he did again now, on the "alternative aspect" of the soldier lying helpless in a bed, "the passive as distinguished from the active" side of the fighting man.[66] When he had recorded this visit some months before in *Notes of a Son and Brother,* he had rejoiced in the way his own youthful experience coincided with that of Walt Whitman, moving tenderly among the wounded of the war, armed "with oranges and peppermints."[67] At St. Bart's in 1914, as an old man talking to the stricken young, the comparison with Whitman must have struck James even more forcefully. What the soldiers felt about the great novelist's slow and solicitous conversation no one will ever know.

Tintner cites James's "growing homoeroticism," evident in his admiration for the young men around him, as one of the reasons for "exposing himself and his feeling to public scrutiny" during the war, and this has become a widely accepted reading of James's war history."[68] However, it seems a faulty use of logic to present this latent desire, whether conscious or suppressed, as the root motive of James's political and literary response to the war. He did enjoy the sight of handsome youths in uniform, and he did believe in the war effort, but that one was the cause of the other is questionable. In his study of touch and intimacy in the war zone, Santanu Das cautions against the "anachronistic" tendency to mark as definitively homoerotic those statements and actions—even apparently explicit actions such as the same-sex kiss—which, when restored to their wartime context, overlap with other deep human instincts such as "sentimentalism, tenderness and aestheticism."[69] James's devotion to his wounded soldiers is similarly difficult to decode. It is perhaps safer to say that James's sexuality, mysterious as this question remains to scholars of his life and work, was only one factor among the many forces propelling him into the public eye in 1914.

James's motives are difficult to fathom. Knowing what we now know about the First World War, his enthusiasm for action and his ever-increasing desire for America to join forces with the Allies seem profoundly out of character for this thoughtful, tolerant, often hesitant man. In 1914, however, social attitudes to war, as to sexuality, were very different to those of the present day. Patrick Devlin notes that "international morality" (a phrase that in another context might sound like the stuff of James's transatlantic fiction) accepted war as a means of settling political differences, but also strictly governed the terms of engagement, protecting the rights of civilians and of neutral nations.[70] The full horror of a "total war" in which civilians and conscripts were the hapless victims of large-scale tactical experiments had not yet been unleashed upon the world, and with his limited access to information about the reality of the front, James was neither unreasonable nor hysterical in imagining during the early phases of the conflict that military force was a workable and noble response to events. Most people in Britain thought the same. Nor was James's response to the war as fixed as it is often portrayed; in truth, his opinions swung around from week to week, and varied subtly in response to different correspondents. As Chapter Two discusses, his essays and letters reveal a mind moving swiftly to accommodate new ideas as they emerge, to employ his imagination and his powers of empathy, to face up to the bewildering scale of the human loss involved, and to find possibilities of creativity in the darkest elements of the conflict. For James, the First World War was about much more than his own emotional baggage.

Through his friends in the political class, such as Edmund Gosse, who was a close friend and advisor to H. H. Asquith, and Edward Marsh, currently private secretary to Winston Churchill, First Lord of the Admiralty, news of James's enthusiasm for the British cause reached Downing Street. Margot Asquith, the prime minister's wife, invited James to lunch, where he found himself suddenly immersed in the inner circle of British leadership. He became a regular guest, but as he wrote to Thomas and Lilla Perry, it was "idiotic" to imagine that lunching with Asquith would allow him "the chance to catch some gleam between the chinks" of the tight controls on public information about the war, "because it's mostly in those circles that the chinks are well puttied over."[71] Nevertheless, he quickly became a close friend of the Asquiths, and was invited to spend a weekend with them at Walmer Castle in Kent in January 1915. Winston Churchill was also present—young, impatient, and sardonic. As James left, he told Violet Asquith, the prime minister's daughter, that it had been "a very interesting experience to meet that young man." It had, he said, brought home to him "very forcibly—very vividly—the *limitations* by which men of genius obtain their ascendancy over mankind." Reaching for a phrase that Churchill himself might have used, James added, "It bucks one up."[72]

There were other experiences that he found equally stimulating, experiences that balanced against the horrors of war and the moods of depression that increasingly swept over him. To a man who had dedicated much of his literary life to dramatizing pluralized viewpoints, his new-found sense of moral and political conviction was oddly exhilarating. Britain seemed to be in "so magnificent a position before the world, in respect to the history and logic of her action," that it came as a surprise to him "to find one can be on a 'side' with all one's weight."[73] He went often to visit Walter Hines Page, the American ambassador to London, in the afternoon, and they had long talks together about the issue of American neutrality. He wrote to Elizabeth Norton that he found himself "sickened to the very soul" by the "*louche* and sinister figure of Mr Woodrow Wilson, who seems to be *aware* of nothing but the various ingenious ways in which it is open to him to make difficulties for us." It was not at all clear whether by "us" James meant those Americans who believed military action was justified or the Allied nations. Swept up as he was in the "rightness" of the Allies' cause, appalled by the loss of "such ranks upon ranks of the finest young human material," and convinced that America held the power to shorten the war by intervention, James had little patience with Wilson's diplomacy, which projected "the meanness of his note as it breaks into all this heroic air."[74]

But politics was never James's métier. He was fascinated by the drama and the intensity of the relationships between the men of power, but it was the question of the personal significance of the war, and how the artist could possibly respond to this which taxed his imagination most.[75] In early August 1914, he had written to Esther Sutro, wife of the dramatist Alfred Sutro, that he intended to keep writing throughout the conflict, despite the smell of blood and gunpowder in the inkpot. James asked her to tell Alfred, "that I hold we can still, he and I, *make* a little civilization, the inkpot aiding, even when vast chunks of it, around us, go down into the abyss."[76] By October, as his own work schedule began to flag, and he became aware of the imaginative difficulties of forming fiction in wartime, he wrote to his American publisher Charles Scribner, with another military metaphor, to explain that it was all he could do to "pretend just to keep in the saddle, sitting as tight as ever I can." Nevertheless, James was beginning to sense that the destructive force of the war also held a strange new kind of creative potential. As he told Scribner, "Those of us who shall outwear and outlast, who shall above all outlive, in the larger sense of the term, and outimagine, will be able to show for the adventure, I am convinced, a weight and quality that may be verily worth your having waited for."[77] Of course, this may merely have been James's eloquent way of negotiating an extension to his deadline, but, by December, he was writing to Scribner once more, explaining that however horrible the conflict was, there was something "infernally inspiring" about it. James felt that "after the first horror and sickness, which are indeed unspeakable, Interest rises and rises and spreads enormous wings," like a great vulture circling in search of the "terrible human meaning" of the war. "It is very dreadful," he wrote, "but after half dying with dismay and repugnance under the first shock of possibilities that I really believed had become extinct, I began little by little, to feel them give an intensity to life (even at my time of it) which I wouldn't have passed away without knowing." He added, "Such is my monstrous state of mind."[78]

As 1914 drew to a close, James felt ready to publish some of his thoughts on the war. He had done little polemical writing in his long and prolific career, and had not written on international politics since the late 1870s, but he felt it was now time to make a public gesture. In November, over lunch with Richard Norton, he offered to write a fund-raising letter for the ambulance unit, describing its work in France and appealing for funds from the public on both sides of the Atlantic.[79] Five days later it was finished, and was published in London as a pamphlet by Macmillan with the sober title *The American Volunteer Motor-Ambulance Corps in France: A Letter to the Editor of an American Journal.* However, it appeared in *New York World*, on 4 January 1915, with the more dashing heading: "Famous Novelist Describes Deeds of US Motor Corps." James may have been appalled or flattered at this decision to trade on his literary reputation—possibly both—but it demonstrated, as the letter read to the Académie Française had done, that his name still carried enough cache to draw some public attention. It is an unusual piece of writing in James's oeuvre. It was clearly produced at speed, and compared to much of his late work, the tone is raw and unfamiliar, although his distinctive intellectual signature is there in his satisfaction at the idea that "the unpaid chauffeur, the wise amateur driver and ready lifter, helper, healer, and, so far as may be, consoler, is apt to be an University man," trained to assimilate and appreciate "the beauty of the vivid and palpable social result."[80] This may have sounded snobbish, but as the following chapters will show, it demonstrated just how shrewd James was about where and how literary responses to the war would originate. The university men of the ambulance services would turn out to be some of the finest writers of their generation. Even when considering the harsh realities of life behind the front, James was determined to see the war in terms of its aesthetic and cultural impact. In reviewing this pamphlet, the *British Medical Journal* paid tribute to what it called "the testimony of a neutral" in corroborating stories of the German army firing on ambulances in contravention of the Geneva Convention—although, to describe James as "neutral" would not, by this stage, be strictly accurate.[81] The most startling feature of this article is the way in which James again experiments with his use of the third-person plural: "we nevertheless pushed on," he writes, as though he was riding in the passenger seat of a converted Model-T through the fields of northern France.[82] He did so in his imagination only, but his sense of who "we" were, and how one could shift one's identity with so small a word was evolving apace.

A Genteel Rebel

After the war, Percy Lubbock would write that in those early days Henry James had provided what everyone lacked: "a voice; there was a trumpet note in it that was heard nowhere else and that alone rose to the height of the truth."[83] But James's voice was speaking with an increasingly British accent. Although still an American citizen, there was no escaping the fact that James, over his many long years in London and Rye, had fallen out of step with many of the changes and demographic shifts in American cultural life—a disjunction that he himself had recognized so vividly during his American tour of 1904-5, and analyzed so minutely in *The American Scene* (1907). Partly as a result of James's own work, and that of others in his generation such as Mark Twain and William Dean Howells, American literary life had acquired a depth and variety by 1914 that would have been hard to imagine even twenty years before. In the 1890s, Boston stood unrivaled as the publishing and intellectual hub of the nation, but by the early years of the new century its intimate, educated atmosphere, which James had found so stifling as a young novelist, was already giving way to new subjects, new styles, new names on flyleaves—many of them foreign-sounding to old New England ears: Theodore Dreiser, Kate Chopin, Gertrude Stein, W. E. B. Du Bois. New publishing houses and new literary and political journals sprang up apace in New York, Chicago, and San

Francisco. Midwest and West Coast lifestyles began to feature in the work of writers such as Willa Cather, Ellen Glasgow, Frank Norris, and Upton Sinclair. It was a very different world from that of James's youth—a world of railroads and telephones, of industrial-scale farming, meat packing, sweat shops, sharp business, theatrical glamor, and political unrest. This too was America.

Like personal motives, however, changes in culture are complex, and are often characterized by interfusion as much as by opposition. Many writers of this new generation were a curious blend of convention and experiment, of hesitation and daring—none more so than the poet Grace Fallow Norton (1876–1962). Norton's life story has never been told outside of her family circle, and her work is not well known. Much of it belongs to the pre-war tradition of "genteel" verse—a style rarely appealing to present critical tastes. However, this was the predominant mode of poetic consumption in prewar America, by a readership that still revered the rhythms and abstractions of Henry Wadsworth Longfellow, read the lyrics of Julia Ward Howe and Josephine Peabody with delight, and found the formal innovations of Emily Dickinson—let alone Walt Whitman—something of a puzzle. As Van Wienen notes, "genteel" has slipped into critical usage as a term which encompasses all "nonmodernist" verse from the early decades of the twentieth century and elides the variety and caustic intensity of these texts, which often provided powerful vehicles for political debate and dissent throughout a turbulent period of American's history.[84] In reality, the use of traditional forms and diction by such poets was often contrasted with unconventional perspectives, daring material, and very un-genteel judgments on society. Norton deserves more attention than she gets for a number of reasons. As a Midwestern, middle-class, college-educated American who had by 1914 traveled widely in Europe, developed liberal views, and immersed herself in the cultural life of bohemian New York, she offers a valuable view of the reactions of the intellectual and creative communities to the war. Caught in Brittany when the fighting broke out, like many other American visitors she fled home, watching events in Europe unfold from a distance with a frustration that found an outlet mostly through words. There are flashes of structural daring in Norton's poems about the war, challenges to the traditional forms of rhyme and meter, which point forward to the innovations of later poets such as Cummings, Borden, and MacLeish. However, her work, like that of the soldier-poet Alan Seeger, more often shows what was possible (and sometimes what was not) within the boundaries of conventional verse.

James might have provided a voice that offered a "trumpet blast." Norton, on the other hand called the American reader's attention to the eerie quiet that the war created in French provincial life. Her long, moving two-part poem about the outbreak of war, "The Mobilization in Brittany," both begins and ends in silence:

> It was silent in the street.
> I did not know until a woman told me,
> Sobbing over the muslin she sold me.
> Then I went out and walked to the square
> And saw a few dazed people standing there.[85]

After the drums and the bells and the shouting and the crying, and the troops at the station singing the Marseillaise, there is silence again and a question that no one can answer:

> The train went and another has gone, but none, coming, has
>   brought word.
> Though you may know, you, out in the world, we have not
>   heard,
> We are not sure that the great battalions have stirred—
>
> Except for something, something in the air,
> Except for the weeping of the wild old women of Finistère.
> How long will the others dream and stare?[86]

The poem's speaker concludes in resignation, "So this is the way of war." Here, it is not the battlefield that defines war, but the quiet despair of ordinary lives disrupted. The irregular lines, the interrupted metrical

patterns and the uncomfortable juxtaposition of harsh contemporary detail and dreamy idealism in her work, show Norton to be a poet working
hard to adapt the rules of her craft to the unsettled, distressing mood of
what she has witnessed. This is poetry with a backstory.

Norton's wartime experience—especially the chain of events by
which the publication of her anthology *What Is Your Legion?* (1916) became caught up with the campaign by many in the intellectual classes
for American intervention—illuminates the means by which writers, and
their publishers and distributors, used their work to attempt to shape
events around them. This attempt has often led to such work, like James's
essays, being characterized as propaganda. However, this term—which in
1914 did not carry such strong overtones of deliberate political deception
as it does now—oversimplifies the relationship between literary and political activity, particularly before April 1917. When one considers that
much material now labeled as "propaganda" was written in criticism of
the U.S. government, and distributed (as Norton's anthology was) in defiance of obstructions to the expression of public opinion about the war,
this issue suddenly seems less straightforward.

Grace Norton was born on 29 October 1876 in Northfield, Minnesota, and grew up in a family of strict Congregationalists affluent with
money made in local banking. Orphaned by the age of ten, Grace was
raised by a succession of aunts and uncles until her older sister Gertrude
married Fred Schmidt, an Episcopalian from nearby Faribault, regarded
by Norton's family as something of a "mythical sin-city," who banished
the censorial relatives from the family home.[87] Gertrude and Fred embraced new ideas—a few years later, they would buy the first automobile in
Northfield—and they encouraged Grace in her musical and literary enthu-
siasms. She was sent to Abbot Academy in Andover, and took piano lessons in Boston in defiance of her Norton and Scriver uncles, who thought
classical music a dangerous worldly pastime. The Schmidts, however, arranged for Grace to travel in Europe, staying with Fred's relatives in Swit-
zerland, visiting Norway, and studying piano in Berlin.[88] She returned to
America in the spring of 1899, and settled in New York City, struggling to
make a living as a piano accompanist, and trying to get her poetry pub-

lished. She once confessed that during this time she was so poor that her main source of income was making marbled endpapers for publishing houses.[89] But life was vivid and full of new contacts. She mixed with writers, painters, academics, and activists, and her friends ranged from the respected publisher Thomas Bird Mosher to the anarchist Emma Goldman. By 1909, she was married to Herman de Fremery, a curator at the Natural History Museum, and living uptown in 177th Street. In 1911, she traveled to France to stay with her husband's relatives. Here, she read avidly, soaking up Guy de Maupassant, Paul Bourget, and Théophile Gautier, "trying to learn the secrets of French poetry."[90] She began to write in earnest, and around this point also changed her name, not to Mrs. de Fremery, but to Grace Fallow Norton, adding the middle name partly for the sound, and also to distinguish herself from Grace Norton of the Cambridge Nortons, whose book *Studies in Montaigne* was published in 1904.

From 1910 until the late 1930s, Grace Fallow Norton's poetry appeared in respected literary journals such as the *Atlantic Monthly* and the *Century Magazine, Scribner's Magazine, Harper's Monthly Magazine, McClure's Magazine, Poetry Journal,* and *Poetry.* She struck up a good working relationship with the Boston publishers Houghton Mifflin, especially the editor and author Ferris Greenslet, who would remain her contact at the firm until 1927. In 1912, Houghton Mifflin published Norton's first anthology, *Little Gray Songs from St. Joseph's,* a series of poems about a young girl dying in an American convent. According to the *New York Times,* the little book was "a revelation of what genius can do with the ordinary and every-day things of life."[91] Modern readers find these poems sentimental and static. But there was something that caught the public imagination in Norton's selection of pain as a subject for verse, and there is a haunting, Dickinson-like quality in her plain vocabulary and in the simplicity of structure. This volume established Norton as a rising writer of promise, someone to watch in the coming years. Amy Lowell would list her in a group of noteworthy poets including Ezra Pound and Nicholas Vachel Lindsay: "poets with many differing thoughts and modes of thought," whose work demonstrated "the great vitality of poetry at the moment."[92] Houghton Mifflin quickly commissioned a second volume of verse.

However, just as Norton's career seemed to be blossoming, her personal world collapsed. No sooner had she dedicated *Little Gray Songs* to "H. de. F.," than their marriage broke down. In the spring of 1912, de Fremery began a relationship with Henrietta Rodman, a high school English teacher. Sometime in the same year, Norton also began a new romance with the young, controversial painter George Herbert Macrum. Divorce proceedings followed, and in February the following year de Fremery and Rodman were secretly married.[93] Macrum, an art student from Pittsburgh, two years younger than Norton, had already caused a stir by daring to exhibit a painting of a nude woman at a students' art exhibition in 1906.[94] He would later make his mark as a specialist in landscapes and urban scenes and would exhibit at a number of distinguished galleries and exhibitions, including the Whitney Museum of American Art, the Pennsylvania Academy, the Corcoran Gallery, and the Appalachian Expo at Knoxville, Tennessee, where he took a gold medal in 1911. His paintings nowadays change hands for up to ten thousand dollars—money that would have been bewilderingly welcome to Norton and Macrum during the coming years.

After the marriage, Norton completed *The Sister of the Wind* (1914), a substantial, second collection of poems, many of which dealt with the emotional upheaval of the previous months, and which also included her best-known poem "Love Is a Terrible Thing." Like so many of her works, this lyric concludes with a cry for personal freedom: "Oh, would I were free as the wind on the wing; / Love is a terrible thing."[95] By the time this book was in print, however, Norton and Macrum, now married and traveling as Mr and Mrs. Macrum, had left America. In May 1914, they sailed to Hamburg on the *Pennsylvania,* with plans to visit Paris and Brittany. Norton wrote to Greenslet from the boat: "Such a chance at France! I intend the most thorough intoxication. Anything less would be utterly ungrateful. . . . All repressed, strangled and mangled ex-Puritans should take the French bath."[96] Associated on the one hand with treasured rebellions from her family upbringing, and on the other with the sense of re-

lease and rejuvenation that accompanied her new relationship with
Macrum, France appeared to Norton a haven of style and creativity. As
she wrote to Mosher, "It's in the Touraine or in Bretagne that I'm hoping
my tongue will blossom without thorns."[97] She arrived with plans for a
third volume of verse, and in July, the couple took a house for three months
in Plomarche, near Finistère, where Macrum could paint in the clear light
of the Brittany coast. Like most other travelers in France that summer,
they had very little warning of what was about to happen next.

When mobilization was announced on 1 August, Norton was stunned
out of her creative reverie, into sharp observation of the situation of the
French people around her. Watching the grim enthusiasm for war and the
overnight militarization of what had seemed a peaceful and placid corner of
provincial France, Norton was both appalled and fascinated at the transfor-
mation. It prompted a series of nine poems, which initially seemed to her a
distraction from the set of lyrics about moods and colors which she was
working on for Greenslet: "Is This the End of the Journey?"; "The Mobilization in Brittany"; "The French Soldier and His Bayonet"; "The Journey";
"In This Year"; "The Volunteer"; "Cutting, Folding and Shaping"; "On
Seeing Young Soldiers in London"; and "O Peace, Where Is Thy Faithful
Sentry?" These poems would later find their ways into that same anthology,
Roads, as a section on the conflict entitled "The Red Road." It contains
some of her strongest work. All trace of sentimentality drops away from her
poetic style as she adopts the rough rhythms of the ancient ballad form in an
uncompromising portrait of the husband-turned-fighter:

The French Soldier and His Bayonet

Farewell, my wife, farewell, Marie,
I am going with Rosalie.

You stand, you weep, you look at me—
But you know the rights of Rosalie,

And she calls, the mistress of men like me!
I come, my little Rosalie,

My white-lipped, silent Rosalie,
My thin and hungry Rosalie!

Strange you are to be heard by me,
But I keep my pledge, pale Rosalie!

On the long march you will cling to me
And I shall love you Rosalie;

And soon you will leap and sing to me
And I shall prove you Rosalie;

And you will laugh, laugh hungrily
And your lips grow red, my Rosalie;

And you will drink, drink deep with me,
My fearless flushed lithe Rosalie!

Farewell, O faithful far Marie,
I am content with Rosalie.

She is my love and my life to me,
And your lone and my land—my Rosalie!

Go mourn, go mourn in the aisle, Marie,
She lies at my side, red Rosalie!

Go mourn, go mourn and cry for me.
My cry when I die will be "Rosalie!"[98]

This uncompromising poem gives a sophisticated reading of many of the racial and gender stereotypes which fuel the business of war. Not only does Norton step into the shoes of the male combatant speaker of the poem, thus abandoning a passive, observing, traditionally feminine perspective; she also appropriates that most phallic of weapons, the bayonet, and personifies it in female form. Here, Norton plays on the name of "Rosalie," the soldier's nickname for the bayonet issued by the French army, a slim, cruel, stiletto-like blade, designed for hand-to-hand fighting in the trenches. The form of the poem carries military echoes too. Its four-foot line with the mix of iambic and anapestic rhythms mimics the relentless

tramp of a traditional marching song, driven forward by direct speech
and repetition. However, Norton is not only appealing to the patterns of
the past. "The French Soldier and His Bayonet" is also a response to the
contemporary French song "Rosalie," by Théodore Botrel, a popular
singer of the belle époche. Botrel's lyrics, which came to prominence in the
fall of 1914, celebrate the French "cult of the bayonet," eroticizing the relationship between soldier, bayonet, and victim in complex and disturbing
ways:[99]

> Rosalie est élégante
> Sa robe-foureau collante,
> Verse à boire!
> La revêt jusqu'au quillon
> Buvons donc!
>
> Rosalie is elegant
> Her sheath-dress tight-fitting,
> Pour a drink!
> Adorns her up to the neck.
> Let us drink, then![100]

The many verses of this song, which Botrel performed regularly through
the war at French military camps during government-sponsored entertainments, explore the sexual connotations of wielding such a weapon: as
a rape, as a seduction, as the release of the heady red wine of the victim's
blood. Botrel's song plays on the French verb *piquer,* which means both to
pierce and to excite or stimulate, but under the surface, there is also a cultural anxiety about the seductive power of women, and a need to distance
the soldier psychologically from the act of killing; through this metaphor,
the grisly, intimate act of stabbing can be displaced and seen as the action
of the personified, female blade instead. Regina M. Sweeney notes that
Botrel's song was much imitated during the war, leading to a whole sub-
genre of "Rosalie" songs, matched by similar lyrics about "Mimi" the machine gun, or "Catherine" and "Nana" the field guns.[101] Yet, the bayonet

appears to have had a particularly vivid place in the French imagination. It was referred to as "the soldier's wife," perhaps because it stood by him when all else had failed. *La Baionette* was also the title of a French wartime journal, which published reports and polemics about the war, designed to rouse national feeling against Germany. Rosalie the bayonet was a powerful symbol of French patriotism, defiance, and hot-headed gallantry.

Likewise, Norton's poem engages with the sensuality of war and its exhilarating physicality. The speaker is a man roused by the adrenaline rush of the battlefield, although the doublings back in his expression, his expansive associations, and the dismissive treatment of his wife, Marie, also hint at intoxication with red wine as much as with the red blood of war. Like later, better-known, anglophone war poems, such as Alan Seeger's "Rendezvous" (1916) or Wilfred Owen's "Strange Meeting" (1919), Norton's poem portrays war as a tryst, an irresistible romantic encounter, but there is little tenderness here. Instead, Norton catches the swaggering, virile tone of the French military songs with their double entendres and forceful exclamation marks. The speaker in this poem has forgotten all sense of purpose or loyalty, and fights only for the thrill of it. Like a consuming, passionate affair, the business of fighting excludes the soldier from all other emotional claims, personal or patriotic. He rejects his role as husband and protector; he also defies the male brotherhood of his fellow soldiers by the shocking, forbidden presence of the female lover in the trenches.

Norton's poem, however, also harnesses conventional perspectives, playing these off the initial violence of the speaker's attitude. The husband chooses between a good wife and a tarnished mistress. The wife is mournful and silent. She does not speak. She only stands, weeps, and looks. The "aisle" of the church suggests her chasteness and virtue, and perhaps a newlywed status. The mistress, on the other hand, is drunken, sensual, and fearless. Virgin and whore—this poem plays on extreme moral archetypes of the kind Norton grew up with. The poem also plays on a racial stereotype. It depicts the *French* soldier and his bayonet, thus exploiting the Gallic reputation for sensuality and infidelity, and revealing a residual Congregationalist distrust, perhaps, of unrestrained sexuality. So, even as she engages with the eroticism of the French songs of the bayonet, Norton also critiques it, drawing attention to the collapse of relationships and communities caused by the war and the dangerous emotions which it arouses. Perhaps this focus on the French setting undermines the brutality of the poem, keeping it at an acceptable distance from its intended readership, in much the same way that the French bayonet songs were themselves designed to humorize and displace the horror of death. A British or American soldier would surely never behave this way? Or perhaps this dark portrayal of the French soldier signals a realization on Norton's part that France was no idealized nation after all, but rather was a complex social construction built up of conflicting social strata and profoundly flawed individuals. Either way, this poem offers a damning indictment of the brutalization of the citizen required by war on this scale, and it raises some powerful questions about the nature and the value of the "civilization" which so many men were leaving their families to defend.

Norton also explores a similar sense of division between male and female experience in her poem "Cutting, Folding and Shaping," inspired by a short stint of volunteering at a dressings workroom. As in "The Mobilization in Brittany," Norton explores new metrical irregularities and half-rhymes in this poem, as though to highlight that the cutting, folding, and shaping of dressings can never shape events, which unfold raggedly in futility and irony:

Cutting, Folding and Shaping

We have made hundreds of oakum-pads and dressings and
    compresses,
Cutting, folding and shaping, amid murmuring women's
    voices.
The woman beside me has lost two brothers, so they tell.
She tells no one. . . . She works well. . . .
The young girl beyond knows her lover will soon be sent;
He goes with the foreign regiment,
But her father is serving Austria at Trente.
They come here and make oakum-pads and dressings and
    compresses,

Cutting, folding and shaping, amid murmuring women's
voices.
I wish I were a great commander of the army,
Strong and rough and stormy.
The spirit of Lafayette would come to me
And I would go over the sea,
Sure of followers, crying, "Who will follow me!"
I am a pale Joan of Arc, seeing visions, hearing no clear
voices,
So I sit here and make oakum-pads and dressings and
compresses.[102]

It is the murmuring voices in this poem that seem the most troubling and
insistent, the quiet, whispering anxiety of lives left behind to wait, and the
frustration of inaction. The images of military glory from the past seem
irrelevant to the cruel, modern ironies of this war, and are remote to the
speaker of the poem, whose role is nothing more (though also nothing
less) than the careful folding of dressings to heal the wounds to come.

Norton, however, would not remain inactive in Brittany. She might
not be Joan of Arc, but she was restless enough to want to be moving,
and it seemed sensible to try to leave France and go home. However,
she and Macrum were not the only ones hoping for a place on a boat. At
the outbreak of the war, an estimated forty thousand Americans found
themselves marooned in Europe, almost eight thousand of these in Paris,
many without money as the banks suspended cable transfers of cash.[103]
Tickets were hard to obtain; trains and boats had been commandeered
to rush troops to the front. Foreign nationals were obliged to report to
the police, and to obtain visas. Even telegrams had to be vetted. It was
the same in Germany, where a young T. S. Eliot, who had enrolled for a
summer of study in Marburg, before undertaking postgraduate research at Oxford, found himself stranded for three weeks before securing a passage via Rotterdam back to England.[104] Slowly, however, an
eerie normality established itself. Those Americans who could made
plans to leave, many helped by the self-made millionaire Herbert Hoover,

whose makeshift agency operated from the Savoy Hotel in London, where he took it upon himself to organize a team capable of "getting the busted Yankee safely home," often lending his own money in order to do so.[105]

Norton and Macrum reached London in October. As there was no prospect of an immediate ship home, they went first to Cornwall where Macrum could paint. But the passage through London had fired Norton's imagination with the images of young soldiers enlisting for death, stories of atrocities in Belgium, rumors of ships lost at sea, and the sense that she needed to wake up and do something. It seemed to Norton that some female, life-giving force must have been sleeping while war was gathering, and that she herself had also been "lost in a murmuring verse." But now, she sensed, it was time to act. The final fourteen-line section of Norton's long poem in seven parts, "On Seeing Young Soldiers in London," offers a stark statement of disillusionment. It presents an apocalyptic image of geographical contraction and collapse, within a poetic form that is itself a ruin of the traditional sonnet structure:

VII

Once I cried, "The world is wide!"
But the world is wide no more. . . .
Shore breaks upon shore,
Tide baffles tide,
Hill rides over hill
Where the high hills were lying,
And on one plain the whole of the world is dying!
Yet up and down my soul, singing still,
(Death has stopped her laughter, can death stop her deeds?)
Life with red lips drives her wild strong steeds,
Denying and crying, crying,
"Go!"

O freedom, freedom, freedom,
I did not know I loved you so![106]

Here the red lips belong not to the hungry bayonet, the agent of death, but to life, a passionate force driving the speaker's soul forward—but to what? On one level, Norton's poetic spirit desired to strike a blow for "freedom" and to "go." Her own personal journey toward emotional freedom seemed to be symbolically caught up with the struggle for military dominance in Belgium and northern France. But like many other poets of the age, Norton was discovering that the noble vocabulary of verse and its symbolic resonances bore scant resemblance to the messy reality of modern mass warfare. For a start, how could one possibility afford "freedom" as a foreign neutral national traveling on scant finances? On consideration, the only sensible option seemed to be to head in the opposite direction. On 7 November, Mr. and Mrs. Macrum sailed prosaically from Liverpool on the *New York;* a week later they were back in America.

1915 — Volunteers

AT FIRST, IT HAD SEEMED A fine thing to be an American. Writing to Richard Norton in September 1914, Henry James felt able to write that the ambulance project made him "proud of your acquaintance, so to speak, and of our common nationality."[1] However, the issue of common nationality was quickly becoming a vexed one. To writers such as James and Wharton, whose cultural sympathies and literary interests were invested so heavily in Britain and France, it seemed natural, even necessary, that America, or at least individual Americans, should support the Allied cause against Germany. The morality of the situation appeared clear-cut. As James declared to Richard Norton, "I *care* unutterably that right should now be awfully achieved & the whole infamy rolled in the dust! Only, alas, what an amount of doing it will take!—not indeed that I doubt for a moment it will *be* done!" By the New Year, however, with military and political positions increasingly entrenched in Europe, it was getting harder to envisage infamy being rolled in the dust. It was also hard to see what America was *doing* to help, beyond the middle-class rush to form knitting circles. Politically, America was far from inactive, though it was operating in the dark. Since September 1914, White House insiders and the State Department had been involved in high-level diplomacy with both Germany and the Allies in the hope of brokering a peaceful end to hostilities. History, policy, and instinct all recommended neutrality to President Wilson: America's long-standing commitment to the Monroe Doctrine of 1823 discouraged meddling with the balance of power in Europe, unless America's interests were directly threatened; the nation was not armed for war on such a scale; it seemed more urgent to protect the interests of America's mercantile trade and shipping; and Wilson, thought-ful academic and devoted Christian that he was, leaned toward the moral high ground. Yet, he was also increasingly attracted to the idea of using America's detached status from the conflict to influence the shape of post-war Europe. In late January 1915, Colonel Edward Mandell House, Wil-son's confidant, adviser, and unofficial envoy, sailed to Europe for secret talks in Britain and Germany. But this was not the moment for peace. Every nation involved had already sacrificed too much to walk away from the conflict with nothing to show for it. Britain and France were planning spring offensives on the Western Front. Germany, having dug securely into the Flanders mud, turned its offensive powers east.[2] Neither side was much in the mood for talking.

In this climate of secrecy and uncertainty, Americans both at home and abroad chose their own loyalties. During 1915, many bitter divisions and frustrations within American society would bubble up to the surface. These often looked like responses to the war, but they were indicative of deeper problems of alienation and conflict across lines of gender, race, and class. The radical, left-wing labor movement the Industrial Workers of the World (known as the Wobblies), which advocated union organiza-tion and socialist reform, and which in 1912 had sponsored the violent tex-tile strike in Lawrence, Massachusetts, had continued to campaign for better conditions for lumber workers in the Northwest, and to raise other strikes and work-force protests. It swiftly denounced the war as a capital-ist money-spinner.[3] This view of events would only intensify later in the war, when the government cracked down on organized labor in reaction to the Russian Revolution.[4] In January 1915, no less than seventeen wom-en's organizations banded together to form the Women's Peace Party, with the social reformer Jane Addams as its national chair, raising a member-ship of over forty thousand within the year. Unlike the defiantly working-class IWW, this organization bridged class categories. It was also generously represented in the millionaire car-manufacturer Henry Ford's ill-starred Peace Ship mission to Europe in November, which collapsed the follow-ing month amid disorganization and infighting among the delegates.[5] Elsewhere, there was talk of "preparedness" by a range of individuals and organizations, some of whom lobbied for the stockpiling of arms, others for the militarization of the public, such as the Plattsburg movement, which organized voluntary summer training camps for the sons of middle- and upper-class families in Plattsburgh, New York. Meanwhile, writing in *Crisis,* W. E. B. Du Bois attempted to persuade the African-American community that, despite its origins in racist and imperialist exploitation and expansion, the war would create an opportunity to restructure modern society, which black people would be unwise to ignore.[6] German and Austrian communities, especially in the Midwest, called for the interests of the Central Powers to be considered alongside those of the Allies. In the pages of the *New Republic,* Randolph Bourne pointed out that "to refuse the patient German science, the collectivist art, the valor of the German ideals would be simply to expatriate ourselves from the modern world," though he saw what had happened to Belgium as the "ruthless hewing-through of might."[7]

This entire spectrum of reaction is visible in what Van Wienen calls the "partisan poetry" of the war, ranging from glib doggerel to experimental free verse, not always of high artistic merit, but consistently illuminating as an index of the ideological firefight that the war sparked in America. In 1915, the most successful of these lyrics was Bryan and Piantadosi's "I Didn't Raise My Boy to Be a Soldier," adopted as the unofficial anthem of the Women's Peace Party, and later countered by many parodies and ripostes, including "I Did Not Rear My Boy to Be a Coward," and the rather less earnest but equally antipacifist "I Didn't Raise My Dog to Be a Sausage."[8] Among protest material, there was also George Viereck's pro-German poem "The Neutral," which urged America to "stop this slaughter if thou wilt"; there was the *Little Red Song Book* of the IWW, whose song lyrics called for the solidarity of international workers against the violence of capitalism at home and abroad; and there were the antiwar poems of Louis Untermeyer and Carl Sandburg in the anarchist magazine the *Masses*—to name but a few.[9] Such breadth of opinion simply could not be voiced in books and magazines printed in the nations at war, governed as these now were by crushing censorship regulations. American poetry and prose, therefore, displayed a much richer variation of political views, and provided more graphic detail about the front line than the literature of the fighting nations—that is, until the curtain of American censorship came down in 1917. It would be a mistake, however, to read this diversity as evidence of public tolerance. Anti-German feeling often ran high, and led to harassment and violence, including lynchings, against German-Americans, especially after the publication in May 1915 of the Bryce Report, by the respected British peer Lord Bryce, which appeared to confirm atrocities against civilians by German troops in Belgium.[10] Printed in every conceivable form of publication, from large-circulation newspapers, to literary journals, school magazines, and church newsletters, the sheer wealth of poetry, fiction, and polemical prose produced in America about the war demonstrated, not only the range of emotions and allegiances it triggered, but also the deep-seated cultural instinct that connected war with literary expression. There never was a battle but someone wrote a song about it.

Less bloody than the fighting in Europe, but in some ways just as fierce, this ideological tussle was a battle about the character and the future of America, and in particular about how it projected its national values abroad. Nor was it clear, in such a swiftly changing society, exactly what those values were. In the later stages of the war, the pro-Allied stance would be equated with "patriotism"—by government agencies at any rate—but this was far from settled in 1915. No voice shouted louder for this equation than that of the former President Theodore Roosevelt. As one of the signatories to the Hague Conventions of 1899 and 1907, which guaranteed the safety of neutral nations, undefended cities, and unarmed civilians, Roosevelt was outraged by Wilson's tame reluctance (as he saw it) to discipline Germany's breaches of international morality: "Force must be put back of justice, and nations must not shrink from the duty of proceeding by any means that are necessary against wrongdoers," he thundered.[11] America's duty was to prepare for conflict, not just to defend itself, but also to be "ready and willing to act as a member of the international *posse comitatus* to enforce the peace of righteousness as against any offender big or small."[12] The Latin phrase fooled no one; Roosevelt's idea was to apply the rough but simple justice of the Wild West to the tangle of European western shore of the Atlantic were precisely those felt most keenly by the Americans who found themselves east of it in 1915. Wilson's policy of neutrality had both its merits and its faults, but for the exiled literary community, it certainly allowed the luxury—unavailable to writers of warring nations—of time to consider a response. Not harried into polarized positions, either for or against the war, as younger writers such as Dos Passos and Cummings would be in 1917, American writers in Europe dispersed across a remarkable range of opinions and activities in 1915. Alan Seeger continued his voluntary service with the French Foreign Legion. Robert Frost and his young family settled in the countryside of the Malvern Hills. T. S. Eliot found little to say about the war in his letters home from Oxford as he worked on his master of arts dissertation on the philosophy of F. H. Bradley—although he would take a closer interest after his marriage to Vivienne Haigh-Wood in the summer.[16] Ezra Pound's energies continued to be devoted to his writing and editorial projects. His main priority, as he expressed it to the collector John Quinn, was "to get on with our Renaissance," and in the poem "Hugh Selwyn Mauberley" (1920) he would later dismiss the "botched civilization" for which so many died as "an old bitch gone in the teeth."[17] Nevertheless, Pound's personal letters also express reservations about the wisdom of American neutrality, and as late as 1918 he could talk about "civilization against barbarism" without apparent irony.[18] The poet Hilda Doolittle (H.D.), married to the British writer Richard Aldington, was thrust into the emotionally exhausting role of war wife when he enlisted, a role which assumed a tragic tone when her first child was stillborn in mid-May 1915—a loss which she blamed on the shock of hearing the news about the sinking of the *Lusitania*.[19] She also worked on her first collection of poems, *Sea Garden,* in which the themes of grief, imprisonment, and conflict lurk under the surface, although the war is never explicitly treated. Gertrude Stein and her companion Alice B. Toklas left their home in Paris and spent the next year touring in Spain.[20] Mildred Aldrich, having seen out the First Battle of the Marne in her farmhouse in Huiry, settled in to wait out the war, and to write up her best-selling memoir, *A Hilltop on the Marne,* published in October 1915, and already in its sixth impression by December. James, Wharton, and

Borden, however, all shared the feeling that this was no time to be an American observer on the sidelines of European history. James would eventually wonder whether this was the time to be an American at all. Disillusioned with American political leadership, attracted by the camaraderie of service, haunted by the scale of suffering, and inspired to help as they could, all three faced difficult choices about where to place their allegiances and their energies. Not least of these was the problem of how, as a writer, one could do something useful with words in a world which seemed to have lost all meaning. James had written to Charles Eliot Norton many years before: "It's a complex fate being an American."[21] This was never more true than in 1915.

Riding into Glory

In her autobiography *A Backward Glance* (1934), Wharton recalls how after the end of the war, on 14 July 1919, she stood on a balcony in the Champs Elysées and watched the victorious Allied armies ride under the Arc de Triomphe and on to the Place de la Concorde. It was all "a golden blur of emotion," and the details would fade, she knew, but astutely she recognized that her response to this demonstration of grandeur had a parallel with her own literary instincts: "As I stood there," she wrote, "high over the surging crowds and the great procession, the midsummer sun blinding my eyes, and the significance of that incredible spectacle dazzling my heart, I remembered what [Henri] Bergson had once said of my inability to memorize great poetry: 'You're dazzled by it.'"[22] This response was characteristic of everything that Wharton wrote about the war. She was dazzled by it, too, but she refused to look away. Just as it seems never to have occurred to Wharton to abandon France during the war, and retire to the safety of Britain or America, it also seems never to have occurred to her that she might not write about the conflict. Others might feel that there was nothing to say about the fighting, but silence was simply not in Wharton's vocabulary.

Early in 1915, the French Red Cross asked her "to report on the needs of some military hospitals near the front."[23] This was by no means

a straightforward request. Civilians, especially foreigners, were not permitted in the militarized zone without special passes, troops were continually on the move, and there was anxiety both public and official about
the role of foreign spies. There was also the physical danger of the war to
consider—not regarded as suitable for ladies. Once Wharton had set her
mind on something, however, not many people could resist her. Percy
Lubbock would later describe her as "the dear great lady to whom none
said nay."[24] If she wanted to visit the front, neither military red tape nor
the bloodiest war in history would stop her. Wharton always had friends
in the right places, and after some diplomacy by the distinguished novelist
Paul Bourget, who was a member of the Académie Française, and an intervention on her behalf by Jules Cambon, the secretary general of the
Ministry of Foreign Affairs, she was given clearance to travel into the territory northeast of Paris.

On 27 February, she packed some medical supplies, and her indispensable companion Walter Berry into the forty-horsepower Mercedes
(affectionately known as *She*), which Berry had worked so hard to keep
out of army hands the previous summer, and set off for Chalons and Verdun, both swarming with troops and ambulances.[25] Cook, her loyal and
laconic New England chauffeur, was in the driving seat; and Mildred
Bliss, wife of Robert Bliss, the secretary of the American embassy in Paris,
and Victor Bérard, both of whom were also involved in Red Cross work,
came too. Wharton wrote excitedly to James from Verdun the next day
about all that she had seen: the miserable hospital in Chalons "with 900
cases of typhoid, where *everything* was lacking"; Sister Rosnet, the un-
flappable nun in the hospice at Clermont-en-Argonne, who had refused to
leave her charges when the Germans invaded; the flashes of firing in the
wood across the valley; the priest in Blercourt who conducted vespers in
the village church as his congregation stood among the rows of wounded
lying in beds on the floor; and the strange wailing hymn that the villagers
sang, "Sauvez, sauvez la France, Ne l'abandonnez pas!"[26] James wrote back
at once, encouraging Wharton to write up her impressions. "Do it," he insisted, "*do* it, my blest Edith, for all you're worth."[27] But by the time his
letter arrived, she had already left for a second trip, returning with supplies

to the region beyond Verduns: shirts, eggs, oranges, gauze pads, dressing gowns. The war-ravaged landscape seemed even bleaker than before, and the little makeshift "ambulances," or medical stations, rigged up in the muddy villages seemed even more pathetic. "Picture this," she wrote to James when she got back, "all under a white winter sky, driving great flurries of snow across the mud-&-cinder-coloured landscape, with the steel-cold Meuse winding between beaten poplars—Cook standing with Her [the car] in a knot of mud-coated military motors & artillery horses, soldiers coming & going, cavalrymen riding up with messages, poor bandaged creatures in rag-bag clothes leaning in doorways, & always, over & above us, the boom, boom, boom of the guns on the grey heights to the east."[28] In one village they visited a church full of *eclopés,*—worn out, exhausted soldiers recuperating after their ordeal in the trenches. They slept in their uniforms on a floor covered in straw. "It is not a hospital," she told James, "but a human stable."[29]

Wharton was beginning to realize the uses to which she could put these impressions and experiences. She saw that, as the war dragged on, American magazine readers would only continue to give money for humanitarian causes if they could be given some vivid sense of what was happening in the war zone. Like many American intellectuals on both sides of the Atlantic, Wharton sided with Roosevelt in viewing Germany's actions as an outrage, not just against Belgium and France, but against America itself. Even James had surprised himself by his sympathy with Roosevelt's position: "Mr. Roosevelt is far from being dear to me," he wrote to his sister-in-law in February 1915, "but I can't *not* agree with his contention that the U.S.'s sitting down in meekness and silence under the German repudiation of every engagement she solemnly took with us, as the initiatory power in the Hague convention, constitutes an unspeakable precedent, and makes us a deplorable figure."[30] Wharton, who had long admired Roosevelt, felt less ambivalence about supporting his calls for decisive military intervention, and about courting popular sympathy for the plight of France. In the opening days of the war, as the French capital plunged into the ordered disruption of mobilization, Wharton had telegraphed her publisher Charles Scribner: "Detained in Paris. Extraordinary sights. Do you want impressions?"[31] He did—but the telegram he sent to her asking for them went awry in the general chaos of early August, and for the next few months, Wharton had been too busy to think much about writing—although she had been sharply alert to what was going on around her. Contractually, she was supposed to be completing a novel for Scribner called *Literature*, about the American world of letters, but like James's novel *The Ivory Tower*, it would never be finished. The pre-war world it described no longer seemed important. In February, she had finally written up her impressions of Paris during the first days of the conflict in a piece entitled "The Look of Paris," which appeared in *Scribner's* in May, but this material was now several months old and much had changed since then. After seeing the war zone, Wharton was inspired with a new and urgent need to capture the immediate situation. Even before James had urged her to put her experiences on paper, she had telegraphed Scribner, alerting him to the fact that she was sending more material his way. But she knew that she needed the cooperation of the military authorities if she was going to see anything of dramatic interest and get to the frontline trenches. M. Cambon talked the matter over with the French top brass, and decided that even if Wharton should discover anything of military sensitivity, "there would be little risk of its betrayal in articles which could not possibly be ready for publication until several months later."[32] Wharton was given permission to visit "the whole fighting line, all the way from Dunkerque to Belfort," although there were some restrictions on giving precise details about people and places. Wharton cared little about that; it was the searing impression that she wanted to capture, in order to "bring home to American readers some of the dreadful realities of war."[33]

The result was a set of three further articles for *Scribner's*, published between June and November, which were then printed along with the Paris piece and two more essays as a single volume, *Fighting France* (1915). It is a difficult book to categorize. The six texts are referred to by different critics as essays, articles, reportage, journals, autobiography, or travel writing, and yet throughout them there are also the linking motifs, the vivid metaphors and causal statements that belong to fiction or political rhetoric. Wharton was not a natural journalist; she was too close to those in power to challenge the veracity of their narratives. She also found it hard to detach her emotions from what she was describing—which is both the strength and the weakness of these texts. As Colm Toibin observes, "Wharton's novelist's eye for the perfect detail is matched in these reports with a sense of moral grandeur and warlike fervour, which makes her book an important document not only about the state of the front but of the state of mind of a woman who passionately and idealistically supported the war."[34] This is something of a double-edged remark; details and moral grandeur are all very well on paper, but most of us live somewhere in between these extremes of scale; and the average soldier or civilian of 1915 may have cared little about either. Strangely, there are few glimpses in Wharton's writing from the front of average human figures, those same figures toward whom her humanitarian response in Paris was so warm. Teresa Gómez Reus and Peter Lauber acknowledge that Wharton avoids "open brutality and bitterness," and has little to say about "the horrific injuries she is bound to have witnessed." However, they ascribe this stance to a respect for French censorship and of the tendency (already observed in Walter Berry) for those who had seen the front to underplay its horrors.[35] Yes, these factors probably did play their part in shaping Wharton's tone, but it may be unwise to make assumptions about what she must have seen. Wharton's travels were all officially sanctioned and, even by her own account, were stage-managed by a military system which had already grown adept at controlling visitors to the trenches and thus the stream of information emerging from the war zone. According to Wharton, she and her party "had always been told beforehand where we were going and how much we were to be allowed to see."[36] As she swept through the militarized zone in her motor car to afternoon tea with officers at a predetermined destination, Wharton was as much a victim of the vast wartime propaganda machine as she was an agent of it.

In May, she took her third trip to the front, a harrowing visit to Lorraine and the Vosges, through the devastated town of Gerbéviller where civilians had been murdered the previous fall, and others had survived only by chance or inventiveness. The mayor's family, trapped in their cellar by a fire which the invading Germans had started in the house above, had fed the flames for three days with every scrap of wood they could find to stop the soldiers getting through to shoot them. In the end, the village was reclaimed by the French, and this family was now back living in that same cellar, trying to rebuild the house and tend their garden. They sent Wharton away with a bouquet of peonies. The next day at Pont-à-Mousson, beyond Nancy, Wharton was shown what she had come to see, but in reality could not even glimpse. "*There* they are," said the guiding officer, "and *there*—and *there.*" But to the untrained eye there was only the rolling countryside. "We strained our eyes obediently, but saw only calm hillsides, dozing farms. It was as if the earth itself were the enemy, as if the hordes of evil were in the clods and grass-blades."[37] Like Norton imagining the earth disordered and contracted, Wharton, protected from the human reality of death and violence in the scene, projected her fears and those of her readers onto the natural environment. However, the lurking sense of inhuman evil and imminent danger which she paints here would have been ironically undercut for subscribers of *Scribner's,* had they already read the March issue of the journal. This carried a piece by the American correspondent James F. J. Archibald, who viewed the very same section of the front, but from the German lines, replicating Wharton's experience, but in a different context and with an opposing political backdrop. Archibald was full of praise for the efficiency of the German army, and their treatment of foreign correspondents. He noted that Richard Harding Davis had recorded the difficulty of reporting from sites of military significance held by British forces, and added, "He should have taken seats in the other grand-stand, for on our side we have been shown all that we could expect and given every possible liberty within military reason."[38] Clearly, in the spring of 1915, this region, where the front largely followed the line of the old border between France and Germany, was not a scene of intense military activity, but a relatively stable sector, showcased by both armies as a model of good practice. Archibald's accounts also suggest that, early in the war, the editorial policy of *Scribner's* was to report even-handedly from both sides of the conflict. However, pro-German and pro-

Austrian pieces, such as those by Archibald, disappeared abruptly from the magazine after the sinking of the *Lusitania* in May 1915.

Three days after the visit to Pont-à-Mousson, Wharton's party was directed to a secret location up in the wooded hills. Wharton saw the dugouts where the French soldiers lived, the *"villages nègres,"* some so established that the semi-underground houses had glass in the windows and flowers growing outside. They seemed "jolly little settlements," but deep bowels cut into the soil led down to the trenches, from which Wharton looked out once more into an apparently peaceful landscape:

> The sharp shooter had stopped firing, and nothing disturbed the leafy silence but an intermittent drip of rain. We were at the end of the burrow, and the Captain signed to me that I might take a cautious peep round its corner. I looked out and saw a strip of intensely green meadow just under me, and a wooded cliff rising abruptly on its other side. That was all. The wooded cliff swarmed with "them," and a few steps would have carried us across the interval; yet all about us was silence, and the peace of the forest. Again, for a minute, I had the sense of an all-pervading, invisible power of evil, a saturation of the whole landscape with some hidden vitriol of hate. Then the reaction of unbelief set in, and I felt myself in a harmless ordinary glen, like a million others on an untroubled earth.[39]

To reassure her of the reality of the war, Wharton is invited to look through the peephole, as though at a fairground show, at "a grey uniform huddled in a dead heap" at the bottom of the glen. Her excited horror at the sight of this single German corpse rather suggests that she has been spared the sight of anything much worse. One should also remember that Wharton has only the captain's word for it that she is at the front line at all. Nevertheless, the sequence of Wharton's travels along the front has clearly crafted a set of powerful responses that she diligently re-creates in her text: outrage, compassion, hope, suspense, fear, reassurance. And this sense of reassurance and faith in the men of France is the tonic chord to which she returns at the end of each of these essays. This moment at the seeming edge of civilization makes her feel "that on the far side of that dividing line were the men who had made the war, and on the near side the men who had been made by it."[40]

Wharton, however, was not only a passive spectator at the front; she was also herself an object of observation, and not just to the soldiers, who were clearly amused and possibly also impressed at the determination of this well-heeled, middle-aged woman to get as close to the danger as anyone would let her. On this third trip, Wharton and Berry were accompanied by the French cartoonist Abel Faivre, who captured them vividly in a cartoon, "Dans les ruines," subsequently published on the cover of the satirical comic *Le Rire Rouge*. Berry sits looking on moodily, as a stout and imperious Wharton stands in the car looking back through a lorgnette at the devastation of the war above the caption, "Ce n'est que ça!"—"Is that all?"[41] Lee observes that the placing of this cartoon on the cover of the magazine suggests what a recognizable figure Wharton had become in Paris.[42] Alternatively, the comedy for many readers may simply have been at the expense of the American trench tourist in the abstract—but the image works either way. The fact that Wharton seems to have taken no offense to this visual satire also suggests that her own attitudes to publicity and self-promotion were shifting dramatically in the context of the war. She also appeared in one of the photographs that accompanied "In Lorraine and the Vosges" in the October issue of *Scribner's*—an incongruous figure in a long skirt, with a parasol and a neatly angled hat standing by a wattle fence with two French soldiers in the background.[43]

By the time of this trip, however, Wharton had a new and pressing need for publicity and for the funds which it could generate. In April, she had been asked by the Belgian Ministry of the Interior to take in sixty Belgian orphans within the next forty-eight hours. Ever quick and capable, Wharton located and equipped a schoolhouse in Sèvres, close to Paris, where the hungry and traumatized children could be cared for. Many of them had been found in the cellars of shelled houses or on abandoned farms. Two little girls had been lifted from the arms of their dead

2. Edith Wharton photographed near French lines on one of her
tours of the front in 1915. From "At a French Pallisade," *Scribner's*.

father. Wharton's response to their needs was so successful that she was
soon asked to take in another six hundred children. This resulted in the
formation of a new charity, the Children of Flanders Rescue Committee,
which Wharton described as "my prettiest and showiest and altogether
most appealing charity."[44] It seems an odd way to describe any activity

born out of such terrible loss and despair, but Wharton was increasingly fixated on questions of presentation and show, and on the ways in which the war made public the most intimate or banal details of so many lives. This was a theme to which she returned again and again in her pieces for *Scribner's*. Traveling in northern France and Belgium in June, she was confronted in Dunkirk with the sight of a "poor bourgeois house that had had its whole front torn away." Only two days before, on 21 June, her party had driven through the town and stopped for tea in the Place Jean Bart. The destruction of this middle-class home seemed worse to Wharton than the fate of the church in the next street, which had been half ripped apart, because a personal, domestic world had been laid bare: "The squalid revelation of caved-in floors, smashed wardrobes, dangling bedsteads, heaped-up blankets, topsy-turvy chairs and stoves and washstands was far more painful than the sight of the wounded church. St. Eloi was draped in the dignity of martyrdom, but the poor little house reminded one of some shy humdrum person suddenly exposed in the glare of a great misfortune."[45] This was a house that had been "thrown open" in a very different way to the intrusion of a paying concert audience into Wharton's private world, but to her the two events overlapped in their disregard for the boundaries and decencies of the past.

It is no surprise that Wharton, with her long interest in living spaces and environments, should react so sensitively to the destruction of houses within the war zone, although readers disagree as to whether she really gave sufficient consideration to the fate of the people who lived in them.[46] Sharon Dean, for example, interprets Wharton's strategy as a preference for "the aesthetics of the scene" over any sense of "empathy" with the people within it.[47] However, one should remember how few people other than soldiers there actually were in the places that Wharton describes. These were the same towns and villages which had been abandoned by the thousands of refugees now flooding into Paris. For Wharton, it was the very emptiness of the buildings in the war zone that made them eerie and poignant, but also weirdly beautiful.

Dean's complaint about Wharton's aesthetic focus is an unusual one, as many critiques of *Fighting France* condemn it for its partisan sentimentality and absence of artistic detachment. So, this judgment is worth a second look, partly because it rests on the assumption so prevalent in literary scholarship since the First World War that the true artist cannot be both empathetic *and* aesthetic. It may be the structural flaw of *Fighting France* that Wharton attempts to hold together these two strands of human response at the very point in history at which they were inexorably pulling apart. It is also what makes the book worth reading. Within its pages, the reader is immersed in the confused emotional world of the early stages of the war; the cultural expectations of an established generation are set cheek-by-jowl against the reinventions of category and expression which the sheer scale of the conflict was beginning to demand. It would have been thrilling to read in 1915 by an audience that had few preconceptions, as modern-day readers do, of the kind of war that was taking place, or of the forms and images in which it should be rendered.[48] If it seems to us now to look back to a more cohesive or conventional moment, it must have seemed at the time to signal a shift forward into new and unsettling literary territories. Wharton's recurring use of the motif of the violated house with its incongruous and trivial contents strewn around it, can be read as a precursor of the absurdist and surreal descriptions of the front that would proliferate in the accounts of later eyewitnesses such as Borden or La Motte, or participants in the war such as Edmund Blunden or Henri Barbusse. Wharton also offers entry points into the strangely attractive landscape of war through the vocabulary of the high culture of the past, the very "civilization" that is worth fighting for. The soldiers silhouetted against the beach at La Panne are like "a black frieze of warriors encircling the dun-coloured flanks of an Etruscan vase"; the bugles sounded for mess issue a call that "was like the call of Roland's horn"; and the Indian soldiers marching to the front wear "delicate, proud faces like the faces of princes in Persian miniatures."[49] This was not yet Eliot's Waste Land, in which the images and forms of a classical past collide with the modern moment and fragment in confusion, as though reflected in a shattered mirror— but there is something oddly similar in Wharton's repeated, and sometimes unwieldy, juxtaposition of ancient and contemporary, a technique she would use to striking effect, and with more irony and disillusionment, in her pears to have encountered a sight worth seeing. This is the sort of passage which Wharton's sharpest critics dismiss as "propaganda," and indeed she uses a technique here that Benedict Anderson identifies as a classic strategy of the propagandist: the shining, archaic imagery offers the reader "intimations of immortality" by linking the present through language to the heroes and idylls of the past.[52] This strategy is repeated and intensified in the final essay, "The Tone of France," in which Wharton attempts to analyze what makes France so distinctive and so admirable. France is worthy of sacrifice, she argues, because its people value intelligence, expression, and courage. Nevertheless, despite the pretense of accuracy, her categories remain abstract and equally applicable to any other nation of the world: "Never for an instant has this people, so expert in the great art of living, imagined that life consisted in being alive. Enamoured of pleasure and beauty, dwelling freely and frankly in the present, they have yet kept their sense of larger meanings, have understood life to be made up of many things past and to come, of renunciation as well as satisfaction, of traditions as well as experiments, of dying as much as of living."[53] Wharton's France is, as Anderson would call it, an "imaginary community" existing everywhere and nowhere, yet appealing to powerful psychological drives— and as such capable of inspiring dangerous actions.

But there is little point complaining about the high color of Wharton's rhetoric. For many writers and readers, this *was* the tone of 1915, the tone of Rupert Brooke's sonnets and Alan Seeger's verse, of Roosevelt's polemics and many a newspaper editorial. Wharton's imagery and language were partly shaped by the controlled nature of her experiences at the front, but they were also subject to the tastes and cultural expectations of her American editors and readership at that particular historical moment. As Noam Chomsky and Edward Herman have noted, in a democratic society the flow of information about controversial events is governed by market forces as much as it is by any centralized process of conspiracy and censorship. It is the "cultural elite" of the publishing world and readers themselves who determine what is printed and read—even to a certain extent what is written in the first place.[54] Inevitably, these tastes and demands look back to the habits and securities of the past, especially in times of turbulence and upheaval. Wharton gave many American readers what they wanted in these pieces, a blend of unease and reassurance, of horror and glory, and appears to have been conscious of what she was doing. She had few qualms about describing her writing as "good propper-gander," and initially at least was not very rigorous in questioning the nationalistic stereotypes and accounts of atrocities which flooded the press after August 1914.[55] However, the expectations of her readers were changing swiftly, as more vivid and violent reports emerged from the front. As the war progressed Wharton's editors, Charles Scribner and Robert Bridges, increasingly tried to steer her back to producing fiction. In response to one of her offers of material from the front, Scribner cabled back tersely, "Prefer short story."[56] For each of her short stories published during the war she was paid a thousand dollars, while her descriptive articles earned only five hundred dollars a piece.[57] Wharton's advocates generally read this response as a symptom of a conservative editorial policy at *Scribner's*. However, some of the material which appears alongside Wharton's essays suggests that the opposite was in fact the case. Indeed, Scribner may have been shrewd in suspecting that Wharton was likely to be protected from the stark realities of trench warfare, and that her real value to his readers lay in her ability to explore the emotional impact of the war on the civilian world behind the trenches. He was certainly willing to publish controversial and graphic accounts of the fighting. For example, in October 1915, E. Alexander Powell's article "On the British Battle Line," which appeared within a few pages of "In Lorraine and the Vosges," gave an unflinching account of shell fire, gas attacks, shrapnel wounds, and the conditions at an evacuation hospital at Bailleul. Powell's account of the horrific injuries inflicted by modern mechanized warfare left little to the imagination, and his sharp, detached voice presented the impact of the war on the individual soldier in a style that would become familiar in later accounts of the war, both fictional and factual. "In the hallway of the hospital," he wrote, "a man was sitting upright on a bench, and two surgeons were working over him. He was sitting there because the operating-rooms were filled. I hope that that man is unmarried, for he no longer has a face. What a few hours before had been the honest countenance of an English lad was now a horrid welter of blood and splintered bone and mangled flesh."[58] Powell's pared down syntax and harsh vocabulary, stripped of any epic allusion, gave *Scribner's* readers a view of the war without heroism or idealism. This was exactly the kind of view which wartime censorship would deny to British and French readers until after the fighting had ceased, and which would be rigorously suppressed by the CPI in America after April 1917. Juxtaposed as it is with Wharton's account, Powell's article throws into stark relief the limitations and absences in her reports. Those who issued Wharton's travel passes, however, had less control over what she could hear, which perhaps accounts for the fact that the most vivid metaphor in her book (also an architectural one) is reserved for the sound of the big siege gun at Dixmude: "a noise that may be compared—if the human imagination can stand the strain—to the simultaneous closing of all the iron shop shutters in the world."[59] Had she been exposed to more of the grim realities of the war zone, who can guess what she might have written? But Wharton was a well-dressed woman in her fifties, busy doing what little she could to alleviate a major humanitarian emergency. She was always going to turn her car around and drive back to Paris, to the world she understood so well. Besides, there were plenty of other younger women willing to volunteer for the front.

Into the Forbidden Zone

In late January 1915, a small, neat woman traveling with two nurses arrived at the casino of Malo-Les-Bains at the seaside resort of Dunkirk. They had not come to play the gaming tables; they had come to dice with death. Inside, amid the dilapidated grandeur, lay over two hundred French soldiers with typhoid, and these three women had come to take care of them. Mary Borden-Turner was from Chicago (Stein once described her as "very Chicago"), and she was twenty-eight years old when she volunteered as a nurse with the French Red Cross.[60] She had left behind in London a complicated and glamorous life: a house in Park Lane; her Scottish husband, Douglas Turner, a former missionary who was shortly to take up a role as an interpreter with an Indian cavalry regiment; three small daughters, the youngest of whom was only eight weeks old; a broken-down love affair with the writer and painter Wyndham Lewis; and a promising career as a novelist.[61] She had no experience of nursing, but she spoke a little French. She was beautiful, she was rich, and, like Wharton, she was used to getting what she wanted. She had not believed that the war would start, but now that it was a reality she wanted to do something about it. However, she soon discovered that what awaited her in the makeshift hospital was not a calm opportunity of service, but "a place of nightmare." Years later she would remember it vividly:

> The sick lay helpless under the great tarnished chandeliers of the gaming rooms, the rows of dingy beds were reflected to infinity in the vast gilded mirrors. There were no nurses until we arrived and nothing to nurse with; no feeding cups, no urinals, no bedpans. Even the dying must crawl out of bed and sit on open pails. The wind howled up the beach beyond the great windows, but the stench in the rooms made one vomit. I would run every so often behind my screen to be sick, go for a moment to one of the broken panes in the glass verandah to breathe the fresh salt air from the sea, then hurry back to that dim purgatory of gaunt heads, imploring eyes and clutching hands.[62]

The women did what they could, and Borden picked up some basic skills from the two trained nurses, whose expenses she was paying from her own pocket, but it was a heartbreaking task. At the start of the war, France had planned for around twenty-five thousand casualties; six months into the war, over half a million men were sick or wounded. The lack of resources and the elaborate bureaucracy frustrated Borden's efforts at every turn—although she found the French soldiers admirable. Eventually, she broke down in tears in front of Colonel Morier, the chief of staff for the French Eighth Army, who offered her an alternative. Would she like to have her own hospital? She should write to the French commander-in-chief General Joffre, "What? Write to General Joffre?" she responded, "But yes, why not?"[63] So, with characteristic flair, Borden found herself, within a few weeks, in charge of a field hospital attached to the Eighth Army. It was a unit of 160 beds, for which the army provided surgeons and orderlies. Borden paid for the equipment and supplies herself out of the private fortune which she had inherited from her father, William Borden, a mining and property magnate, who had left her assets worth around ten thousand pounds a year. Like Wharton, she also enlisted her friends and family in America as sponsors and fund-raisers. She stipulated that, as *directrice* of the hospital, she should have authority over the women employed there, and the right to appoint her own nurses—despite the reluctance of the French army to allow foreign nurses to tend to French patients. It was an immense undertaking, but as Borden wrote to her mother back home, it was also "the thing that every woman in England would give her eyes to get and can't get."[64] She was exaggerating, of course, but there were indeed many women who would gladly have taken Borden's place. So confident was the War Office in London of its own male-dominated facilities and procedures, that it refused offers of medical help and organization from a number of British women, perhaps most famously from the pioneering Scottish surgeon Elsie Inglis, who on volunteering to provide a hospital at the front for the British army was told, "My good woman, go home and sit still."[65] Undaunted, Dr. Inglis went on to establish the Scottish Women's Hospitals for Foreign Service, which ran fourteen field hospitals with all-female staff in France, Russia, and Serbia during the war. Dr. Inglis, however, was a trained professional in her fifties, with twenty-five years of medical experience. Clearly, Borden had some catching up to do. Nevertheless, she had energy and passion, she was a quick learner, and her years in India with Turner had given her a belief in her own resourcefulness.

By July 1915, Hôpital Chirurgical Mobile No. 1 was ready for service, and was set up in a green field near Rousbrugge in Belgium, between Ypres and Dunkirk, some seven miles behind the front but still within "la zone interdite," the militarized "forbidden zone" off-limits to civilians. There were seventeen members of staff, including twelve nurses recruited from America, Britain, Canada, and Australia. These included Agnes Warner, the apparently frail but redoubtable, gray-haired, head nurse, a graduate of New York's Presbyterian Hospital, who would stay with Borden's unit till the end of the war; and Ellen La Motte, who had trained as a tuberculosis nurse at Johns Hopkins in Baltimore and had been working for several months at the American Hospital at Neuilly. In the first six months, the hospital accommodated over eight hundred critically wounded men, with only sixty-eight deaths. It was the best survival rate of the entire front, and Borden was told that wounded French soldiers pleaded to be sent to her hospital.[66] As it was a mobile unit, the entire hospital, including the huts and the operating theater could be packed up onto trucks and take to the road within a few hours. But so static had the military situation at the front become that the green field near Rousbrugge would be home for over a year. The field, however, would not stay green for long. When Borden, with her literary instincts sharpened to intensity by the experience of war, came to write about the hospital, what she began with was the mud:

Mud: and a thin rain coming down to make more mud.

Mud: with scraps of iron lying in it and the straggling fragment of a nation, lolling, hanging about in the mud on the edge of disaster.

It is quiet here. The rain and the mud muffle the voice of the war that is growling beyond the horizon. But if you listen you can hear cataracts of iron pouring down channels in the sodden land, and you feel the earth trembling.[67]

These lines would become the opening of *The Forbidden Zone,* Borden's startling and experimental account of her impressions of the war. Bitter and vivid, yet lyrical, this book is rarely celebrated as one of the great texts of the First World War—but that is what it is. Borden witnessed and endured a dramatic series of military crises: Ypres, the Somme, and the Nivelle Offensive at le Chemin des Dames. Few war writers, combatant or observer, have struck such a fine balance between the intensity of personal recollection and the exacting demands of art. Borden's book, like its author, is remarkable. As with Wharton's *Fighting France,* it does not

fit readily into any standard genre: memoir, autobiography, fiction, poetry, prose. It is easy enough for a careful reader to map the technical devices by which Borden unsettles the narrative progression of her text, but
it is not so simple to explain why these devices produce such a powerful
effect on the reader. Nor can one confidently use this text to locate Borden's ideological position on issues such as national identity, gender, or
even the legitimacy of the war itself. Her words conceal as much as they
reveal. Moreover, *The Forbidden Zone* confronts the reader with an odd
mix of immediacy and retrospect, which makes it difficult to disengage
the composition of the text from the scenes that it describes. Although
published in 1929, much of the book was written while Borden was working at the front, in snatches between shifts or during her periods of leave in
Paris or in Brittany with her daughters. Five sections (four poems and one
prose item) appeared in the *English Review* in August 1917.[68] At that stage,
she had completed a draft of the book, which she sent to Collins for
publication—but the manuscript was refused. The stark hospital scenes
and the cynical portrayal of military procedures were too controversial for
the current, highly censored, publishing climate, even though Borden had
not yet tackled her most shocking material.[69] The text was revised and extended in the 1920s, to include the five longer narratives: "Enfant de Malheur," "Rosa," "Blind," "The Priest and the Rabbi," and "Two Gunners."
However, these new stories were partly reconstructed from letters and diaries written at the front, and therefore also carry lingering traces of the moment of their inception—words and images conceived in the heat of the
moment and matured over time.[70]

   The Forbidden Zone demonstrates the difficulty of drawing a neat
line between art and life. Far from operating as a passive receptacle of perception, writing for Borden was an active process, and her literary sense
determined the ways in which she assimilated the events around her.
Many female volunteers at the front, like their male counterparts in the
trenches, came into the war with hopelessly unrealistic ideals and expectations formed by the sanitized images of recruiting posters and by popular literature such as Florence Barclay's *My Heart's Right There* (1915) or
Berta Ruck's *Khaki and Kisses* (1915), tales that Jane Potter describes as

"part of the public's fantasy investment in the war."[71] As a graduate of Vassar College (1907) and a voracious reader across a range of genres, as well as across the transatlantic divide, Borden brought a more sophisticated literary luggage to the front than most—materially as well as intellectually. She had packed volumes of Gertrude Stein and Gustav Flaubert in her suitcases, but resonances of nineteenth-century American classic texts also echo persistently throughout her war writing: Nathaniel Hawthorne, Walt Whitman, Herman Melville, Stephen Crane.[72] As Christine Hallett demonstrates, accounts of nursing at the front by educated and self-conscious upper-class volunteers with a literary education tend to be more "reflective and sometimes assertively opinionated" compared with those produced by trained nurses, whose interpretation of events was likely to be "factual and pragmatic."[73] Borden was perhaps the most educated and self-conscious of them all—but like the young trench poets Robert Graves, Siegfried Sassoon, Charles Hamilton Sorley, and many others, her education also provided her with an important coping mechanism. Words allowed her to objectify traumatic scenes and sensations, to place them at a distance, to find beauty or humor where they had no right to exist. Like Henry James, she sensed that the conflict offered new possibilities for the writer, monstrous and terrible, but interesting and exhilarating nevertheless.

The opening of *The Forbidden Zone* confronts the reader with a complex and disturbing voice, very different both from the earnest artistry of Wharton or Norton, and from the bare reportage of correspondents such as Davis or Powell. This is a different kind of literary voice, apocalyptic but also ironic, detached and yet strangely tender in its sensuality. Borden engages her reader on new, unstable terms, presenting the inexplicable sights of war with a theatrical flourish, like Virgil showing Dante around purgatory. Her narrative voice lists from past to present tense, and from first to third person and back, sometimes addressing the reader with a disconcerting directness, as though they too have arrived among the disorientating images of the war zone:

This is what is left of Belgium. Come, I'll show you. Here are trees drooping along a canal, ploughed fields, roads leading

into sand dunes, roofless houses. There's a farm, an old
woman with a crooked back feeding chickens, a convoy of motor lorries round a barn; they squat like elephants. And here is
a village crouching in the mud: the cobblestone street is slippery and smeared with refuse, and there is a yellow cat sitting
in the window. This is the headquarters of the Belgian Army.
You see these men, lolling in the doorways—uncouth, dishev-
elled, dirty? They are soldiers. You can read on their heavy
jowls, in their stupefied, patient, hopeless eyes, how boring it
is to be a hero.

The king is here. His office is in the school-room down
the street, a little way past the church, just beyond the dung
heap. If we wait we may see him. Let's stand with these people
in the rain and wait.[74]

Borden provides few names, places, or dates by which one can locate her
impressions, but this village in the mud is La Panne, the base of the belea-
guered Belgian government. Anything less like Wharton's description of
the flashing regiment riding "straight into glory," or of the Belgian king
and queen as staunch and noble souls, whose defiance of Germany represented "Liberty enlightening the world," would be hard to imagine.[75]

Part 1 of *The Forbidden Zone,* entitled "The North," replicates the
strangeness of encountering the sights of war for the first time. It begins
with a series of sharply ironic, unsentimental sketches: from the mud of
the opening scene; to the laughing, golden airplane that visits destruction
on the homes of "the ant people swarming through the gates of the city"
and then darts off into the clear, morning sky, watching from a great height
as the "big gun hiding in the sand-dunes" roars into action, making a
ragged hole which "yawned in the open square in the middle of the town."
There is the observation balloon "like an oyster in the sky, keeping an eye
on the Germans"; the uneasy juxtaposition of masculine, military routine
with the daily chores of the women shopping in the market square; the in-
scrutable ritual of a medals ceremony; the intimate misery of the young
couple on the beach whose future is blighted by mutilation and regret.[76]

These images flash by without explanation or context, like scenes glimpsed on the road to the front, although this impression is within the mind of the reader. The organization of Borden's sketches is not chronological, as "The North" contains at least two sections "The Regiment" and "Enfant de Malheur," that are based on events from the summer of 1917. So, this effect of moving through disparate images to a point of focus is carefully constructed by the arrangement of the text. It is not until the section "Moonlight" that the reader encounters Borden in her hospital environment, an environment that will become increasingly absurd and claustrophobic as the book progresses. By the time the reader arrives there, it has already become abundantly clear that this is a world in which recognizable categories of judgment have been overturned and normal emotional responses suspended. This section of the text inverts Hawthorne's well-known celebration of moonlight, in "The Custom House" section of *The Scarlet Letter,* as the ideal medium of imagination and romance.[77] For Borden, the moonlight and the smell of new-mown hay in the field beyond the hospital remind the battle-hardened nurse of things beyond the routine of the war, but so attuned to the demands of her role has she become that these echoes of normality are unsettling and disruptive, rather than transcendent. "The little whimpering voice of a man who is going to die in an hour or two" is a familiar and comprehensible sound, like the rumble of the trucks going up to the front, and the tramp of men marching up the line to be killed. The roar of the guns is the lullaby which sends her to sleep; if it stopped, she would wake disconcerted. The smells of bleach and blood and mud are all known and welcome, but the "lovely lunatic moon" and the "lovely scented love-sick earth" seem unreal and untrue. They are "not a part of the routine."[78]

On one level, the routine of Borden's hospital was impressive. Not only was the 5 percent mortality rate the lowest along the front, but the hospital quickly developed a training role for new doctors and later opened a dentistry unit. New huts were added, doubling the number of beds. Visitors came, including King Albert of Belgium, and there were regular appearances by generals pinning medals on the wounded. For the nurses, alongside the duties of assisting at operations, there was an end-

3. Mary Borden, standing on the right, with recuperating patients at her hospital in Rousbrugge. From Warner, *My Beloved Poilus*, 103.

less cycle of the small repetitive tasks of the wards, administering painkillers, changing dressings and sheets, filling hot water bottles, trying to clean up the mud that seemed to leach into the buildings through every opening. But this routine was also full of pathos and absurdity. As Borden relates in "Moonlight," exceptional things became commonplace. The roof of her hut would blow off in a high wind, and she would not even get out of her bed but slept on, waiting for the orderlies to come and put it back. Every night at midnight, the staff would gather in the sterilizing room by the operating theater to drink hot cocoa among the piles of bandages and surgical instruments: "Sometimes legs and arms wrapped in cloths have to be pushed out of the way. We throw them on the floor—they belong to no one and are of no interest to anyone—and drink our cocoa. The cocoa tastes very good. It is part of the routine."[79] But Borden also sensed older, more abstract forces within the routine: Life, Pain, War, and

Death. Echoing Virgil's account of Aeneas's trip into the underworld, Borden gives these elements personalities and forms.[80] Like the sights and sounds in the night around the hospital, these figures belong in a world of disrupted values. Life is a helpless, quarrelsome animal. Pain is a "harlot in the pay of War," who lies in bed with the wounded men, pinching, caressing, teasing, and exhausting them.[81] Only Death, the beautiful angel, can release them from Pain's clutches, and as Borden waits in the moonlit night for the sound of the whimpering man to stop, she is in no doubt which of these figures she prefers.

Borden's use of Virgil's pagan iconography distances her text, refreshingly so, from the religiosity of many of the contemporary debates about the justness (or otherwise) of the Allies' cause. Indeed, her engagement with biblical imagery is often bitter and sarcastic, flouting religious sensibilities with almost Yeatsian disdain. "The war is the world," she writes. "It had no beginning, it will have no end. War, the Alpha and the Omega, world without end—I don't mind. I am used to it."[82] Borden had profound but conflicted views about Christian belief, and it is probably no accident that the following chapter, "Enfant de Malheur," balances this defiant tone, with her portrayal of the quiet but epic struggle of Guerin the chaplain to redeem the soul of a young Apache, a desperate, blasphemous, Parisian criminal, conscripted into the Battalions d'Afrique. However, Borden's uncertainty about religious values is only a part of the general instability that this text explores, an instability that undercuts the long-revered classical-Christian base of Western culture. Borden is less voluble than James or Wharton about the collapse of "civilization," but the deliberate misfiring of words and images within her work offers a powerful sense of a world where old values no longer hold meaning and everything (as Yeats himself would say) is falling apart.[83]

The reference to Virgil's *Aeneid*—itself a propagandist text glorifying combat and nationalism—would have been much more obvious to Borden's classically trained contemporaries than it is to most readers today, and locates her text within the tradition of war literature from classical times onward. Like the traces of Walt Whitman in her poetic structures and her celebrations of the beauty of the male body, or the echoes of Stephen

Crane's novel *The Red Badge of Courage* (1895) in her impressionistic prose descriptions of the expanded vistas of war, Borden's use of Virgil suggests her need as a writer to find models on which she can build a structure out of her chaotic impressions of war. However, her engagement with the texts of the past is neither nostalgic nor repetitive, partly because Borden was keenly aware that her position as a woman inside the military system was unusual and opened up disruptive perspectives, hitherto largely unexplored within the tradition of war literature. Indeed her engagement with the issue of gender is as difficult to summarize as her literary style. There are many points in her text where Borden embraces the traditional nurturing female role with its qualities of empathy, responsiveness, and patience. In *The Forbidden Zone,* the act of nursing is often portrayed as defiance, or as Margaret Higonnet puts it, as "a kind of resistance to the physical and spiritual destruction of the war."[84] However, Borden's portrayal of the nurse's role is complicated and contradictory.[85] Although an idealized model of femininity, the nurse must also assume practical, active, and decisive qualities traditionally associated with masculinity. She is strong and capable, while the wounded soldier lies passive, helpless, and childlike in her care. Borden's disruption of gender can be read as an attempt to cut through the dead wood of social convention, creating what Ariela Freedman calls "a sequestered zone between the home front and the front line," where "gender itself has been wounded" and people are "reduced to bodies and functions."[86] In "Moonlight," Borden articulates this reduction of the socially constructed self to a raw, almost animal state: "There are no men here, so why should I be a woman? There are heads and knees and mangled testicles. There are chests with holes as big as your fist, and pulpy thighs, shapeless; and stumps where legs once were fastened. There are eyes—eyes of sick dogs, sick cats, blind eyes, eyes of delirium; and mouths that cannot articulate; and parts of faces—the nose gone, or the jaw. There are these things, but no men; so how could I be a woman here and not die of it?"[87]

Borden defied prewar stereotypes; nevertheless, her life and letters reveal a reluctant feminist. In 1913, she was arrested for throwing a cobblestone through the window of a government office in Whitehall, London,

as part of a suffragettes' protest. However, even in the heat of her moment
of political rebellion, she felt the absurdity of her situation, accompanied
by a sense of relief at being escorted away from the scene by two, large,
protective police constables. She wrote later: "I felt, as I have said, very
silly. I disliked the whole business. I had made a fool of myself for a principle, but I had no sense of self-satisfaction. I believed in votes for women,
and it hadn't seemed sporting to let the other women who believed as I did
do the dirty work of collecting and throwing stones; so I had made my
feeble feminine protest, had thrown my stones as only a feeble woman can
throw, and was now being politely conducted to the police station by two
indulgent and chivalrous giants in uniform."[88] Borden spent five days in
custody at Bow Street Police Station, sustained by the lunch baskets and
novels which her family delivered. Her sense of embarrassment and futility about the whole situation was compounded when her husband paid
the twenty-five shilling fine to release her, without consulting her first.
This was a long way, as she wryly noted, from hunger-striking in Hollo-
way prison, as other female protesters did. Borden held progressive views
about contraception, divorce, and family finances as well as voting rights.
However, she was astute enough to recognize that for many women, the securities of traditional roles were often as attractive as the freedoms offered
by modern alternatives. Changes to society come slowly in both British and
American society, she writes, "because most women are, like myself, half-
hearted about this business of their rights."[89]

Nursing may have been perceived as a safely feminine role for women
after 1914, but as Borden quickly discovered, nursing within a military
command structure during a time of war created all kinds of untenable
paradoxes.[90] The act of caring made the nurse complicit in a wider agenda
of destruction. Soldiers were to be restored to health, simply so that they
could be returned to the trenches. Like the cocoa served up among the
amputated limbs and the cries of the whimpering man in the moonlight,
this was all part of the routine: "Just as you send your clothes to the laun-
dry and mend them when they come back," she wrote, "so we send our
men to the trenches and mend them when they come back again. . . . We
send our men to the war again and again, just as long as they will stand it;

just until they are dead, and then we throw them into the ground."[91] Sometimes, participation in the processes of war created even stranger dilemmas. In "Rosa," Borden tells the story of a soldier brought to the hospital at Rousbrugge with a bullet in his brain, having attempted suicide by shooting himself through the mouth. The surgeons and the nurses are required to save his life, so that he can be court-martialed and shot as a deserter. The initial surgical operation is a success, but "Rosa," as Borden calls the man in recognition of the woman's name that he cries out so persistently, tears off his bandages night after night, determined to prevent his wound from healing. Borden speculates that behind this riddle of military regulations there is a human story more complex than a cowardly refusal to fight. There is, she suspects, a tragedy of passion and loss that makes the soldier's life unbearable. Flouting both military and medical protocol (she had been trained, remember, in neither), Borden instructs the night nurse not to replace the man's bandages when he removes them. There is a moment where the nurse hesitates, constrained by "her traditions, her professional conscience, the honour of her calling," but both women know that the decent thing is to allow him the dignity of choosing his own fate.[92] Two days later he is dead.

This story throws up so many contradictions about male and female roles at the front that it is hard to unravel it. Initially, it offers a neat reversal of stereotypes: the helpless, passive, emasculated soldier, known by a woman's name, is redeemed by the active, assertive female, prepared to take responsibility for ending a life. In the end, however, it is the soldier who makes the decisive move of ripping off his bandages in one "last fumbling desperate and determined act," while the nurses conspire to observe and do nothing—a response that affirms their feminized intuitive sympathy. Neat patterns of social behavior do not emerge clearly from such a scene, and The Forbidden Zone refutes as much as it supports Claire Tylee's suggestion that women's writing from the front heralds a new kind of female consciousness.[93] Although Borden's book upsets conventional views of gender, it offers little to put in place of these, and seems increasingly concerned with other kinds of problems about the nature of perception and expression. It is sharply unlike many war texts by women writers, and strangely akin to certain texts by men.[94] As the fighting continued, Borden would find her position as a female observer and a willing participant in the machinery of war increasingly problematic. It was one thing to be an American and another to be a woman, but such categories of identity seemed to matter less and less. The real question was: how could one remain human amid such engulfing inhumanity?

Beyond Words

On New Year's Eve 1914, Henry James had lunch with Richard Norton in London. He found him "unmitigatedly magnificent" with his "intelligent force, his energy and lucidity, his gallantry and resolution." James particularly liked Norton's defiance of rules that barred him from offering assistance to civilian refugees or armed troops. Norton had said that "when the Germans ruthlessly broke every Geneva Convention by attempting to shell him and his cars and his wounded whenever they could spy a chance, he was absolutely for doing in mercy and assistance what they do in their dire brutality, and might be depended upon to convey not only every suffering civilian but any armed and trudging soldiers whom a blest chance might offer him."[95] James was impressed. Norton's attitude seemed to sum up many of the elements of his own emotions about the war and give them an outlet: the outrage, the sympathy, the defiance, the desire for action without violence. Amid the confusion of conflicting voices and opinions, here was a cause with which he could align himself. Buoyed by the success of his little pamphlet, James volunteered over lunch to write another piece in support of Norton's operation. He did not expect that someone else would write it for him.[96]

A few weeks later, James agreed to give a newspaper interview about his support for the Ambulance Corps. This was probably at the instigation of Sir Gilbert Parker of the War Propaganda Bureau, working with Charles Masterman at Wellington House. Parker, whose remit was to ensure that the Allied cause made a good showing in America, organized a series of interviews by American newspapers with a succession of literary lions, including Thomas Hardy, Arthur Conan Doyle, G. K. Chesterton,

Arnold Bennett, Mary Ward, and Israel Zangwill.[97] James mistrusted journalists, and regularly cast them in sinister or comic roles in his fiction.[98] He had given only two previous interviews, both times reluctantly: one to Florence Brooks for the *New York Herald* in 1904, the other to the poet Witter Byner for the *Critic and Literary World* in 1905. As Matthew Rubery notes, James's avoidance of publicity appeared to be "at odds with his long-standing ambition to achieve popular success as a novelist," but was thoroughly consistent with his sense of the inner self as a separate entity from the persona projected through art.[99] James's short stories, such as "The Private Life" or "The Middle Years," often explore this split in the writing self between the personal and public. Nevertheless, James agreed, perhaps because he wished to be seen to be doing what he could, or perhaps because he was disarmed by the young journalist Preston Lockwood (1891–1951), who was sent to do the interview. Lockwood had grown up in St. Louis and had done some journalistic work before coming to Britain. He also had ambitions as an author. Like many young Americans of his age and class, he was currently working through a dilemma about the relative merits of writing or enlisting—a dilemma which may have endeared him to James, full as he was of memories of the troubled start of his own literary career during the Civil War in the 1860s. Like James, Lockwood also had anxieties of identification. In the one-act play *Sham,* which he cowrote with Lincoln Eyre in the autumn of 1914, Guy Armstead, "a journalist of sorts, a press agent, and minor mender of plays" is berated by the woman he loves after reading the paper and exclaiming, "By Jove! We're giving them hell on the Aisne." "*We!*" cries Phyllis, the young American starlet, "Who do you mean by *we?* . . . You who sit here in London and think only about whether the news from the front makes good reading—news that's written in the blood of men who are real men—not the pen-fighters of Leicester Square!" Emasculated and embarrassed, Guy contemplates action: "Wonder how *I'd* look in uniform," he muses in the play's final line, as a Scottish regiment marches under the window, bagpipes skirling.[100] However, it is left open whether the "Sham" of the title indicates his earlier avoidance of military service, or his later participation in the war as a device to impress Phyllis. In February 1915, Lockwood was not yet in uniform, but by May he had joined the American Field Service as a driver, and would later serve as personal assistant to its director A. Piatt Andrew. Lockwood would publish a vivid account of his work in Alsace in 1916, and would go on to join the French army and then the U.S. army in 1917.[101] However, the experience of interviewing James may have been almost as daunting. Theodora Bosanquet, James's secretary to whom he dictated most of his work and letters, described the interview in her diary:

> Monday, 1 March 1915: I've had several days of holiday for a rather funny reason. Mr James consented, for the first time in his life to be "interviewed" the other day in connection with the American Motor-Ambulance Corps, by a representative of the *New York Times*. His consent, however, was only given on the condition that he might see the Copy produced. That the young journalist brought round last Thursday. But H.J. finding that it wouldn't do at all from his point of view, has spent the last 4 days re-dictating the interview to the young man, who is, fortunately, a good typist. I should love to see the published result. I think the idea of H.J. interviewing himself for four whole days is quite delightful.[102]

This was "pen fighting" of a rather different sort.

The result was the misnamed "Henry James's First Interview," printed on 21 March 1915 in the magazine section of the paper. In it, James described himself as "Chairman of our Corps Committee," a role that had fallen to him "for no great reason that I can discover save my being the oldest American resident here interested in its work." But he went on to say, "if I render a scrap of help by putting on record my joy even in the rather ineffectual connection so far as 'doing' anything is concerned, I needn't say how welcome you are to my testimony." James was not just being modest. His actual involvement in the running of the corps appears to have been minimal. His surviving date books contain surprisingly few references to meetings or activities at the headquarters of the corps, where

Lockwood originally interviewed James. There are only two surviving letters from James to Richard Norton, though it is likely that they also corresponded by telegram.[103] Beyond his general admiration for Norton's activities, there is little in James's letters to other contacts implying inside knowledge of the organization, and he seems grateful to the Norton family in Cambridge for scraps of information about it.[104] This may not have been James's fault. One of the things that people appear to have liked about Richard Norton was that he was not much of a committee man. He made his own decisions in much the same way that he would get out a spanner and fix his own ambulances. Whatever was happening in London, and whatever James's role in it was, the real headquarters of the corps was wherever Richard Norton was—usually in a makeshift depot somewhere in northern France.

The importance of James's association with the corps was symbolic, both to the public and to James himself. In allowing the organization to cash in on his cultural capital, James was simultaneously reassuring himself that this cultural capital was still worth something. Many, some might say *most*, of James's actions late in life were outcomes of his desire to control his relationship with the reading public. His time-consuming (and as it turned out unremunerative) labor of revising his fiction and writing the lengthy prefaces for the collected New York Edition of his novels and tales (1907–9) was first and foremost a conscious act of self-presentation—a project which Michael Anesko describes as "patenting a style for futurity."[105] Likewise, the intended volume about his brother's life and letters that he had begun after William's death in 1910 quickly transformed into the first two volumes of Henry James's own self-reflective autobiography, the third volume of which was still a work in progress in 1915. James's identification with wartime projects is often, as noted in the previous chapter, interpreted as a reflex governed by his neuroses about the past. But even if one is determined to interpret his motives as solipsistic (which is an ungenerous judgment on this generous man), it is much more interesting to see James's wartime ardor as a symptom of his anxiety about the future—both the future of his own legacy, and that of the culture in which that legacy would operate. What, he must have wondered, would happen to his fiction in a world where armies burned down libraries?

Certainly, James's own instinct to control and revise Lockwood's text would suggest that futurity was much on his mind in early 1915. From the outset of the article, he asserted his literary independence, making clear that the very act of being interviewed was a sacrifice to the war effort. "I can't put," he said, "my devotion and sympathy for the cause of our corps more strongly than in permitting it thus to overcome my dread of the assault of the interviewer." Not even "the most suggestive young gentleman with a notebook" could help him to say anything better than he felt he could say it himself—as Lockwood already knew to his cost. Almost half the interview was given over to James's consideration of the failings of the interview as a means of communication, and to Lockwood's attempts to draw James into discussion about his literary methods and his idiosyncratic punctuation. James was thus careful to present himself first and foremost as an author, a measured man of words, but he also wanted to present himself very clearly as an American. Germany's invasion of Belgium, he said, was "the most insolent 'Because I choose to, damn you all!' recorded in history," and one which had far-reaching implications.[106] He went on: "How can one help seeing that such aggression, if hideously successful in Europe, would, with as little loss of time as possible, proceed to apply itself to the American side of the world, and how can one, therefore, not feel that the Allies are fighting to the death for the soul and the purpose and the future that are in *us*, for the defence of every ideal that has most guided our growth and that most assures our unity?"[107] Growth and unity—this was once more the language of the Civil War, and the emphasis on "*us*" implied a desire to put the divisions of that war firmly in the past, to imply a cohesive American identity in which James was willing to participate. But James had an eye on transatlantic unity too, and expressed his desire to transform "the indifference of Americans at large" into "intelligent human pity."

In the end, however, he came back to the theme of silence, and his haunting fear of the future. Like Grace Fallow Norton, he was coming to understand that silence could be a powerful response to the clamor of conflict. James said that there was really nothing one could say about the war—although, self-evidently, this was not true. These were the very words that Hemingway would find so resonant in later years: "One finds it in the midst of all this as hard to apply one's words as to endure one's thoughts. The war has used up words; they have weakened, they have deteriorated like motor car tires; they have, like millions of other things, been more overstrained and knocked about and voided of the happy semblance during the last six months than in all the long ages before, and we are now confronted with a depreciation of all our terms, or, otherwise speaking, with a loss of expression through increase of limpness, that may well make us wonder what ghosts will be left to walk."[108] In this statement of bewilderment, it was again unclear who was included in "us," or whether indeed this was one of those words which was beginning to lose any semblance of meaning. Like Wharton and Borden's absurdist warscapes, James's vision of a world haunted by frayed language is an early version of the kind of futility and thwarted articulation that would resurface in later years in poems such as T. S. Eliot's "The Hollow Men"—who might indeed be James's limp ghosts of language, characterized as they are by "Shape without form, shade without colour,/Paralysed force, gesture without motion."[109] To James, whose identity was defined by authorship, and whose legacy depended on the resilience of language, the prospect of the failure of words must have seemed an absolute of despair. Still, words had served him for over seventy years. He had learned well how to sharpen them to his purpose. Overstrained and knocked about they may be, but he was not quite ready to lay down his best weapons—not when it was all so "interesting," as he remarked increasingly in his letters. Something beautiful, he felt, could come of this war yet.

Leaving Everything Else Behind

Throughout the spring of 1915, James produced a remarkable series of essays about the war. Having broken his silence, suddenly he could hardly stop writing. Working on his prefaces and his autobiography over the previous decade had given James a range of strategies for examining his own emotional and mental processes, and this preoccupation with how and why he felt as he did pervades his war writings. In February, around the time of his *New York Times* interview, he began work on "Within the Rim," an essay about his reactions in the opening days of the war.[110] This was swiftly followed by "France," included in Winifred Stephens's publication *The Book of France* (1915); by "The Long Wards," published in Edith Wharton's own charity fund-raising volume *The Book of the Homeless* (1916); by "Refugees in England," which appeared in American newspapers in October and then as "Refugees in Chelsea" in Britain the following March; and by *The Question of the Mind,* published as a pamphlet in London and reprinted in the *Philadelphia Ledger* and the *New York Sun* in August as "The Mind of England at War."[111] In addition to these, he wrote a short obituary for Allen D. Loney, one of the financial backers of Norton's Ambulance Corps, who was killed in the sinking of the *Lusitania,* and an appreciation of Rupert Brooke, published as the introduction to Brooke's *Letters from America* (1916). If one defines "propaganda" as all published materials which sanction or provide a rationale for military action, then that is exactly what these essays were—but that is a simplistic definition of the term, and James's statements on the war are far from simple. He was eager to support "charitable" causes, but, as Borden was quickly realizing at the front, the boundary between charity and politics was a muddy one. In 1915, he allowed a short paragraph from a private letter to be reprinted in *Sixty American Opinions on the War,* an edited volume produced under the auspices of the War Propaganda Bureau, although such was the secrecy of this operation that Buitenhuis doubts whether any of the contributing authors knew that the book had been "made, published and distributed by a propaganda agency of the British Government."[112] Other than this contribution, only *The Question of the Mind* (an essay which, incidentally, barely mentions the war) was published by an organization that was involved in generating materials and staging public meetings to encourage enlistment and support military activities. Even in this case, however, the relationship of James's work to the official British war effort was not straightforward. The Central Committee of National Patriotic Organisations, founded in August 1914 by Henry

Cust, the editor of the *Pall Mall Gazette,* and James's friend G. W. Pro-
thero, was a voluntary body with the stated aim of promoting "reasoned
knowledge among all classes" in order to "sustain the wills and sacrifices
of the British people through the blackest days of weariness and dis-
couragement."[113] The committee operated independently of the British
government's own War Propaganda Bureau, which also employed many
prominent authors during the conflict, including Arnold Bennett, G. K.
Chesterton, Ford Madox Ford, Hugh Walpole, and Wyndham Lewis.
One of the original aims of the committee was to promote the Allied cause
in neutral nations, but the government was clearly uneasy about this project, and in the spring of 1915 Asquith himself wrote to Cust discouraging
him from exporting materials abroad.[114] James clearly did have powerful
political opinions about the war, and took whatever opportunities came
his way to put these into public circulation. However, he was a long way
from working directly for the British government, as is sometimes in-
ferred; indeed as a citizen of a neutral nation he would have been legally
barred from any such employment, certainly before July 1915.[115] Significantly, he continued to use his own literary agent James Brand Pinker to
place his articles and handle his public and financial affairs throughout
the war, rather than operating through any official routes on either side of
the Atlantic. The charge of "propaganda" against a writer is always a serious one, especially against an artist as self-conscious and scrupulous
about the methods and purposes of art as James was. It implies a willingness to sacrifice independence and integrity to political ends and financial gain. Then again, there is something equally wrong about the
writer who has nothing to say about a social crisis on their doorstep.
Suffice to say if James *was* attempting to write the kind of propaganda
that governments encourage in wartime, the kind that reduces the contradictions of war into a tidy struggle between good and evil, and rouses
the citizen to passionate, defensive action, then he did not appear to understand his brief.

   James's war essays are introspective and uncertain, as much concerned with his own imaginative world as with the outer arena of conflict
and charity. He does admit himself to be horrified at the prospect of "a

world squeezed together in the huge Prussian fist and with the variety and spontaneity of its parts oozing in a steady trickle, like the sacred blood of sacrifice, between those hideous knuckly fingers," but these essays also reveal his deep distaste for violence, and his sharply modern awareness that many of the emotions roused by war are merely social and cultural constructions.[116] In particular, the problem of how to locate or define national character was the running thread on which James's war writings were strung. As a long-term observer of international mores, he was far from accepting the "manifest destiny" of the British peoples to govern, or indeed any essentialist view of national traits.[117] Perhaps it was his cosmopolitan upbringing, or perhaps it was his highly developed aesthetic sense of the subjective nature of experience, but certainly James was more conscious than many of his contemporaries of the mutability of the self, whether in relation to stereotypes of nationality, class, or gender. As Peter Walker remarks, these essays highlight "something of the perils of trying to reduce James's sense of himself to a single national identity," or more generally of "characterizing his identity as having a stable, essential core."[118] James had long dramatized the susceptibility of the consciousness to external influences through his fiction, and he had mused openly on the question of American identity in *The American Scene* (1907), where he asked provocatively: "Who and what is an alien, when it comes to that, in a country peopled from the first under the jealous eye of history?" In a nation of immigrants, how was it possible, he wondered, to "put a finger on the dividing line" between American and non-American identity?[119] The individual, he saw, could choose to identify with or reject a cultural position aligned by convention or tradition to one particular country, but such positions were subject to change, development, and internal negotiation. This was not only true of American identity; it was also the case with the British people, whose response to the war so fascinated James.

"Within the Rim" begins, like so many of James's own tales, with observation—with James himself as the "restless watcher" scanning the horizon and wondering about what lies out of sight across the English Channel: "the bright mystery beyond the rim of the farthest opaline reach."[120] However, the "rim" of the title is also the limit of James's own perception, which is really the subject of the essay. What he tries to articulate here is not just his sense of England, but the sense of his sense of England. James acknowledges the social and psychological factors that shape his response to the war and to his adopted home. As though laying a blueprint for later retrospective studies of how propaganda operated during the war, such as Walter Lippman's *Public Opinion* (1921) or Harold Lasswell's *Propaganda Technique in the World War* (1927), James identifies the key triggers for emotional response in wartime: the sense of history, the personal past, the power of narrative, and the desire for community. That these are constructed elements, not revealed qualities, is articulated through his metaphoric description of his consciousness as a built space. As war begins, James finds that his "house of spirit" must be remodeled and extended to accommodate his new ideas about the English: "I found myself before long building on additions and upper storeys, throwing out extensions and protrusions, indulging even, all recklessly, in gables and pinnacles and battlements." Eventually this mental construction becomes "a fortress of the faith, a palace of the soul, an extravagant, bristling, flag-flying structure which had quite as much to do with the air as with the earth."[121] This castle in the air, James freely admits, is an imaginary construction, which has "more to say to one's state of mind" than any external reality.[122] But in a characteristic reversal of the concrete and the abstract, James notes how this mental structure seems believable, while the material threat which war presents to English history and tradition seems little more than a fiction. "We might all have resembled together," he writes, "a group of children at their nurse's knee disconcerted by some tale that it isn't their habit to hear."[123] But James is unembarrassed by the imaginary quality of his English feeling. He concludes that the power of "Englishness" to inspire the imagination is the very reason that one should want to defend it.

Words, as James himself pointed out, deteriorate over time. Like "propaganda," terms of nationality carry different overtones to present-day readers than to those of 1915. To a twenty-first-century ear, "Englishness" denotes a narrow, formal, and limited conception of the British Isles, one so parochial that it cannot even acknowledge the existence of Scotland,

Ireland, or Wales. However, this term belonged to a different cultural register in the early twentieth century. Stefan Collini, Peter Mandler, and J. H.
Grainger all note that, in the years between the Boer War and the First
World War, a difference emerged between blustering, expansionist, imperial "Britishness," usually associated with Conservative, Unionist, and colonial interests, and a more rural, cultured, and anti-imperial "Englishness,"
associated with Liberal or socialist agendas, a smaller-scale and more nostalgic form of national culture.[124] James's political friends and connections
were largely on the center-left of the political spectrum, and throughout his
wartime writing it is usually "Englishness" that he champions—particularly
the domestic, rural, and literary qualities of "Little England," as it was often termed in opposition to imperial "Great Britain."

This fascination with Englishness is also evident in *The Question of
the Mind,* where James works through his complex reactions to, and relish of, the untamed nature of the English intellect, which he sees steeped
in a characteristic "good-nature." Of course, affirming national character
through traits such as good nature, which might be applied to almost any
country in the world, merely highlights the projected nature of national
identity. But unlike many others writing during the war, James does not
develop this point into a rationale for violence, or even into a eulogy on the
British character. As ever, he seems more interested in charting how he
arrives at his conclusion, tracking the twists and turns of his emotional
consciousness, and asking how it is that he looks so fondly on the many
flaws and irritations of British intellectual life. This is hardly a text to
send the reader running to the recruiting office. In "The Long Wards,"
where James considers his impressions of the "citizen soldier" comparing
the remembered Union soldiers of his youth with the British "Tommy" he
had encountered on his hospital visits, the good nature and the amiabil-
ity of the English draw James's attention once more. He admires the lack
of philosophy or rhetoric in the response of the injured soldiers who
"content themselves with *being*" and "have no use for any imputed or
derivative sentiments or reasons."[125] But James is troubled by the endless
stream of changing faces that he has visited over the months. In a surreal
image, like something out of a Salvador Dali painting, he envisages the long

ward of the hospital as an "incalculable vista" disappearing into futurity: "The perspective stretches away in its mild order, after the fashion of a tunnel boring into the very character of the people, and so going on forever— never arriving or coming out, that is, at anything in the nature of a station, a junction or a terminus, bordered with the thick-growing flower of the individual illustration."[126] It is a disturbing image, which reflects both James's anxiety about the dark future and his growing awareness of the real scale of the human cost of the war—not a subject to which a professional propagandist would direct the reader's attention. James can applaud the resilience of these young men on whom "the stress of carnage" appears to have left "so little distortion of the moral nature."[127] Nevertheless, he is uncertain about the society in which they have grown up "ignored and neglected," and about what would happen if they were "tended and fostered and cultivated" instead. "For I believe in Culture," he concludes—a rare statement of faith from this usually cautious and ambivalent writer.[128]

James may have doubted the staying power of words, but by mid-1915 he had reasserted his faith in the relationship between experience and expression. Although James was an increasingly public presence, his most vivid statement about his own artistic identity during the war was a private one. In July, his long friendship with the novelist H. G. Wells came to an abrupt end, after Wells published an unkind parody in *Boon,* a light-hearted collection of satiric papers, in which he notoriously described James's literary style as that of "a magnificent but painful hippopotamus resolved at any cost, even at the cost of its dignity, upon picking up a pea which has got into a corner of its den."[129] This on its own, James might have let pass as a difference of taste, but more galling was the accusation that his work had no connection with reality: "In all his novels you will find no people with defined political opinions, no people with religious opinions, none with clear partisanships or with lusts or whims, none definitely up to any specific impersonal thing."[130] In the exchange of letters that followed, Wells insisted that art was not really relevant to life, not at least to the extent that James appeared to think. James replied with intensity. Art was, he said, "relevant in a degree that leaves everything else behind." He went on: "It is art that makes life, makes interest, makes importance, for our consideration and application of these things, and I know of no substitute whatever for the force and beauty of its process."[131] It is a much quoted passage, but usually in the context of James's long interest in the complexities of realist fiction. It is a much more powerful statement in the context of war. Consistent with his role in the National Propaganda Bureau, Wells believed, as his alter ego Boon makes clear, that "the novel is to follow life," that literature was at the service of political, social, and military aims. James did not—which is why, however his war essays were appropriated at the time, and however they have been construed since, he could never really be a "propagandist." James's view of "Culture" was much more like Eliot's than Arnold's; culture was an internal organizing principle, not a social project. It was not that international economics and the drama of the front did not matter—far from it—but these things were vivid to James as events that were experienced, explored, and understood within the individual human consciousness. Art was the means by which they took form and became communicable.

James, however, was about to make a very public statement about his individual feelings about the war. In late June, around about the same time that he was falling out with Wells, he decided to renounce his American citizenship, and to adopt British nationality. He had learned that if he wanted to go down to his house in Rye, near the coast, for the summer, he would have to register himself as an alien and report regularly to the police, which was both inconvenient and disconcerting. He had lived in Lamb House for almost twenty years. However, as he told his friend Edmund Gosse, this was "only the occasion" of his decision and was "not in the least the cause."[132] He took the Oath of Allegiance on 26 July. Privately, he wrote to his nephew Harry, that his move was "determined by the War and what has happened since, also more particularly what has *not* happened. . . . I certainly shouldn't have done it, under the inspiration of our Cause, if the U.S.A. had done a little more *for* me." It was, he felt, an indispensable act: "Like Martin Luther at Wittenberg, 'I could do no other.'"[133] Publicly, his reasons were set out in the press release which he sent out through his literary agent James Brand Pinker (the only time in his life that James resorted to such a method of self-publicity), and published in the *Times* on 28 July 1915. They were: "Because of his having lived and worked in England for the best part of 40 years; because of his attachment to the country and his sympathy with it and its people; because of the long friendships and associations and interests he has formed here—these last including the acquisition of some property; all of which things have brought to a head his desire to throw his weight and personal allegiance, for whatever they may be worth, into the scale of the contending nation's present and future fortune."[134] James was required to give four sponsors who could vouch for his sincerity and, as he noted wryly to Gosse, testify to his "speaking and writing English decently."[135] Through Gosse, James approached Asquith himself to sign as one of his sponsors. For someone who had lived so privately for most of his life, James knew how to make a grand gesture when he wanted to. This gesture drew both praise and censure, and compounded the problem of categorizing James as British or American, which had already exercised his critics and admirers alike, and would continue to do so long after his death—though as Ezra Pound noticed, even that debate was a sure mark of James's standing on both sides of the Atlantic: "No other American," wrote Pound in 1918, "was of sufficient importance for his change of allegiance to have constituted an international act; no other American would have been welcome in the same public manner. America passes over these things, but the thoughtful cannot pass over them."[136]

James's new relationship with England and his returning confidence in the power of literature were vividly explored in the essay on the young poet Rupert Brooke, which he wrote in the weeks following his change of nationality. When Brooke died of blood poisoning on a troop ship on his way to the Dardanelles in April, James responded with disbelief and sorrow. On hearing the news, he replied to Brooke's friend and mentor Eddie Marsh: "If there was a stupid and hideous disfigurement of life and outrage to beauty left for our awful conditions to perpetrate, those things have been now supremely achieved, and no other brutal blow in the private sphere can better them for making one just stare through one's tears."[137] James had first met Brooke in 1909 on a visit to Cambridge University, but saw little more of him until the summer of 1914. The acquaintance was

encouraged by Marsh, who was increasingly close to James around this
time, and who was eager to introduce Brooke to established literary contacts.[138] However, the lunches and dinners in London stopped abruptly
after Brooke volunteered with the Royal Naval Division and was posted
first to Antwerp, then to a training camp in North Africa, and then to Gal-
lipoli. One of the last letters he received was a long correspondence from
Marsh, dated 31 March, in which was folded a letter from James to Marsh
praising Brooke's "1914" sonnets about the outbreak of war, published in
New Numbers in January 1915, and a clipping from the *Times* reporting
that one of these poems "The Soldier" had been read by Dean Inge in St.
Paul's Cathedral on Easter Sunday.[139]

Before sailing, Brooke had named Marsh as his literary executor.
Eager to capitalize on the extraordinary public attention which the young
poet's death attracted, Marsh lost no time in arranging the publication of a
volume of Brooke's poetry, *"1914" and Other Poems,* with Sidgwick and
Jackson in early June. James wrote to Marsh in admiration: "Immense the
generosity of his response to life and the beauty and variety of the forms in
which it broke out, and of which these further things are such an enrich-
ing exhibition. His place is now very high and very safe—even though one
walks round and round it with the aching soreness of having to take the
monument for the man."[140] As James had predicted to Scribner the previous November, here was writing of "weight and quality" that would "outwear and outlast" the war, though Brooke had not outlived it. Marsh was
also working on a memoir of Brooke, to serve as an introduction to a collected edition of Brooke's work. He aimed to provide a more realistic portrait of his friend than many of the saccharine and patriotic testimonials
that appeared up and down the land in the weeks after his death. For this
memoir, Marsh gathered comments and anecdotes from a number of
Brooke's friends—though the endeavor sparked a protracted row with
Brooke's mother, who wanted a more conventional image of her son projected to the public, one which concealed his left-wing politics, his dislike of authority, and his very un-Edwardian attitudes to friendship and
romance.[141] James offered to contribute to Marsh's memoir, but Marsh
suggested that instead he should write a longer piece as the introduction

to *Letters from America,* a collected edition of the travel essays that
Brooke had written while traveling in the United States, Canada, and Ta-
hiti in 1912–13.[142]

James frames his comments about Brooke within a discussion of poetic "identity," asking what it is that makes "the first spark of the flame" of
the poet.[143] What is the torch, James wonders, that has passed through the
hands of Dante, Keats, Shelley, Whitman, Byron, and Tennyson? Thus,
when James notes that Brooke's image is of "the stuff poets may be noted
as made of," he sets him among the great poets of the past—although for
the majority of this essay, James is more concerned with the future, and
with Brooke's persona as the "wondrous modern."[144] The identity of the
poet in an age of travel, change, and war clearly troubles James. Like others
who paid tribute to Brooke, James notes the timeless quality of his physical
beauty and poetic character. However, in the modern age, it seems that this
beauty is no guarantee of truth or artistic integrity. His "beautiful crown-
ing modernness" made him, James writes, "the heir to all the ages" (not
exactly a compliment in Tennyson's 'Locksley Hall') and one who may
have been corrupted by popularity and sociability into "the spoilt child of
history."[145] Nevertheless, James finds something reassuring in his connection to "the English tradition." He admires Brooke's "natural accommo-
dation of the English spirit, this frequent extraordinary beauty of the
English aspect, this finest saturation of the English intelligence by its most
immediate associations, tasting as they mainly do of the long past, this
ideal image of English youth."[146] This lavish tribute echoes Winston
Churchill's obituary to Brooke in the *Times,* as a young man embodying
"all that one would wish England's noblest sons to be in the days when no
sacrifice but the most precious is acceptable."[147] However, James meant
something slightly different by his sense of "Englishness" than Churchill
did. In James's tribute to Brooke, as in "Within the Rim," England is not
only about tradition and social responsibility, but is also powerfully connected to the flux of modernity, to liberal attitudes to class and morality,
to a democratic sense of individuality, and to the infinite possibilities of
art. The essay on Brooke helps to make sense of James's switch of national
allegiance in 1915, as it articulates James's sense that the literary spirit was

defined by "the art of living inward"—an art that was more possible to sustain in the atmosphere of early twentieth-century "Englishness" than in the more demonstrative and yet culturally insecure environment of contemporary America.[148] James also recognized that Brooke represented no absolute, immutable values; rather he was something of a work of art himself, the site of many conflicting readings and perspectives, a highly synthesized construction. Yet, as James already knew from his own career, the construction of a literary persona is a creative act, and a gesture of faith in the future.

James would not see that future. The essay on Brooke was his last completed piece of work. In early December, only a few days after he had reviewed the proofs of the essay, he suffered a series of strokes from which he would not recover. His sister-in-law Alice Gibbens James rushed from America, braving the dangers of submarine warfare in the Atlantic, to be at his bedside; Edith Wharton kept in touch with his condition through the devoted Bosanquet. On 1 January, Edmund Gosse brought the news to James that he had been awarded the Order of Merit—a prestigious royal award for high achievement in the fields of the arts, learning, literature, and science. Marsh, now a secretary at Downing Street, Gosse, and Asquith himself had all played a part in arranging the honor. Only very rarely has the O.M. been awarded to non-British nationals. This was not just a formal recognition of James's literary identity but also of his new national identity, and of his support for Britain's position in the war. James rallied a little after this, but his strength was fading. He had not really been well for almost a decade; heart trouble, indigestion, and depression, compounded over the past year and a half by the anxiety and grief of war, had worn him out. He died peacefully, aged seventy-three, on 28 February 1916.

Letters from America was published a few days later, on 8 March. The following day, the *Times Literary Supplement* carried an unsigned review of the book by James's young friend Percy Lubbock, who also wrote a long obituary defending James's literary method in the same issue. As Lubbock noted of *Letters from America*, "There are many good pages in this book, but the real book is without doubt its title-page." The juxtaposition of the names of James and Brooke, of the old and the young, of the

past and the future, the novelist and the poet, spliced together in this volume seemed to Lubbock to promise some powerful narrative about art,
beauty, and loss which was not easy to articulate: "Rupert Brooke, who
appeared and vanished like a song—Henry James, whose years were one
great monument of the labour of art, brought, so far as an artist's work may
be brought, to completion—both are already a legend; and the two leg-
ends, so diverse in all but the fact of their beauty, here run into one. Every
one who reads this book will be aware of this other unwritten book which
is mingled with it; but it is too soon for any reader to speak of it fully."[149]
As James's essay on Brooke had made clear, Lubbock understood that
identity is a complex construction, especially in the case of the author,
whose image survives in "legend." Over the next decade, Lubbock would
contribute in no small way to shaping the legend of James's own authorial
identity by editing his unpublished works and letters for publication.[150]
However, early in 1916, as James had predicted, it did not yet seem possible
to give voice to what it was that these two writers had come to represent.
With James and Brooke both silenced, it seemed indeed as if the real book
of this war might never be written.

THREE

1916—Books

BEFORE THE WAR WAS MORE than a few weeks old, Ferris Greenslet, commissioning editor at the Boston publishing house Houghton Mifflin, realized that it would be good for business. Without domestic radio, with only occasional access to moving images of the conflict, and with newspapers full of political positioning, the public would want books "telling not only what the war was about, but what it was like." Producing "war books," he decided in the fall of 1914, should be the firm's top priority. A reasonable man, Greenslet was willing to publish a range of views, from what he termed "Allied propaganda" to arguments for the German point of view. Like Charles Scribner in New York, he was initially tolerant of Austrian and German perspectives, finding room on Houghton Mifflin's 1915 list for Fritz Kreisler's *Four Weeks in the Trenches: The War Story of a Violinist* and the anonymous *Journal of a German Submarine Commander.* Yet he grew increasingly hostile to Germany as a military and political power, especially as U-boat attacks continued intermittently on American merchant vessels on "Periscope Pond." The sympathies of Houghton Mifflin's readers were similarly shaped and reshaped by events. Greenslet, who ventured across the Atlantic several times during the war in search of new British and French literary talent, often with the help of Gilbert Parker or John Buchan at Wellington House, discovered early that "the best time to publish a war book is the day you accept it," as its contents might be out of date by sundown.[1]

Nevertheless, the public appetite for war-related texts, both fiction and nonfiction, appeared insatiable, and Greenslet's strategy paid off. Toward the end of 1915, Mildred Aldrich's eyewitness account of the early days of the war, *A Hilltop on the Marne*, proved a runaway success, notching up seventeen printings in all, and two follow-up texts, *On the Edge of the War Zone* (1917) and *The Peak of the Load* (1918). Greenslet would also publish Leslie Buswell's memoir of volunteer service, *Ambulance Number Ten* (1915), closely followed by Ian Hay Beith's *The First Hundred Thousand* (1916), Charles W. Eliot's *The Road to Peace* (1916), and James Norman Hall's *Kitchener's Mob* (1916). The manuscripts kept on coming, and the books kept on selling. Between 1914 and 1918, Houghton Mifflin would issue over a hundred war books with a total circulation of nearly 1.5 million copies—and this was only one of hundreds of publishing firms across America.[2] Wartime industry was booming; and the book trade was no exception. However, Greenslet's stake in the war was not merely economic: "The chief aim," he admitted in 1943 as another war was waged, "was to try to help educate America to a full knowledge of the evil ambitions that were loose in the world, even if in the end it should lead us to join in fighting them."[3]

This apparently bland remark is revealing, and not just for the moral confidence that underpins it, or the educative purpose of literature that it assumes. Here is another reminder that for the American reader, the First World War was a cultural and intellectual event long before it was a practical reality. Most European readers were thrust into conflict, or at least into a social environment focused obsessively on that conflict, with little cultural preparation—certainly with no sense of the kinds of images, both verbal and visual, that it would produce. On the other hand, American readers had almost three years to think and read about the war before it became their national business. It is probably no coincidence that *The Great War and Modern Memory*, the study which so decisively claimed the war as a cultural event, should have been by an American author. Paul Fussell has little to say about the American literature written during the war, or even after it. However, his premise that its events should be understood primarily through their impact on the collective cultural consciousness probably stems from this prevailing American perspective on the war as a site of intellectual and artistic conflict, rather than as a social and political fault line in the historical landscape—though it was that too for the United States. Greenslet clearly had no embarrassment, even in hindsight, that he deliberately put his readers in the mood for fighting. He was also good enough at his job to know that this was increasingly what the public wanted. As Charles Genthe points out in his survey of almost four hundred nonfiction American war narratives printed during the war, the overwhelming numbers of such books took for granted that military action was justified, and extolled the virtues of "sacrifice and inspiration." Such texts, Genthe insists, should not be seen as proof of naivety or ignorance on behalf of their authors, but rather "as evidence of the romantic orientation of the American reading public."[4] Despite the present-day habit of equating the experience of the war with innovative literary practice and the expression of disillusionment, in reality, daring and cynical texts were slow to emerge, and were vastly outnumbered by those which took a more idealistic line. These enthusiastic texts clearly made their mark. The energy with which many Americans embraced the declaration of war in April 1917, shows how well the cultural ground had been prepared in the early phases of the conflict by Greenslet and others like him. Nevertheless, before condemning this alliance of publishing and politics, one should remember how informal, at times even antagonistic, this alliance was, especially in the early stages of the war, when much of what he published was directly in conflict with Wilson's policy of neutrality. Greenslet clearly felt that the literature came first, and the politics had better catch up if it could. His effectiveness as an opinion maker, however, would be officially recognized later in the war. After April 1917, Greenslet worked closely with George Creel and provided a publishing outlet for the activities of the Vigilantes.[5] He was also offered a post in the U.S. navy in communications in London. "It was a terrific temptation," he wrote, "but after a conference in Washington, the consensus of wise men was that I would better keep on doing my bit where I was."[6]

Not everyone saw it that way. Later in the war, Randolph Bourne would survey this entire process with characteristic disgust: "If our intellectuals were going to lead the administration, they might conceivably have tried to find some way of securing peace by making neutrality effective. They might have turned their intellectual energy not to the problem of jockeying the nation into war, but to the problem of using our vast neu-

tral power to attain democratic ends for the rest of the world and ourselves
without the use of the malevolent technique of war. They might have
failed. The point is that they scarcely tried."[7] But even Bourne had to admit that the writing and publishing classes were largely responding to
public taste, though this taste for dramatic foreign crises over less exotic
troubles closer to home struck him as bitterly complacent: "Numbers of
intelligent people who had never been stirred by the horrors of capitalistic
peace at home were shaken out of their slumber by the horrors of war in
Belgium. Never having felt responsibility for labor wars and oppressed
masses and excluded races at home, they had a large fund of idle emotional capital to invest in the oppressed nationalities and ravaged villages
of Europe. Hearts that had felt only ugly contempt for democratic striv-
ings at home beat in tune with the struggle for freedom abroad."[8] Despite
their different political sympathies, both Greenslet and Bourne make it
all sound straightforward—which it wasn't. Had the reading public responded wholeheartedly to the arguments for war, there would have been
no need for George Creel's inventive and expensive Committee on Public
Information (Greenslet's "wise men" in Washington) to market the conflict
to America in 1917. Alternatively, had the cultural elite, of which Bourne
was himself a prominent member, uniformly supported military intervention, there would have been no cause for the restrictions on freedom of
political expression put in place once America mobilized. Clearly, the publishing environment of the midwar period was a complex one, and general-
izations about readers and writers were, and remain, treacherous. To
engage with the First World War in print was to take on a set of inconsistencies and contradictions which at times defied expression.

The rest of this chapter looks at three texts which dared to engage
with the war in this turbulent publishing context. Wharton's edited collection *The Book of the Homeless,* which was sold in aid of her refugee
charities, came out early in 1916, featuring a stunning international cast of
writers, artists, and composers from Thomas Hardy to Igor Stravinsky.
Here was a clear piece of evidence, were any needed, of Wharton's elite
cultural status and her enviable personal connections in both America
and Europe. It was also evidence of the willingness of the intellectual and

creative classes on both sides of the Atlantic to direct their abilities toward the "war effort." Likewise, Norton's pamphlet of patriotic poems *What Is Your Legion?* (1916), deftly handled by Greenslet at Houghton Mifflin, appears at first glance to be exactly the kind of text which Bourne blamed for heedlessly "jockeying the nation into war." On closer inspection, however, this text reveals an agenda deeply concerned with social reform and left-wing international politics. But the most remarkable text of 1916, perhaps the most remarkable text in English published during the war, was Ellen La Motte's memoir of her months spent nursing at the Western Front, *The Backwash of War.* This slight, dark book finds little to say about the political scenery of the moment, and offers nothing to the debate about American neutrality or intervention—unless pointing out the grim consequences of conflict can be seen as taking a stance. Its steely exposé of the moral ironies of war struck a new note among the war books of 1916, a note which the establishment would later be keen to silence, but which would sound again and again in later texts. None of these three books was a runaway success, either commercially or critically, although the reasons for their obscurity are in themselves interesting. Nevertheless, these works offer glimpses into the complexities and inconsistencies of the midwar book world, and show the difficulties of persuading readers to think about the war in any but the simplest terms.

A Book for the Homeless

Henry James described it as an "inspiring appeal."[9] In July 1915, Edith Wharton wrote to a number of her friends and contacts, outlining her plans for a collaborative book to be sold in aid of her wartime charities. She was by no means the first to take on such a project. In 1914, Wharton had contributed a poem to *King Albert's Book,* edited by Rudyard Kipling and sold in aid of the Belgian Fund of the *Daily Telegraph.*[10] Samuel Honey and James Muirhead's *Sixty American Opinions on the War* appeared in 1915 "to show how many friends we have in America."[11] Winifred Stephens's anthology *The Book of France,* to which James had contributed the opening essay, came out in July 1915. James sent Wharton a copy, presumably so that she could survey the competition, though he insisted that the "B. of F. doesn't amount to much (such things, *con rispetto parlando,* never do!)"[12] Wharton, however, was determined that her book would amount to something, and with characteristic energy and ambition, she set about amassing a dazzling list of almost sixty contributors, and arranging with her publisher Charles Scribner to produce the volume on a nonprofit basis. Within a couple of weeks, she had secured offers of artwork from Claude Monet, Auguste Rodin, Jacques-Émile Blanche, Charles Dana Gibson, Leon Bakst, designer for the Ballet Russe, and Pierre-August Renoir, who sent a charcoal sketch of his son, who had been recently wounded at the front, one of the finest items in the book. James, despite his reservations about the genre, turned out to be a willing and effective assistant, liaising with his literary and artistic contacts such as Joseph Conrad, William Dean Howells, Thomas Hardy, and John Singer Sargent. However, still smarting from their recent quarrel, James drew the line at corresponding with H. G. Wells, and Wharton had to deal with him directly. Laurence Binyon, John Masefield, Paul Bourget, Arnold Bennett, Mary Ward, Max Beerbohm, John Galsworthy, Edmund Gosse, Josephine Preston Peabody, Sarah Bernhardt, Eleanora Duse, and Claude Debussy: the list of contributors provides a vivid snapshot of the cultural landscape of the moment—or at least of Wharton's carefully composed landscape, which is not quite the same thing. Edward Marsh gave permission for a poem by Rupert Brooke to be included posthumously. André Gide, who was closely involved in the Foyer Franco-Belge, also provided a piece, but there were few representatives of the younger, or more experimental generation of writers and artists: no Gertrude Stein, no Roger Fry, no T. E. Hulme, no Ezra Pound, certainly no Wyndham Lewis. W. B. Yeats, at James's request, provided a short but pithy six-line poem, "A Reason for Keeping Silent," voicing dissent at the whole project. Wharton, to her credit, printed it anyway.[13]

She did not agree with Yeats that the poet had "no gift to set a statesman right." Indeed, the point of the venture was to allow her poets a platform to speak over the heads of the statesmen, society figures, or religious leaders, who were notably absent in this volume—certainly in comparison with the competition. *The Book of France* had a decidedly aristocratic tone. The London branch of the French Parliamentary Committee's Fund for the Relief of the Invaded Departments which had benefited from the book was headed by an honorary committee which boasted five British government ministers, including Winston Churchill, and a number of peers of the realm. While most of the articles were contributed by prominent French writers, many of the translations were provided by the wives of the great and the good of the British Empire: Lady Randolph Churchill, the Duchess of Sutherland, Lady Frazer, Lady Glenconner. However, this society gathering was nothing compared to Kipling's bewildering list of over two hundred contributors in *King Alfred's Book*.[14] In that introduction, Hall Caine, one of the most popular novelists of the day, boasted that the volume had been created "by the pens of a large number of representative men and women of the civilised countries," though one has to wonder exactly who or what this select cast represented.[15] Alongside a rich array of writers, artists, and composers (many of whom also contributed to Wharton's book), sat the names of the British prime minister, H. H. Asquith; the chancellor of the exchequer, David Lloyd George; the former U.S. president Howard Taft; the former viceroy of India Lord Curzon; plus Lord Kitchener, Lord Bryce, and a score more of earls, admirals, members of Parliament, and public figures, including Emmeline Pankhurst, the chief rabbi, and no less than six archbishops. In contrast, Wharton's book was self-consciously, if not quite exclusively, artistic. The French generals Joffre and Humbert found their way into the volume, as did her old friend the Boston judge and novelist Robert Grant—although when he sent a caustic anti-Wilson essay about the trivialities of the upper classes at Newport, Rhode Island, for inclusion, Wharton asked him to withdraw it and submit a thoughtful poem instead. As is obvious from her preface, *The Book of the Homeless* was not intended as an overtly political text—though it is often read as such. Apart from one reference to the "senseless and savage bombardment" of southwest Belgium in April 1915, Wharton's preface makes no direct allusion to the war, focusing instead on the stories of the refugees and the activities of the relief workers. This was a volume dedicated to those willing to "carry the burden of humanity," and which was

to impress through the "beauty and variety" of the work of Wharton's col-
laborators.[16] With her famous good taste, selecting and directing the finest
cultural talent of her era, she clearly believed she was creating, or at least
curating, a work of art.

So, it seems ill-judged that Wharton should have commissioned an
introduction from Theodore Roosevelt. Scribner was initially in agreement with this choice, but when Roosevelt caused a public stir with his
attack on Wilson's administration in *America and the World War,* which
Scribner himself published 1915, he became nervous that a highly politi-
cized introduction might give the book "a somewhat controversial character." Scribner reminded Wharton that the former president was "so much
disliked in some quarters and has hit the Administration so hard" that
Wilson's supporters might be put off from buying the book.[17] These fears
were not allayed when Scribner saw Roosevelt's copy, in which he noted
pointedly that Wharton's relief work went some way to atone for "our national shortcomings."[18] But Scribner could no more say "nay" to Wharton
than anyone else could—and as usual she got her way. Wharton knew
Roosevelt personally, and admired his pro-Allied stance on the war. She
was also captivated by his energy, eloquence, and charisma. After his
death in 1919, she would write to his sister Corinne Roosevelt Robinson:
"When I write of your brother my heart chokes in my throat & I can't go
on. No one will ever know what his example & his influence were to me."[19]
His sense of urgency and responsibility, his appeal to duty, and his conviction of the ennobling influence of service to one's nation chimed forcefully with her own ideas. Nevertheless, it is hard to imagine that Wharton,
with her nuanced opinions on social manners and transactions, could
ever have fully taken on board his aggressive nationalism or his essentialist attitudes to gender roles.[20] What they did share, however, was the conviction that the war with Germany was the supreme test of their society, that
it was not just a conflict about geopolitical boundaries and international
economics, but of ideals and moral absolutes. Hence, Wharton's willingness to include Roosevelt in what was fundamentally a cultural project.
His visionary rhetoric made him, in Wharton's eyes at least, more than a
mere politician. He spoke for the values of civilization.

And what better way to declare one's belief in the future of civilization than by creating an object of aesthetic and cultural value that would
bear witness to the suffering of the war being fought to sustain it? Wharton is sometimes accused of degrading her art for fund-raising purposes
during the war. However, the production of *The Book of the Homeless* suggests the opposite: here was a women determined not to compromise on
artistic standards. Every inch of *The Book of the Homeless,* and every element of its production spoke of Wharton's discrimination and her faith in
the ability of the reading public, or at least an elite strata of it, to appreciate
the quality of the object in hand. Scribner's was the perfect publisher for
such a project. Since the 1870s, the firm had been acquiring a reputation as
a publisher of deluxe editions of classic writers such as Stevenson, Kipling,
Carlyle, and Hawthorne.[21] These series—often available by subscription
only, which prevented the purchase of single volumes, thus putting these
items firmly out of the financial reach of a whole class of readers—were cal-
culated to appeal to the image-conscious nouveau riche of Gilded Age
America, for whom book-owning was often more important than reading
itself. Henry James's New York Edition (1907–9) had been just such a project, offering beautifully crafted books printed on specially watermarked
paper with photographic plates and elegant, hand-finished bindings—but
many of the copies circulating today still have uncut pages. These were
books to be displayed, handled, and admired, rather than actually read.[22]

Wharton herself had grown up in a house which boasted a "gentleman's library" of several hundred books, mostly just such sets of calf-bound
volumes: Macauley, Victor Hugo, Sainte-Beauve, the Brontës, Ruskin,
Coleridge, and assorted French and English classics. "Were these latter
ever read?" she asked in her autobiography, "Not often, I imagine; but
they were there; they represented a standard."[23] Wharton, therefore, well
understood the material role of books in upper-class American life as sym-
bols, not simply of conspicuous leisure and consumption, but also as to-
tems of some governing, if remote, cultural "standard"—the standard of
civilization. She was capable of mocking this attitude, as she had begun to
do in the unfinished novel *Literature,* which she abandoned at the outbreak of the war, but she also participated in it. Witness her lavish con-

struction of a personal library of several thousand volumes at her house, The Mount, in Lenox, Massachusetts, which significantly was also one of her favorite rooms for entertaining visitors.[24]

Wharton *did* read her books, voraciously, throughout her life, but she knew that for many of her class, the look of the thing was what mattered— and it was from her own class that she hoped to eke out more funds for her relief work. So, early in her planning for *The Book of the Homeless* with Charles Scribner, she asked him to engage the services of Daniel Berkeley Updike, the Boston book designer and director of the Merrymount Press, to oversee the production of the book. Wharton knew Updike from her years living in Newport and Lenox, admired his work, and had consistently sent business his way when possible, insisting that her Scribner's books be printed with Updike in the years before the company had a press of its own. However, the production of *The Book of the Homeless* was much more complicated than a novel. There were artworks in a number of media to reproduce, some in black and white, some as photographic plates, and several in color. The standard edition was to cost five dollars, but there were also to be small runs of limited editions, priced at twenty-five and fifty dollars, aimed at the bibliophile market, not just with different covers, but also printed on special high-quality paper.[25] Wharton had originally hoped that the book would be on sale by October 1915, but her specifications required meticulous planning. With her own sense of urgency and with the astonishing amount of energy that she mustered for all of her war projects, she found it hard to understand why others could not instantly meet her demands. Various contributions came in behind schedule, including Wharton's own translations of the French contributions, slowing down the editorial process. At one point, James feared his essay had found its way to the bottom of the Atlantic with the American ship the *Arabic*.[26] Nor was Updike moving as fast on the production side as Scribner would have liked. To Wharton, Scribner voiced his frustration at having to send everything to Boston, "and not be able to crowd the work, as we could do in our own factory or if done under our direction." Writing to Grant, who had offered to collate the American contributions, he noted more candidly that Wharton's expectations were unrealistic: "It is a more difficult matter to get such a book into shape than she perhaps realizes, but we shall pull through in some way."[27]

Scribner did pull through, but not in time to catch the Christmas gift-book market, which had been the main target of the project—an outcome which, as Lee suggests, contributed to Wharton's decision to shift to Appleton as her publisher after the war.[28] This was a bitter disappointment for Wharton, compounded by the news of James's debilitating series of strokes in early December, and the upheaval of finding new premises for her sewing workroom when the French government requisitioned the building in which it had lodged. The book finally came out on 22 January 1916 and was, Scribner assured her, "a very fine example of bookmaking."[29] Good taste had triumphed, but this taste was also the Achilles' heel of the project. By late April, Scribner could report to Wharton that sales of the book had been satisfactory, largely through the tireless efforts of Wharton's sister-in-law Minnie Jones, who had coaxed and bullied the ranks of New York society into purchasing the volume. However, the production of the book had been so lavish that of the nine thousand dollars of sales, seventy-five hundred dollars had been eaten up in costs, mostly incurred by Updike.[30]

Fortunately, Wharton was not only relying on sales of the book. Through Minnie, she had arranged an auction of the original artworks and manuscripts at the American Art Gallery in New York on 25 January. Authors, including James and Roosevelt, who had submitted typescript copy for the printers, had also laboriously copied out their own words by hand to create a more marketable commodity. James's manuscript of "The Long Wards" sold for $500; Scribner himself paid $575 for General Joffre's contribution; Wharton's short poem "The Tryst," a hastily written, emotive piece, which she described to Minnie as "doggerel," sold for $350. The auction was exactly the sort of society charity event that Wharton would lampoon in her novel *A Son at the Front;* but the numbers added up. After expenses, the auction netted almost seven thousand dollars— more than four times what the book itself raised in the first few months.[31] Wharton had been right that the New York upper classes liked their culture in collectible form—as shown by the fact that the deluxe fifty-dollar edition of *The Book of the Homeless* had been the first to sell out. She also relished, no doubt, the verdict of the *New York Times* on the book, which praised her preface for its "direct, simple and graphic style, its personality and singleness of heart." Like almost every other contribution, it was, the reviewer added, "a piece of real literature."[32]

Wharton had not pitched the book as a political statement, but this did not mean that she wished to avoid the controversial aspects of the war within its pages. And as her own poem "The Tryst" demonstrates, accounts of the suffering of civilians, especially children, were not only powerfully poignant but also fairly effective at extracting dollars from the public—or at least they had been up until now. But as Ferris Greenslet had discovered, the best time to publish a war book was the day it was accepted by the publisher. By the time *The Book of the Homeless* came out, the mood both in American and Europe had shifted from that of mid-1915. Images of Belgian atrocities no longer had quite the shock value or even the credibility that they had commanded six months before, and most Americans were hoping that Wilson would negotiate both sides into peace. *Ars longa, vita brevis*—a phrase which in this context translates as the somewhat obvious truth that the production of beautiful art books could never keep pace with the rapid events, the fickle tastes, and the brutally short lives of the midwar period.

Slow though it was, the push to get the book through the printers meant that Wharton, overstretched with her relief work in Paris, did not take as much time over the placing of the different contributions as she might have. The book is grouped generically, with poems and artworks all placed together in the opening section, and all the prose works together at the back of the book. Opportunities to highlight many of the book's recurring themes and motifs have been missed. Monet's beautifully executed crayon sketch of boats on a beach might have sat dynamically alongside Conrad's account of his escape with his family from Poland through Austria at the start of the war, full as this is of reminiscences of his life at sea and his interest in the underwater war of the U-boats. Renoir's sketch of his young son could have illustrated James's elegy for wounded youth in "The Long Wards." The scattered references to homes and houses seem almost accidental, which they evidently were not in a book sold in aid of the homeless; some judicious placing would have illuminated this central image. Wharton either did not understand or did not leave time for the creative possibilities of editing, which could have fused this collection into an elegant statement about the war. The raw material was good enough; certain pieces, at least those by James and Yeats, have become canonical texts. Despite this, *The Book of the Homeless* offers a less satisfying and lively read than contemporary issues of *Scribner's Magazine* or the *Atlantic Monthly*, in which poems and pictures are placed for maximum effect, and the pieces jostle against each other for attention. Nevertheless, despite the slightly wooden placement of the items (or perhaps because of it), the crush of voices and perspectives gathered in *The Book of the Homeless* aligns the volume with a technique that would become increasingly useful for representing the war and its aftermath: montage.

Wharton was the figure who linked everything in the project together. Yet, seen on paper without an intimate knowledge of the book's production history, the contributors would have appeared as an unlikely, almost a surreal, grouping of disparate voices. Where else could one possibly find André Gide sharing pages with Theodore Roosevelt, or the actress Sarah Bernhardt within the same cover as the great Harvard philosopher George Santayana? The spectrum of political hues runs from pacifist to belligerent, with every shade in between. As with the potential thematic connections, Wharton has not made the most of these startling contrasts—although this failure also creates, perhaps unwittingly, a democratizing effect in which the words of the actress, the general, and the man or woman of letters are presented in flat series and without hierarchy, as though to underscore that the war described in this volume defies expression by the single voice, and can only be apprehended in fragments. This effect is also intensified by the mix of French and English in the book, and by the fact that most of the artworks are either studies for other works or unfinished sketches, thus showing artistic expression in process—in stark contrast with the lovingly produced material object in which they were embedded. The majority of these visual images are informal pencil or charcoal sketches of contributors to the volume, so that many of the named figures within the book are encountered from Two angles, as both a speaker and a subject, as both a voice and a face. Each of these faces, the volume silently reminds us, sees the war through its own eyes and from its own point of view.

Fragmentation, brevity, mixed media, diverse voices, conflicting perspectives, anticlimax: over the next two decades, these would become standard devices of the self-conscious literary text—although Wharton herself would continue to deliver her carefully controlled narratives, and readers would continue to devour them. At first glance, *The Book of the Homeless* has little in common with the radical, collaborative literary ventures of that decade on both sides of the Atlantic, such as *Blast, New Numbers,* or the *Seven Arts.* These publications are often seen as the rightful precursors to the multimedia format of the experimental yet fashionable literary periodicals of the 1920s such as the *Little Review,* the *Dial,* or the *Criterion,* in which many later responses to the war, including poetry by Cummings and Eliot, were published. However, as a sustained look at *The Book of the Homeless* shows, many of the distinctive elements of these journals were also employed in established and elitist literary circles such as those around Wharton—partly out of necessity. The story of her book reveals how multiplicity, fragmentation, and paradox were all produced in this text by the conditions of the war, and the exigencies of producing collaborative art in the midst of cultural confusion. As such, it provides one of those missing links in the narrative of *how* the war shaped the literature which followed it. Wharton's volume bears the hallmarks of a rushed job, but even that rush can be seen as a defining element of modern life, and her loss, or dispersal, of editorial control can be read as an experiment in a less individualistic, author-centered way of creating text. In her search for a format in which the bewilderment and fragmentation of war might be communicated, she had clearly struck on something that had potential.

What Is Your Nation?

On Friday 6 May 1916, John Purroy Mitchell, the mayor of New York, had a bad day at the office. He decided to request the postponement of a memorial service in Carnegie Hall the following day, organized by the American Rights Committee to mark the anniversary of the sinking of the *Lusitania*. It was billed as a memorial service, but there was no disguising the political intent of the event. Three thousand tickets had been issued, a program of organ music, including Chopin's "Funeral March" and the patriotic song "America" was planned. A "*Lusitania* Declaration," calling for the severance of diplomatic relations with Germany, had already been drafted. A small book of poetry had been specially printed for sale at the event. Mayor Mitchell was worried. On 4 May, the U.S. government had asked the German government to suspend submarine warfare against neutral shipping, and Mitchell claimed that the meeting would jeopardize negotiations and cause scuffles in the streets with pacifist protestors. He called in the organizers and "suggested" that they defer it. His actions were taken, he claimed, "to avoid possible embarrassment to the national government or anything which might produce disorder in the city."[33] But if he was hoping to divert attention away from the anniversary of the sinking of the *Lusitania,* he had miscalculated. The *New York Times* gave the story of the postponement front-page coverage, reported the planned program, and printed the draft "*Lusitania* Declaration" in full. It also gave front-page prominence to the event when it was finally allowed to go ahead two weeks later on Friday, 19 May, and printed the main speeches. However, by then most of the three thousand ticket holders had drifted away to other entertainments, and a crowd of only a few hundred showed up. The "*Lusitania* Declaration" was redrafted to include a condemnation of Mayor Mitchell's "suppression" of the original meeting as well as the failure of Germany to respond satisfactorily to the U.S. request for safe passage at sea. Public outrage was successfully motivated, and letters to the editor of the *New York Times* about the violation of American free speech flew thick and fast. The government was unmoved. Wilson, already planning his presidential reelection campaign, which would run in the fall of 1916 on the slogan "He kept us out of the war," was unlikely to rethink his position in the light of these events.

Caught in the middle of this debate was the small red paperback booklet of verse, sold by ushers at the Carnegie Hall event for twenty-five

cents. *What Is Your Legion?* by Grace Fallow Norton comprised twenty-
one poems calling openly for America's involvement in the war. It sold 240
copies on the night of the meeting, which was not a bad showing considering how few people turned up. Over the next six months it would sell a
further thousand copies across the United States and in Canada. Norton
donated her profits from the book, in the end only a few dollars, to the
American Rights Committee. But unlike *The Book of the Homeless,* this
pamphlet was never about the money. It was a statement of allegiance.

After Norton and her husband George Macrum sailed home in November 1914, they had spent the following months between their little
house in Woodstock and a rented apartment on East 31st Street in New
York. Macrum gave art classes, continued painting, and tried to sell his
pictures from the Brittany trip to pay the bills. Norton took her time finishing the poems for *Roads,* drafting and redrafting them carefully in
spare evenings between her engagements as a piano accompanist. Writing
about the war was a draining and seemingly futile process: "I felt like a
butterfly barking at a cyclone," she wrote to Greenslet as she sent him a
section of the manuscript.[34] In April 1916, just as *Roads* was going to the
press, Norton wrote again with a suggestion for another volume of verse.
"I had a writing fit about a month ago and wrote 23 poems in about three
weeks, having mostly dreamed it out first in a very curious way. . . . And I
daresay the work is as crude as though it were not so divinely inspired."[35]
She had shown it around to friends and literary contacts in New York, including Professor Franklin Giddings, a sociologist at Columbia University
and a key member of the American Rights Committee. This Committee,
closely aligned with the Preparedness movement, was chaired by the publisher and Civil War veteran Major George Haven Putnam, and included
Hamlin Garland, Booth Tarkington, Josiah Royce, and many more writers and academics within its ranks. It was bankrolled by some of the most
respectable surnames in America: Adamses, Abbotts, Curtises, Emer-
sons, Hales, Longfellows, and Wendells.[36] Despite his sympathy with the
content, Giddings was unable to undertake to publish a pamphlet of poems, but he showed them to Putnam, who pronounced them "well deserv-
ing to come into print."[37] Meanwhile, Norton had enlisted Greenslet. He

was a little wary of the "slap-dash" quality of the verse, but still felt it was "pithy and timely stuff, and ought to see the light."[38] If a backer could be found to underwrite the project, Houghton Mifflin would, wrote Greenslet, "be very glad indeed to handle them both on poetic and patriotic grounds." He signed off from this letter, "Belligerently yours."[39] Three days later, on 24 April, Norton sent the revised copy of the poems, along with the news that Elizabeth Stillman Chamberlain, wife of a Columbia professor, had taken an interest in the project and would back the project against any losses to the publisher. Would it be possible, Norton asked, to have the pamphlet for 7 May, for the meeting at Carnegie Hall? Could the books have a red paper cover? "It would please me enormously to have just the right shade." She concluded, "The word 'patriotic' in your last letter brings its usual thrill. It is a fine, beautiful word and we may have to pay a big price for it. Who knows?" Greenslet wrote back, promising to set up the type at once, apparently undaunted by the two-week turnaround, although there was one minor disappointment: "The fact seems to be that owing to the war it is impossible to get red paper. It's an aniline dye or something, and the Germans, among their other atrocities, have prevented its exportation."[40] Norton, however, insisted on the color, offering to "pay for that lovely red dress, if it must be paid for, out of my pocket."[41] Greenslet, patiently attentive to detail, and probably aware from Norton's correspondence how little she could afford such a gesture, tracked some down in the end.

What did it matter—the color of the cover? Norton's anthology *Roads* had been closely attuned to the moods and associations of color. Her earlier war poems in the section of *Roads* called "The Red Road" had played on the passionate, violent, even diabolical connotations of red, like a lit fuse running from poem to poem. But *red* was a term that was also beginning to carry political overtones, and which would become one of the most contentious epithets of postwar America. With her wide spectrum of friends and contacts in anti-establishment circles, Norton would certainly have known of the *Little Red Song Book* of the Industrial Workers of the World, in which the organization's ambition to "form the new society within the shell of the old," was set to music. Despite the antiwar stance of the organization, the rhetoric of militarism was regularly adapted to voice the aspirations of the working class to struggle for victory over capitalism. This was quite literally the case in the appropriation of the Civil War song "Hold the Fort," which appeared in the 1914 edition of the *Song Book* with revised, labor-friendly lyrics:

> We meet today in freedom's cause
>   And raise our voices high;
> We'll join our hands in union strong
>   To battle or to die.
> *Hold the fort for we are coming—*
>   *Union Men, be strong.*
> *Side by side we battle onward.*
>   *Victory will come.*[42]

Even before the First World War broke out, lyricists such as Joe Hill, the most widely published of the IWW songwriters, was rejecting national allegiance in favor of anticapitalist radicalism. "Should I ever be a soldier," he had written in 1913,

> 'Neath the Red Flag I would fight;
> Should the gun I ever shoulder,
> It's to crush the tyrant's might.[43]

In this song, as Van Wienen notes, class war became "the justifiable, even necessary, alternative to national defense," and the violent wartime repressions of IWW activities were ominously prefigured.[44] Hill would not witness this. In November 1915, he was executed by firing squad in a Salt Lake City jail, convicted of a murder that very few people believed he had committed. The IWW masterminded a high-publicity campaign to secure him a new trial, in which Wilson himself had attempted to intervene, but the Utah Supreme Court would not be swayed. Throughout his confinement, Hill had carried on making up songs in prison, where his songs had so often been sung by others. In *1919*, the middle volume of *U.S.A.*,

John Dos Passos would characterize Hill as "forming the structure of the new society within the jails of the old."[45]

Norton's determination to issue *What Is Your Legion?* in the format of a blood-red pamphlet established both a kinship and a contrast with the *Little Red Song Book,* so recently the focus of intense public attention. Her book was the same size, weight, and color, but the opening poem, "O Say, What Is Your Legion?" announced a very different response to the war. This was a call to the American people not to stand aloof but to choose a side; and the conclusion of the poem left no doubt about which side Norton recommended:

> My people, O my people, whose towns the sea has spared,
> O say, what is your legion? How has your legion fared?
>
> And the music of your marching,—is your music surging
> shrill
> Where the world rocks and shivers, uttering its will?
>
> My land, eyrie of eagles whose wings beat by the sea!
> When shall we cry to Belgium, "Our hearts are with
> you—free!"?[46]

Unlike Wharton, Norton does not labor the plight of Belgium as an incentive for action. Instead she appeals to the past—most specifically the shared republican past of France and America. "When Lafayette Came" recalls America's debt to the French general who defied King Louis XVI to serve against the British in the Revolutionary War. She also aligns the reader's sympathy with Daniel Webster, whose powerful speech in favor of Greek independence in 1824 was an open criticism of the newly minted Monroe Doctrine, and with Germany's failed revolution of 1848,

> that dear lost year, so great,
> So brief, so black, so bright—
> When your soul yearned for liberty.[47]

Defiance of a misguided government, these poems suggest, is often the noblest route. The obvious implication, especially given the context of the book's debut at Carnegie Hall, was that these instances from the past served as models for speaking out against Wilson's policy of neutrality. However, there are also poems in the booklet which betoken a more radical attitude to government. In "Blunders and Faults" and in "Vast Russia" she condemns the tyranny of czarist Russia, while celebrating the "young noble students crying, 'Liberty!' "[48] In "Come to the Door of Your Heart" she berates the captains of American industry, the very class of people who had put up the money for the *Lusitania* rally, for growing rich on the proceeds of the wartime economy:

> O come to the door of your heart!
> Your servants would send me away;
> They say you are sitting apart,
> Counting your gold all the day.
> They say your tills overflow,
> That your bright gold rings and chimes,—
> That its chiming covers so
> The din of these warring times![49]

The speaker of the poem stands at the door, Christ-like, unregarded, offering redemption and wholeness through engagement with the fate of the wider world. Norton's depiction of Germany seems cartoonlike in "Blood and Iron," where she characterizes "An iron land with an iron god / and no faith in man save under an iron rod."[50] However, her invective is all for the kaiser, and ultimately her justification for the Allied cause is that France and Britain are fighting to topple "an armed and iron monarchy," to free the German people (although she does have to do some fancy footwork to excuse Britain its king and its empire).[51] Perhaps the most vivid statement of Norton's position is in the coda to the collection, "This Book":

> I saw this book in a dream.
> I held it within my hands;

The cover of it was red;
I waited my soul's commands.
Red is the color of blood,
The color of brotherhood;
Red is the color of flame—
I saw this book in a dream.[52]

This poem makes no secret of its political sympathies. However, there are other resonances at work here too. There is more than an echo of the "Author's Apology" which opens the second volume of John Bunyan's *The Pilgrim's Progress*, another work of conscience, also based on a dream, also defiant of political authority and insistent on the rights of the individual—but ironically also a text which had become widely accepted as an exemplar of sound moral and cultural values in the prewar era.[53] Indeed, this is a text that resonates through other poems of Norton's both in this collection and in *Roads*, which is so clearly structured around the idea of a spiritual journey, though not an explicitly religious one, through the turmoil of emotional change and war. Norton deftly maneuvers her reader into, at the very least, acquiescence with her aspirations for international political change by her apparent acceptance of mainstream values. However, woven through certain familiar and bland points of reference are those other more radical sentiments, which would not have been at all out of place in the *Little Red Song Book:* "The brothers of our souls! Who are they? When / The cry is 'Men or Kings?' our brothers answer 'Men!' "[54] In 1916, this sympathy with international socialist ambitions did not appear to present Norton or—perhaps more tellingly—her publisher with any dilemma about her commitment to American nationalism. As her comments to Greenslet show, Norton considered herself "patriotic," and her poems express a blend of Emersonian individualism and socialist comradeship that would have been impossible to market even a few months later to an American public suspicious of Bolshevik designs on Western democracy. However, in May 1916, this position dovetailed neatly with the rhetoric of benevolent expansionism that was quickly becoming the most convincing argument for American intervention in the war. This was certainly the tone of the *Lusitania* meeting. Putnam's speech, reported the next day in the *New York Times*, offered a rationale for action which has an oddly familiar air for modern-day readers:

> We have a State gone mad to deal with. The other States of Europe are trying now to curb this mad State, and I declare that the time has now come when the United States should act with France and England and Belgium and their allies in the cause they are fighting for. They are fighting for principles which every American should hold dear. They are fighting for democracy against autocracy. Germany believes that the United States is her enemy. The German people have been fed lies concerning the United States and its attitude in this war. If at the end of this war the Teutons win we will have the job on our hands of fighting for our lives. We are sure of one enemy. Let's be careful to keep the friendship of those who are still our friends.[55]

The fear of the "rogue" state, the sense of alliance with a common international cause, the promotion of democracy and founding principles, the distinction between foreign states and their peoples, but the unity between the American state and hers, national security, special relationships: these have become familiar arguments for American intervention overseas throughout the past century. Woodrow Wilson and his advisors are often accused of inventing these tropes retrospectively to justify a decision to act in 1917, when neutrality became politically untenable. However, these ideas were clearly well-rehearsed among the American intellectual classes many months before they became White House policy.

After America entered the war in 1917, Norton's husband, George Macrum, volunteered to work with wounded soldiers with the YMCA in France. Later, he was seriously ill during the Spanish flu epidemic of 1919. Norton tried to get back to France too, but her poor eyesight and a recurring cough barred her from volunteer service. The little house which she had built in Woodstock burned to the ground, destroying many of Macrum's paintings from the months in Brittany, and many traces of her childhood.

4. Grace Fallow Norton's passport photograph, c. 1920.
Photograph courtesy of Ellen Weiss.

Norton increasingly earned a living through translation work, and in 1917 found herself caught up with a bestseller as the translator of *The Odyssey of a Torpedoed Transport,* a series of anonymously published letters supposedly written by a French merchant seaman, "Y.," but really the fictional work of Maurice Larrouy (1882–1939). In 1919, Norton joined Macrum in Paris after his discharge, and around the time of the Paris Peace Conference, which she found profoundly disillusioning, she was translating political pamphlets for the League for International Conciliation. One of these recounted the German workers' revolution of 1918; another called for more lenient treatment of postwar Germany in the Treaty of Versailles, warning that a harsh settlement would store up trouble for the future. The couple were largely based in France through the 1920s and 1930s, but by the outbreak of the Second World War, Norton and Macrum were back in the United States, living in Sloatsburg, New York, and voting for F.D.R.

During the 1940s, Macrum abandoned his painting because of a shake in his hands caused by a palsy; Norton gave up writing in solidarity. However, she never gave up her left-wing views. Her great niece Ellen Weiss recounts the story of an elderly Norton in the 1950s on a family visit to Washington, DC, asking to be taken to the visitors' gallery in the Senate but having to be hastily ushered out when it became clear that what she planned to do when she got there was to lean over the balcony and spit on Senator McCarthy's head. It would have been a dramatic gesture of contempt for his treatment of the creative community, but not even that would have made Grace Fallow Norton "un-American." Hers was a view of nationality that transcended party politics.

Backwash

Across the Atlantic, another aspiring writer was experiencing the disillusionment of war, but this time at closer quarters. Ellen La Motte had arrived in Paris in November 1914, eager to put her extensive nursing skills to good use, but soon found herself asking: "Was it not all a dead-end occupation, nursing back to health men to be patched up and returned to the trenches, or a man to be patched up, court-martialled and shot?"[56] She had been determined to work at the front, although she was, as her friend Gertrude Stein noted, rather "gun shy."[57] It was probably Stein who sent what La Motte called the "cryptic message" which brought her to France in the first place. It said simply, "Come—American Ambulance," a phrase which called up images of "service on the battlefield, gathering in the wounded on stretchers and conveying them to a waiting ambulance," or working night and day for eighteen-hour shifts in a dressings station without time to eat or sleep.[58] Gun shy or not, La Motte accepted the challenge, but she was quickly to discover that little in this war would be as expected. The "Ambulance" turned out to be the spacious and lavishly equipped American Hospital in the suburb of Neuilly. There were ten-hour shifts and regular days off; there were wealthy volunteers who showed up for work wearing the family pearls with their uniforms; there was tea every day at three o'clock; and there was an overabundance of clean sheets and medicines, of dressings and cigarettes for the patients.

It was only the patients themselves who were in short supply. During the Battle of the Marne, earlier in the autumn, the wounded had come in twenty a day and more; now there were barely twenty a week. There were 350 patients in a hospital that could hold 400. La Motte heard that over thirty thousand hospital beds in the city lay empty. Since the Germans had retreated, Paris was too far from the front to serve as a major medical clearing center; the hospital was now, she noted wryly, nothing more than "a clearing house for sentiment."[59] Anyone who wanted to help was taken on, regardless of their experience or skills: aristocrats, both American and French, artists, painters, opera singers, writers. Some were hardworking and adaptable. Others seemed more intent on "gathering experiences which will tell well in next year's ball-rooms." Many came for the regular meals and the company. "Do come down to tea," an upper-class auxiliary urged La Motte one afternoon. "Why, one meets all the smartest people in Paris down at tea!"[60] There were, of course, terrible injuries to be treated. As La Motte quickly surmised, those patients who had lived long enough to make it to hospital were not so likely to die of their wounds, as of the gangrenous infections that set in from lying too long in the mud of no man's land, or waiting for days in railway stations or hospital trains on the way to Paris. What was needed, she could see, was more effective care closer to the front. "Somewhere off, outside of Paris, there is Hell let loose, and daily we hear tales of wounded men lying in hundreds in the market place of some little French village, neglected and uncared for; but that is another story."[61]

La Motte's exasperation with the amateur, thrill-seeking volunteers of the American Hospital was to be expected, perhaps. Its patrician atmosphere offended both her nonconforming views about the position and potential of women in society, and her long years of medical training and experience. Ellen Newbold La Motte was born in Louisville, Kentucky, in 1873. Her father, Ferdinand La Motte, was from French Huguenot stock, and her mother, also Ellen, was a Newbold—a name which figures regularly in Wharton's family tree.[62] La Motte had studied at the Johns Hopkins

Training School for Nurses in Baltimore, graduating in 1902, and then
serving as a supervising nurse for the Johns Hopkins Hospital. It was during these years that she had struck up a friendship with Stein, who was
studying there for a medical degree, which she never completed. From
1904 to 1905, La Motte was assistant superintendent at St. Luke's Hospital
in St. Louis, but in 1905 she returned to Baltimore to work as a tuberculosis nurse with the Instructive Visiting Nurses Association. In 1910, she
took up a role as the superintendent of the Tuberculosis Division of the
Baltimore Health Department, a position she held until 1913.[63] Her methods were modern and radical. Shortly before leaving for France, she wrote
a handbook for TB nurses, dismissing the established modes of treating
the disease via home care, and advocating the voluntary segregation of patients in isolated hospital wards to halt the spread of the disease.[64] It was a
characteristically unsentimental solution to a difficult and emotive issue.
The *British Medical Journal* praised her approach, but this was a controversial stance, which set La Motte at odds with her own colleagues, many
of whom had long campaigned for a greater reliance on visiting nurses.[65]
However, the picture that emerges of La Motte through her own writing is
one of a woman who rarely flinched from telling an uncomfortable truth.

La Motte's public health role was also characterized by an awareness of the potential of women professionals in a heavily male-dominated
field. So, it was no surprise that on her arrival in Paris she engaged with
another of the careers increasingly opening up for women: journalism.
Buoyed up by the completion of her book on TB, and sharply aware that
as a nurse she would have access to places and scenes which professional
correspondents would never be allowed to see, La Motte was keen to capitalize on this privileged viewpoint. Unlike Borden, she had limited literary experience, although in her thirties she had published essays on
European hospitals, each of which was a curious blend of public-health
research and travel writing; she also edited the *Johns Hopkins Nurses'
Alumnae Magazine* in 1908.[66] She had always wanted to write, and a
monthly stipend paid to her by a cousin, the wealthy industrialist Alfred I.
DuPont, had encouraged her to resign her nursing post in Baltimore in
1913 with a view to developing her literary abilities. La Motte was always

and on 20 June, she set off with a group of nurses for Dunkirk. It took ten hours to complete a journey that before the war would have taken three. Papers had to be checked and rechecked, and La Motte had the sensation "of being locked in" to the military zone like "a prisoner at large."[69] They were met at the station by "B.," who drove them to a little, wooden seaside hotel. In the morning they sat on the beach and explored the bustling town. There were plenty of signs of the war, pasted strips of paper in the windows, distant guns, an occasional damaged house, but the sun was shining, the sea wind was sweet, and the water in the bay glittered and sparkled. "After the fever, the rush, the gossip and intrigue of Paris, this war zone seemed restfulness and peace."[70]

It was all different the following day. After six weeks of relative quiet, Dunkirk faced a fourteen-hour bombardment. It began at three in the morning, with a bomb dropped by a German plane, and all day at forty-minute intervals seventeen-inch shells fell on the town. The residents hid in their cellars, or fled to the beach, but nowhere was safe. This was the same bombardment that Wharton heard as she drove to La Panne to meet the Belgian king, the bombardment that ripped apart the Church of St. Eloi and the bourgeois house nearby. This was the work of the siege gun at Dixmude that had sounded to Wharton like "the closing of all the iron shop shutters in the world," announcing the end of domestic and mercantile normality.[71] Like Wharton, La Motte was both fascinated and appalled at the contrast between "the peaceful workaday life of yesterday and this sunlit, silent, stricken scene of today."[72] Caught in the town center as a new round of firing began with her fellow nurse "W.," La Motte felt utterly outwitted by the situation: "In that fearful moment, there was not one intellectual faculty that I could call upon. There was nothing in past experience, nothing of will-power, of judgement, of intuition, that could serve me. I was beyond and outside and apart from the accumulated experience of a lifetime. My intelligence was worthless in this moment of supreme need. Every decision would be wrong, every movement would be in the wrong direction, and it was also wrong to stand still."[73] It was a sharp and vivid lesson to La Motte that the war would test her capacities in ways that she could not previously have imagined.

A local family took the two nurses down to their cellar to shelter until the firing paused, and then they scrambled back to the hotel. But there was nowhere to hide and nothing to do. La Motte sat on the shuttered balcony with the other nurses, drinking tea and eating chocolate, "six of us, calm, smiling, apparently indifferent." Meanwhile the shells whistled overhead or struck nearby, once less than a hundred yards away. They could have asked an ambulance to drive them away into the countryside, but it seemed an admission of failure before they had even reached their hospital. "The authorities," she reasoned, "would consider it an indication of how we would stand by our patients under fire." So, to calm her nerves, La Motte picked up her pen, composing the account of the bombardment that she would later send to the *Atlantic Monthly* with the title "Under Shell-Fire at Dunkirk." "I am writing this to kill time," she wrote, "yet as each shell strikes I spring to the window, and my chair falls backwards, while the others laugh. . . . And so we sit on the balcony and watch the bursting shells—and wait."[74]

Did she really write an elegant eight-page journal article as shells whistled overhead? The final result seems too polished; the beginning of the piece gives no clue of this origin; the admission of her paralyzing fear under fire for the first time seems too considered. The task would have required incredible composure. However, it is not at all unlikely that something, which later became the article, took shape on that day and in that place—in the same way that many of Borden's sketches were drafted on location. There are too many accounts of soldiers and other service personnel turning to reading and writing as a way of distracting the mind during shelling for La Motte's claim to be dismissed as fanciful. Siegfried Sassoon writes vividly of repeating verse to himself during shell bombardments, and of reading to maintain his sense of identity during the endless, impersonal hours of boredom and waiting that army life induced.[75] Captain, later Lieutenant Colonel F. J. Roberts, MC, founding editor of the trench magazine the *Wipers Times* (named after the pronunciation of Ypres by the British troops), even copyedited under fire. "Have you ever sat in a trench in the middle of a battle and corrected proofs?" he would write after the war, "Try it."[76] But whatever she put on paper that day, La Motte's presentation of herself in the act of writing is significant. Like James, she wished to present herself to the world as an author, as an independent consciousness. Her tactics here are also like those in Mildred Aldrich's stylized "letters" from her house on the Marne, or in Borden's present-tense internal monologue in "Moonlight." The reader is invited to step into the immediate instant of the writer's experience, as the distance between events and the moment of reading is collapsed by the use of present tense, of small sensory details, and a stream-of-consciousness blend of external and internal data. But there is more to it than that: writing is also presented as antithetical to the destruction of war. The violence and fear cannot be halted or reversed, cannot even at times be made to make sense, but if they can be put into words, they can to some extent be controlled. That, as James might have said, is one of the ways in which "art *makes* life," and shapes experience. The act of writing in the face of death seems in some ways a trivial defiance—hence the laughter of La Motte's companions, perhaps—but in a war where civilization seemed at stake to so many, it was a powerful statement of the cultural worth of text. Writing is always an attempt to cheat mortality, especially in a war zone, where the author both hopes and fears that the words committed to paper may outlive him or her. So, there is something doubly resonant in La Motte's expression that she is "writing this to kill time"—before time can kill her. This was her attempt to "make a little civilization," with "the inkpot aiding," as James had suggested to Alfred Sutro.

La Motte's intimate and confessional account of her experience at Dunkirk is stylistically very different from Borden's sketch "Bombardment," which narrates a scene of destruction from an aerial perspective, looking down like the insouciant plane on the antlike people of the "human hive" who "swarmed out onto the sands."[77] However, the two accounts fit closely together: the early-morning plane, the crowds on the beach, the siege gun in the distance, and the crater in the town square. It seems remarkable enough that Wharton and La Motte should both have witnessed and written about the same attack on 22 June 1915, but Borden's account suggests that she, perhaps, was there too and used the same event in her writing. Of course, Dunkirk faced bombardment many times during the war, and Borden had worked there for several months earlier in 1915. Moreover, she does not name her bombarded town in *The Forbidden Zone*. It could be anywhere. High up where the plane flits about in the early-morning sunshine, names of towns, let alone of people, do not very much matter—which is exactly her point. Alternatively, she could have worked up her piece from firsthand accounts of the bombardment by La Motte or the other nurses. Her imagination was equal to that. Nevertheless, it also seems likely that Borden would come to Dunkirk to greet her hospital team. Who was "B." who met them at the station with the motor car and drove to the dock to pick up supplies during the shelling? Was Borden one of the six sitting on the balcony watching the explosions all around them in the dusk? Did she recognize in La Motte's compulsion to write under stress an instinct like her own?

Borden and La Motte would work closely together over the following year, often confined for weeks at a time in the claustrophobic world of the hospital compound, but their relationship remains something of a mystery. Borden makes no specific mention of La Motte in her writings, and does not appear to have corresponded with her after the war. La Motte's correspondence with Stein and DuPont has been archived, and further unpublished material is still held privately, but no letters to Borden appear to have survived.[78] In *The Backwash of War,* Borden appears as the *directrice* of the hospital, a cool, detached figure in an immaculately starched white uniform, level-headed in an emergency, but also capable of arguing with generals. In "A Joy Ride," published in the *Atlantic Monthly* in October 1916, La Motte describes her as "the *Directrice,* who is my friend"—but even here the *directrice* gives orders, which La Motte must follow.[79] It is tempting to think that the two women might have shared ideas and read drafts of each other's work—but no real evidence of this has emerged, and there must have been little time for such niceties at the front. The writing of both women becomes markedly more daring after the summer of 1915, but whether this is due to an innovative lead given by one to the other, or the recent impact of Stein's work on both of them, or is simply a reaction to the intensity of their war-zone experiences is impossible to say. Probably all of these factors were at play to some extent.

Despite this uncertainty about the impact of their shared context on their writing (or perhaps because of it), Borden and La Motte are often discussed together, under one chapter heading, as though two sides of some war-minted coin—the writer turned nurse on one side, and the nurse turned writer on the other.[80] Margaret Higonnet describes their complementary accounts of the Rousbrugge hospital as like the "double X-ray" technique developed during the war for locating foreign bodies, usually shrapnel or bullets, hidden deep within the human form, by coordinating two X-ray pictures taken from different angles.[81] This effect is most striking in those places where their narratives overlap—as they apparently do in their accounts of the bombardment at Dunkirk. But texts are never comprehensive—though, like X-rays, they do at times offer a view of what lies below the surface—and these contrasting verbal accounts create as much uncertainty and dislocation as they do precision. The apparent symmetry of Borden's and La Motte's binary view of the hospital at Rousbrugge is also further complicated by the perspective of Agnes Warner, who joined the unit in September 1915, and whose letters home describing the unit were published as a fund-raising collection *My Beloved Poilus* in 1917. Here Borden appears as Mrs. Turner, the capable manager, organizing concerts and paying for Christmas dinners. The intensity of experience voiced in La Motte's and Borden's texts is veiled by Warner's optimism about her patients' chances of recovery, and in conventional aspirations of service and resilience. "Good night, mother," she writes, "these are sad times, but we must not lose courage."[82] Nevertheless, even Warner described in detail the grim injuries which flooded into the casualty clearing station, and began to question her nursing vocation under the stress of action at the front: "I think I shall have to find a new job when the war is over," she wrote in April 1916, "for I don't think I shall ever do any more nursing."[83] Warner's letters, which were never intended for the public and were published without her knowledge, might have been expected to provide the most immediate view of Hôpital Chirurgical Mobile No. 1. However, the censoring of letters by military authorities, and the self-censorship of those who wrote home, often constrained by a desire to spare relatives and friends the full horrors of war, make these letters oddly less vital than the highly stylized and depersonalized texts of Borden and La Motte. Among other things, Warner's letters serve as a reminder of Genthe's point that the experimental litanies of futility, which have become accepted by many present-day readers as the definitive texts of the war, were only a tiny portion of the material published at the time: "Bitter narratives such as Ellen La Motte's *The Backwash of War* were exceptions," he writes. For Genthe, La Motte's book is "the most bitterly disillusioned" of them all.[84]

One should also remember that for all their similarities of scene and even at times of tone, Borden and La Motte were sharply individual personalities, and responded to the war in different ways. Borden's writing, like her life, is characterized by warmth, engagement and passionate determination, sometimes to the point of obsession. La Motte's response to the war, both written and personal, is marked by reserve and irony. If they agreed on the fact that something was wrong with the running of this war and that readers had a right to know about it, this did not necessarily demonstrate how much they had in common, but rather that the great futility of the waste of human life at the front was so enormous as to override their differences. The persistent critical habit (which I am, of course, repeating here) of presenting Borden's and La Motte's work in tandem, although rewarding in so many ways, also runs the risk of fusing them into a composite figure, something like both of them, but not exactly either of them, a representative type—a daring, articulate, cynical yet dedicated war nurse, but a type nevertheless. However, if research into women's accounts of the First World War has achieved anything in recent years, it has been to expose the dangers of creating such types, of attempting to generalize about women's experience of the conflict—indeed about anybody's experience of it.[85] As La Motte's writing demonstrates, one of the most insidious traits of war is the way in which it strips the individual of his or her particularity, and presents them as the arbitrary emblem of some group or cohort: a nation, a class, a gender, a regiment, an illness, or an injury. Their personalities, situations, and injuries are blurred, their features smoothed over, like those of a patient after clumsy plastic surgery. It is perhaps for this reason that her sketches of hospital life in *The Backwash of War* are so often titled with these labels which prove again and again, on a closer reading, to have so little to do

Like Borden's story, "Heroes" features a night nurse, although here she appears as a woman "given to reflection" who muses on the wastefulness of squandering valuable medical supplies on a man who is later to be executed. "However," remarks the narrator, "the ether was a donation from America, so it did not matter." This night nurse initially seems to stand in for the narrator, implying, as Higonnet suggests, that La Motte herself is the night nurse of Borden's tale, the one who colludes in allowing the patient to rip off his dressings and thus hasten his own death.[87] But La Motte's decision to distance her night nurse into third-person narrative makes the equation of the author with her own character problematic. There is no "I" in this sketch, as there is in several others. If the thoughts or actions of the night nurse were ever those of La Motte, she has her own reasons for wanting to detach from them: perhaps so that the reader encounters these ideas not as the opinions of the narrator, but as floating questions to be tackled on their own merits; perhaps so that the division between character and narrator can be used to convey a range of conflicting responses to the situation; perhaps so that she can stand back and observe her own reactions. It is this sort of technique that distinguishes La Motte's book from the vast majority of the nursing memoirs published both during and after the war, and makes her writing function as literature rather than reportage—even though many of the tactics of reportage also persist in her writing, the short sentences, the paucity of adverbs and adjectives, the plain but vital details. The indeterminacy of viewpoint in this sketch mirrors the ethical uncertainly posited by the events it portrays. La Motte does not answer the complex questions that she raises in "Heroes." Is the attempted suicide more or less of a hero than the other wounded soldiers in the ward? Here is Alexandre, who smokes in his bed, making the other patients nauseous; vain Felix who is more concerned about his mustache than the fistula "which filled the whole ward with its odour"; Alphonse, who eats a box of pears sent from home without offering a bite to anyone else, then vomits up the whole lot; Hippolyte, with his filthy jokes. Are these men heroes? They have been forced to fight by ideals not their own. Is there not also something heroic in the attempt at escape from the pointlessness of military service? And is there anything heroic about the "dead-end occupation" of patching men up to be shot at again?

La Motte's book and its title are predicated on the awareness of a deep ambiguity in everything connected to the war. As she writes, "everything has two sides," and any nobility of action is balanced by the "dirty sediment at the bottom of most souls." La Motte's sense of her role as a writer is as one who takes on the task of exposing that sediment: "Well, there are many people to write you of the noble side, the heroic side, the exalted side of war. I must write you of what I have seen, the other side, the backwash. They are both true."[88] Thus, *The Backwash of War,* betrays her increasing disquiet at her own part in a medical and military system that can celebrate as a "surgical triumph" the medical treatment of a quadruple amputee, sent home to his father, blinded, without hands or legs, wishing only to be allowed to die. As Hallett notes, for many nurses at the front, writing, in its many forms, offered a means of "containing" the trauma of war, which threatened at times to overwhelm them: "Effective, efficient and disciplined, their compassion cloaked by their apparently closed and impenetrable personalities, nurses poured their own trauma into the pages of their letters, diaries and semi-fictional accounts, where it survives to haunt us today."[89] However, one of the troublesome and distinctive elements of La Motte's work is her apparent anxiety about the inability of words and texts either to "contain" experience, or to generate purposeful meaning from it. Her own expression is weighted with heavy irony, constantly establishing double readings and reversals of reference: the inconsiderate "heroes"; the "surgical triumph" which is so far from triumphant; the assurance that "France is democratic," despite the fact that the load of the war is so unequally spread between social classes.[90] "Finished here!" cries the surgeon on one side of the surgical screen to announce to the nurses that his operation is a success. "Finished here," replies the *directrice* from the other side of the blood-spattered sheet to relate that his patient is dead.[91]

The Backwash of War explicitly voices unease about the nature and purpose of writing in the war zone, partly to underscore the difficulty of articulating the reality of war, but also to allow La Motte to explore her own growing sense of the contradiction between the demands of literature and of nursing. Marius the dying taxi driver shouts out his fury at the American volunteers who drive him to the hospital in the ambulance: "Strangers! Sightseers," he sobs, "Do I not know how to drive, to manage an engine? What are they here for—France? No, only themselves! To write a book—to say what they have done—when it was safe!"[92] The book to which Marius objects is presumably exactly the kind of book that La Motte herself was writing, a set of wartime sketches, a memoir, a book that suddenly seems heavy and uncomfortable in the reader's hand. There are other forms of writing in the hospital too, though it is striking how seldom these represent genuine communication. In "The Interval," a chapter concerned with the "gross, absurd, fantastic" interval between life and death, La Motte describes a soldier with a head injury, who writes continually, compulsively, but whose writing makes no sense to anyone:

> Always and always, over and over again, he writes on the paper, and he gives the paper to every one who passes. He's got something on his mind that he wants to get across, before he dies. But no one can understand him. No one can read what he has written—it is just scrawls, scribbles, unintelligible. . . . Once we took the paper away to see what he would do and then he wrote with his finger upon the wooden frame of the screen. The same thing, scribbles, but they made no mark on the screen, and he seemed so distressed because they made no mark that we gave him back his paper again, and now he's happy. Or I suppose he's happy. He seems content when we take his paper and pretend to read it. He seems happy, scribbling those words that are words to him but not to us. Careful! Don't stand too close! He spits.[93]

Like La Motte writing under fire at Dunkirk, the scribbling man finds consolation in the act of putting pen to paper. However, the desire to cheat mortality by communicating the "something he wants to get across, before he dies" is cruelly frustrated by his inability to articulate his ideas in words that anybody else can understand. His written marks are no more effective than the tracing of his finger over the wooden frame of the screen. These words are words to him, but to no one else. He is appeased when others take his paper and "pretend to read it," but in this case both writing and its counterpart of reading are worthless. The action of pouring out written signs parallels the action of spitting—an expulsion, a compulsion, not a signal from one consciousness to another. Nothing is passed on. The soldier's thoughts, confused and fractured as they are, go unrecorded. Death engulfs them.

La Motte's description of the scribbling man suggests a level of doubt in her own mind about the impact of the written word. What is most poignant about this anecdote is the urgency of the soldier's activity, the evident importance of the material that must be relayed but cannot be understood. Something similar takes place in the sketch entitled "At the Telephone," in which a delirious patient on the operating table imagines himself back in the trenches, trying to convey or receive a message over the telephone: "He struggled hard to get the connection, in this mind, over the telephone. The wires seemed to be cut, and he cried out in anxiety and distress. Then he grew more and more feeble, and gasped more and more, and became almost inarticulate in his efforts. He was distressed. But suddenly he got it. He screamed out very loud, relieved, satisfied, triumphant, startling them all. *"Ça y est, maintenant! Ça y est! C'est le bon Dieu à l'appareil!* (All right now! All right! It is the good God at the telephone.)"[94] Like the papers handed out by the scribbling man, this message is delivered yet remains incoherent to those who receive it. The broken telephone connection and the scrawled, indecipherable text: both offer powerful metaphors for the breakdown of the individual consciousness and for the difficulty of conveying the reality of war to those who have not witnessed it for themselves.

At times, the distortions and incoherencies of the messages of the war zone are intentional. In "Women and Wives," the heavily censored letters that travel back and forth between those working in the hospital and their wives deliberately conceal the horrors and hardships of life at war or at home, and the infidelities of the men with the sexually available women of the front. Letters must function as substitutes for wives, who are prohibited in the militarized zone. Indeed, it is the very inefficiency of these written letters as forms of communication which makes them desirable in a climate where the authorities would prefer certain truths not to be told: "Letters can be censored and all the disturbing items cut out, but if a wife is permitted to come to the War Zone, to see her husband, there is no censoring the things she may tell him. The disquieting, disturbing things. So she herself must be censored, not permitted to come. So for long weary months men must remain at the front, on active inactivity, and their wives cannot come to see them. Only other people's wives may come. It is not the woman but the wife that is objected to. There is a difference. In war, it is very great."[95] La Motte goes on to muse about the corruption of a system which prefers the men of the front to have sex with the women of the war zone, to whom they have no commitments, than to be allowed visits from their wives who might bring tales from home, reminding the men of domestic obligations—thus inviting them to question the validity and necessity of their wartime roles. La Motte's language here is striking. It is not just the letters that are censored, but the wife herself. The woman is not just debarred from writing freely, but is effaced, shut out—because she might tell the truth.

Such questions of censorship and access would acquire an immediacy of their own for La Motte in the months to come. By July 1916, the French line near Ypres had largely been taken over by the British army, and the hospital at Rousbrugge, now expanded to eighteen huts, including a specialist dental unit, was relatively quiet. Borden wrote to Colonel Morier, her main ally within the bureaucratic system of the French army, suggesting that the unit be moved to the Somme, where the British-French offensive that would generate over a million casualties was beginning. However, this was not straightforward. The French commander in the region was keen to keep a medical presence at Rousbrugge. There were also issues of red tape concerned with moving international nurses from one part of the front to another. New military regulations forbade non-French nurses from entering *la zone interdite* to nurse French soldiers—but Borden was not happy with the level of training which most French volunteers had received, and was furious that the service she and her nurses had given over the past year had not earned them more trust and respect from this point by American and European governments alike, would form the backdrop to two books which she would write before the end of the war, a collection of short stories, *Civilization* (1919) and a book of travel writing and polemic *Peking Dust* (1919). This contentious issue would be the main focus of her writing for the rest of her career. She continued to publish books and magazine articles on the subject right up to her late sixties, and took an active role campaigning for international regulation of the opium trade.[99] In the 1920s she advised the League of Nations on this problem, but became deeply frustrated at its inability to broker an agreement between the key nations. She was awarded the Lin Tse Hsu Memorial Medal by the Chinese Nationalist government in 1930 for her efforts. She also received the Order of Merit from the Japanese Red Cross, of which she was a special member. She remained active in the Johns Hopkins Nurses Alumnae Association as well as the Huguenot Society of America, the Authors League of America, the Society of Women Geographers, and the Women's National Republican Club in New York. If anyone had imagined that redefining herself as a writer would distance La Motte from the world of public health and politics, they could not have been more mistaken.

Early in 1918, La Motte and Chadbourne were back in New York, preparing for the publication of La Motte's collections of short stories and making plans for a second trip to China. However, passports were hard to obtain now that America was fully involved in the war, and much more sensitive than before about the political opinions of its citizens traveling abroad on nonmilitary business. La Motte enlisted the help of DuPont, who was willing to vouch personally for her loyalty to the United States— though not for that of Mrs. Chadbourne. He also warned the two women that in the current political climate any evidence of a proneutrality stance would immediately veto any chance of a passport to travel.[100] Something else was about to happen which was to suggest to La Motte that her opinions and activities were being viewed with some suspicion. For several months *The Backwash of War* was advertised in the radical journal the *Liberator,* which had been conceived as a replacement for the *Masses,* which had collapsed in the wake of the unsuccessful trial of its editorial team in November 1917 on charges of obstructing enlistment. News vendors had refused to carry the paper, and soaring postal charges had made subscriptions unviable. The title folded. However, its charismatic editor, Max Eastman, was unwilling to keep out of circulation, and in March 1918 he launched a new venture which resurrected the name of William Lloyd Garrison's anti-abolitionist paper the *Liberator*. Ellen La Motte was listed as a "contributing editor" and among the book notices in the back pages of the journal *The Backwash of War* appeared, price one dollar, with the description: "A Masterpiece."[101] In July, however, the publication of the *Liberator* was delayed. It appeared that something had caught the eye of the censor and had to be blacked out before the paper could be distributed. It was the recommendation of *The Backwash of War*. La Motte suspected that it would not be long before something went amiss with the publication of the book itself. As she wrote years later:

> No official notice was ever sent to me. After several weeks I ventured to inquire of the publishers what had happened. The Government, it appeared, did not care for the book.
>
> "But why not? It reveals no military secrets. These sketches, while written of a French hospital, could apply equally well to any other hospital back of the lines—whether German, Russian or Serbian. They are true—"
>
> "That is exactly the trouble," I was told. Truth, it appears, has no place in war.[102]

Eager to avoid further official scrutiny or surveillance, La Motte abandoned her attempt to acquire a U.S. passport until the war was over, spending the final months of the conflict in the Catskill Mountains, New York State, with Chadbourne, writing and learning to drive a Ford car.[103] G. P. Putnam issued a British edition of *The Backwash of War* in 1919, but it would be 1934 before it was available again to American readers. By the 1930s, perceptions of the war had changed radically—partly due to the emergence of many more disillusioned accounts of the war, such as those by Remarque, Sassoon, and Graves. La Motte's text found its place among these, though it was difficult for readers even in the 1930s to remember

how shocking this material had been in 1916 when it first emerged. One
1934 review compared the book to Henri Barbusse's *Le feu*, also published
in 1916.[104] It was a shrewd comparison—not just because of the brutal hon-
esty of both texts, but also because each of these works had, in their own
ways, developed new strategies for writing about violence on an unfamiliar scale, and had laid the tracks on which later, more celebrated, narratives would run.

Nothing quite like *The Backwash of War* had been written in English
before. It was the text that first caught the distinctive note of the conflict,
and demonstrated how its brutality and pathos could be handled in prose.
As an emerging writer, self-conscious about the role of literature in war
and about her own developing voice, La Motte was perhaps more open to
being shaped by her circumstances than those writers who arrived in the
war zone with a set of ready-made literary strategies, which had to be un-
learned before they could find words for what they wanted to say. As an
American, representing an ostensibly neutral nation, she was able to offer
a devastating critique of the war's systems and practices without compromise to her own sense of national identity. Moreover, access to an American publisher and readership allowed La Motte to publish while the
conflict was ongoing. She seems an unlikely figure to break new literary
ground: a forty-two-year-old nurse arriving in Dunkirk in 1915 with a suit-
case and a notebook. Nevertheless, La Motte was perfectly placed to produce a new kind of text in that narrow window of opportunity for plain
speaking and plain writing, before the publishing climate of the United
States changed so dramatically in April 1917. In *The Backwash of War*, she
created a something stark and unflinching which, despite its anxieties
about the limitations of language, showed a sharp edge of authenticity in
its depiction of the human cost of war. Other writers would follow.

FOUR

1917—Perspectives

FOR THE ALLIES, 1916 WAS A long, dark year. On the Western Front, the French army exhausted itself defending Verdun, and the British advanced doggedly into the mud of the Somme. Meanwhile, in the east, Germany gained ground against Russia in Poland, and marched through Romania in a matter of weeks. The human cost of the year's fighting was absurd: a million French and German casualties at Verdun alone, half of these fatalities; similar numbers at the Somme, where the British army suffered fifty-eight thousand casualties on the first day of the offensive; more slaughter on a massive scale on the Eastern Front. The financial cost of the war was also rising and the Allied governments were running out of resources. It was becoming clear that borrowing from Wall Street was the only way to continue the war, and the American administration allowed the issue of both commercial credits and bonds to the British government. No sooner had this money left U.S. banks, than it was flowing back in; sales of wheat and munitions were quickly making America the world's largest single market as well as "the banker, arsenal and warehouse for Britain and France." By the midpoint of the war, U.S. trading with the Allied nations had quadrupled, and one third of the world's gold was in the hands of American bankers.[1] It was becoming clear that if politics did not draw the U.S. government to into the conflict, then economics would.

Late in 1916, President Wilson decided to use his financial ascendancy and the moral authority which he felt derived from his neutral position and his recent reelection to put pressure on the European powers to talk. In December 1916 and January 1917, a series of "Peace Notes" changed hands. Wilson wanted the European governments to clarify their political objectives as a first step toward a deal that would end hostilities, a deal to be arbitrated by a newly formed League of Nations. However, Wilson failed to recognize the extent to which his timing suited the agenda of the Central Powers—or at least was seen to do so by the Allies. Having given little ground on the battlefields through the year, Germany and Austria had the most to gain from a swift conclusion to the fighting. The stalemate on the Western Front was such that despite the appalling loss of life on both sides, the front itself had barely moved since November 1914, and Germany still occupied most of Belgium. Wilson also failed to see how sections of his rhetoric were expressed in terms which neither side could possibly accept. As Colonel House recorded in his memoirs, the underlying principle of Wilson's plan for Europe was "the right of nations to determine under what government they should continue to live."[2] However, this principle of self-determination, such an unassailable idea from an American perspective, appealed neither to the German and Austrian autocracies, whose own peoples had no such right, nor to the colonial centers of Paris and London. If Belgium and Poland were to determine their own fate, what then for Ireland, for India, for Senegal, for Syria? Then, in his address to the Senate on 22 January, the president urged the world to accept "Peace without Victory," a phrase which may have reflected Wilson's sensible desire to avoid postsettlement recriminations, but was hardly a crowd-pleasing refrain. Page, in London, warned that this wording would alienate the Allies and suggested "Peace without Conquest." Wilson went ahead regardless. Even now, he seemed to believe that a brokered peace was possible, but it was too late: Germany had already made two moves that would make retaliation inevitable.

On 9 January, while Count von Bernstorff, the German ambassador to Washington, was still talking up the possibility of a negotiated settlement, the generals Erich Ludendorff and Paul von Hindenberg persuaded the kaiser to allow them to embark on a program of unrestricted warfare against shipping in the Atlantic. Their aim was to blockade British ports, and starve the nation into submission; the 1916 harvest had been poor, and Britain was more reliant than ever on imported grain. The German generals gambled that even if unrestricted marine warfare were to force the United States into the war, the nation would not be able to respond swiftly enough to make any decisive impact before Britain was brought to its knees in July. America was given just eight hours' warning of the change of policy, which took effect on 1 February. Wilson severed diplomatic relations with Germany on 3 February, but characteristically he determined to wait for some overtly aggressive act before declaring war. Meanwhile, British Naval Intelligence had intercepted and deciphered a telegram, dated 19 January, in which Arthur Zimmermann, the German foreign secretary, instructed the German ambassador to Mexico City to discuss the possibility of an alliance between the two nations should America enter the war. In the event of such an alliance defeating America, Texas, New Mexico, and Arizona would be returned to Mexican rule. Japan was also to be invited to join the fray. To make matters worse, the coded message had been transmitted via several routes, including one via the State Department to the Germany embassy in Washington, thus riding roughshod over a courtesy which the U.S. government had extended to the Germans for the purposes of mediating peace, by allowing Berlin to correspond with its Washington embassy directly without using British-controlled cable routes. "Good Lord!" Wilson is reported to have exclaimed when told of the message and its mode of delivery—an unusually vociferous form of self-expression for this pious and methodical man.[3] It was perhaps not a particularly friendly gesture toward America that British operatives had tapped this source, but the White House was grateful all the same. The British had hesitated to share the inflammatory message with Page in London for nearly a month, wanting first to check its authenticity, and then hoping perhaps that America would declare war before it was needed, thus allowing British intelligence to conceal their access to certain wire routes and ciphers. The Zimmermann message was deliberately leaked to the American press, where it fueled public enthusiasm for military action, although many people thought it was a hoax. Nevertheless, Wilson was still reluctant to ask Congress to declare hostilities. His Armed Ship Bill, licensing civilian vessels to carry weapons for self-defense, was facing a blockade of its own in Senate by a group of twelve world must be made safe for democracy. Its peace must be planted upon the tested foundations of political liberty. We have no selfish ends to serve. We desire no conquest, no domination for the sacrifices we shall freely make. We are but one of the champions of the rights of mankind. We shall be satisfied when those rights have been made as secure as the faith and the freedom of nations can make them."[7] It was one of the great presidential speeches, greeted by tumultuous applause and cheers—but Wilson did not feel triumphant. He is reported to have said later that evening, "Think what it was they were applauding. My message today was a message of death to our young men. How strange it seems to applaud that."[8] The resolution was debated in both houses. Senate endorsed it on 4 April; the House of Representatives followed suit the next day. On 6 April, Easter Sunday, Wilson signed the resolution at the White House. Immediately, an aide rushed out to the lawn and semaphored to an officer in the Navy Department across the street. The signal was relayed across the nation and to every U.S. ship at sea: W-A-R.[9]

Thinking about these events from a literary perspective, it is fascinating to see how many of them were concerned with words, and with the ways in which those words exposed or entrenched the positions of those between whom they flowed: the misdirected diplomacy of Wilson's war notes; his failure to grasp the difference it would make to settle for "Peace without Victory" rather than "Peace without Conquest"; the confidential letters and memoranda passed between Wilson and his advisers; the scrambled, ciphered, and intercepted language of the telegraph; the great eloquence of the president calling his nation to war. As Dos Passos would later point out in his analysis of Wilson's actions, here was a man who had been brought up to a Presbyterian faith in the moral and spiritual power of language: "Like any oldtime Covenanter," wrote Dos Passos, "Wilson believed in the efficacy of the word. By the right word men could be brought to see the light."[10] Unfortunately, in 1917, force and economics were speaking much louder than words. The sequence of events that brought America to war highlighted the limitations of language as a means to bridge ideological differences, or to unify fragmented perspectives. Certainly, the traditional constructions of political discourse proved inadequate for this task in the winter of 1916–17. Great orator that he was, even Wilson could not find words that would express with sufficient clarity and persuasion his vision of a world governed by principle and dialogue. Perhaps the language of authority could not halt the fighting because this very discourse had been discredited by its role in setting the war in motion. Rejecting the "German Note" of December 1916, which set out a basis for negotiation, the newly appointed British prime minister, David Lloyd George, gave a speech in the House of Commons pointing out that verbal guarantees from Germany held no value, because they had been comprehensively violated in the past. "The mere word that led Belgium to her destruction will not satisfy Europe any more." he asserted. "We shall put our trust in an unbroken army rather than a broken faith."[11]

The contexts were different, but the problems facing the politicians in 1917 of how to make language accommodate antithetical viewpoints, also beset anyone attempting to write the personal chaos of the war. Just as new military and diplomatic strategies were deployed in attempts to break the deadlock, so innovations of structure, narrative and tone increasingly came into play in the literature of the latter half of the conflict in an attempt to give voice to the chilling contradictions of life—and death—in the war zone. Among these innovations, the most striking are those which introduced new perspectives, as though their authors were in search of a vantage point from which the conflict could be seen to make sense, even while they felt that such a search might be futile. Revising her manuscript of *The Forbidden Zone* for publication in 1929, Mary Borden would articulate the difficulty of asserting an authorial point of view about the war: "To those who find these impressions confused, I would say that they are fragments of a great confusion. Any attempt to reduce them to order would require artifice on my part and would falsify them. To those on the other hand who find them unbearably plain, I would say that I have blurred the bare horror of facts and softened the reality in spite of myself, not because I wished to do so, but because I was incapable of a nearer approach to the truth."[12] It is a paradoxical, almost disingenuous statement, coming as it does in the preface to one of the most stylized accounts of the war in the English language. Borden's text is nothing if not full of artifice, narrative

manipulation, and effect. Even in their earliest manifestations, the fragments of perception which Borden assimilated into text were carefully
crafted and arranged.[13] Nevertheless, only by such means can she con-
struct a version of the truth—a truth which she has already admitted to be
out of the grasp of her language. As the following pages show, Borden's
account of her time at the Somme through the winter of 1916–17, which
constitutes the second section of *The Forbidden Zone,* is dominated by her
textual experiments in perspective, just as her letters and poems from 1917
were also focused on problems of observation and distortion.

Likewise, the young volunteer ambulance drivers John Dos Passos
and E. E. Cummings would find the conventional mode of linear narrative
unworkable as a means for recording their impressions of the "great confusion," which they were experiencing firsthand in their deployment among
the first wave of Americans to arrive in Europe after Wilson's declaration of
war during the summer and autumn of 1917. As Malcolm Cowley wrote in
his autobiography *Exile's Return* (1951), so many future authors, including Ernest Hemingway, William Slater Brown, Robert Hillyer, Dashiell
Hammett, William Seabrook, and Cowley himself, served as volunteer
drivers in 1917 that one could almost view the ambulance services and the
French military transport as "college-extension courses for a generation of
writers." (Alfred Kazin called the Norton-Harjes unit "the most distinguished of all the lost generation's finishing schools.")[14] Cowley explains
that such courses offered vital life instruction for inexperienced college
graduates: "They taught us courage, extravagance, fatalism, these being
the virtues of men at war; they taught us to regard as vices the civilian
virtues of thrift, caution and sobriety; they made us fear boredom more
than death." These lessons could, perhaps, have been learned in any
branch of the army. However, the endless hours of waiting, and the sup-
portive status of driver, like that of nurse, instilled in these young minds
"a lesson of its own," something that Cowley termed "a *spectatorial* attitude."[15] Certainly, the work of these witness-participants is characterized
by a fascination with the surface appearance of events, and a distinctively
plain, unflinching tone, shorn of idealism and generalization. This is often
described as a tone of "detachment," which is curious, as it is at its most

intense in those writers of the war who remained alert and analytical at the front. Consider for example Thomas Boyd's *Through the Wheat* or William March's *Company K,* both of which present uncluttered, matter-of-fact accounts of the battlefield, sometimes withering in their parody of military language. The frank, plain-speaking tone of these works is, perhaps inevitably, less evident in the work of writers such as Cather and Wharton, or the "high" modernists, such as Eliot, Pound, and H.D., who viewed events at a distance and with a higher level of abstraction—although these depictions of conflict also have a place and, very often, a beauty of their own. However, the persistent use of "detachment" as the hallmark of authentic experience in the war zone suggests that critical responses to eyewitness accounts of the war have somehow come at this issue upside-down, or at least with an oddly unregenerated set of assumptions about what would or should constitute the language of engagement. As the work of Borden, Dos Passos, and Cummings demonstrates, some sort of emotional containment was indeed required to continue functioning in the high-stress atmosphere of the military zone, but no one could really be a detached spectator in the theater of war. Simply to be there was to participate in some role, whether of violence, victimization, or complicity—sometimes all three, as Dos Passos's fictional characters would so vividly discover. So, the tone that is often interpreted as detachment in war writing is perhaps better understood as a strategy evolved by veteran or volunteer writers to make sense of, or atone for, their intimate *involvement* in events. Those truly detached from the action, had no need for such a strategy. In the most inventive works of 1917–18, this need to negotiate personal involvement shapes a range of narrative perspectives—sometimes external to the self, sometimes obsessively internalized, sometimes juxtaposing two or more viewpoints. Like the cubist painters of the period, these writers saw that distortion and fragmentation could be more effective, perhaps even more honest, than traditional realist representation, and created a vehicle for conveying the political and moral contradictions of war. In so doing, they developed a set of narrative and poetic techniques, and a tone of quiet contempt, that would shape the writing of their generation.

At the Somme

This is the song of the mud,
The pale yellow glistening mud that covers the hills like satin;
The grey gleaming silvery mud that is spread like enamel over
    the valleys;
The frothing, squirting, spurting, liquid mud that gurgles
    along the road beds;
The thick elastic mud that is kneaded and pounded and
    squeezed under the hoofs of the horses;
The invincible, inexhaustible mud of the war zone.

Mary Borden's poem "The Song of the Mud" appeared in the August 1917 issue of the *English Review* alongside "The Hill" and "Where Is Jehovah?" under the heading "At the Somme." Another poem, "Unidentified," and the prose poem "The Regiment" also appeared in the same issue. These five works are startling pieces of writing, especially in the context of the midwar period; the content is harsh and the technique daring. Like "The Hill," with which this book opened, "The Song of the Mud" articulates a world where human figures have become secondary details within a warscape that is elemental and mechanical, without color or hope or purpose. Traditional poetic form is abandoned as the crowding stimuli of the war zone jostle up against each other and spill out over the page in their desolation. It is tempting to imagine that Mr. Eliot, conscientious young banker at Lloyds, who kept up assiduously with the London literary magazines of the day, may have picked up a copy of the *English Review* on his walk to work, opened it over lunch, and had the beginnings of an idea. But it is perhaps safer to say that Borden's poems, like La Motte's *Backwash of War,* were among the earliest examples of works which explored the war from an angle which would later become familiar: stark, uncompromising, self-conscious, unconventional, focused on futility, incompatibility, and absurdity. From such a perspective the human self, so confidently expressed in earlier responses to the war, even when suffering or broken, becomes a doubtful and marginalized element within a world of random and unstructured events. Thus in "The Song of the Mud" the soldiers who flounder and drown in the mud of the battlefield have neither identity nor voice. Like the guns and the horses and the detritus of battle, they are merely objects in the landscape and will be consumed by that landscape, sucked down into the "thick bitter heaving mud." Only the mud, active and ubiquitous, vital but not sentient, has agency or personality; but ironically only the homicidal mud also has the power to stop the fighting:

> This is the song of the mud that wriggles its way into battle.
> The impertinent, the intrusive, the ubiquitous, the unwelcome,
> The slimy inveterate nuisance,
> That fills the trenches,
> That mixes in with the food of the soldiers,
> That spoils the working of motors and crawls into their secret parts,
> That spreads itself over the guns,
> That sucks the guns down and holds them fast in its slimy voluminous lips,
> That has no respect for destruction and muzzles the bursting shells;
> And slowly, softly, easily,
> Soaks up the fire, the noise; soaks up the energy and the courage;
> Soaks up the power of armies;
> Soaks up the battle.
> Just soaks it up and thus stops it.[16]

While the layout and syntax of Borden's poem are self-consciously like those of Whitman, this is no "Song of Myself." The confident human identity of Whitman's verse epic has vanished into the mud; consciousness is obliterated, and the song is soaked up into silence. For Borden, as for James and Norton, the words of war were haunted by silence, the silence of death, or the silence imposed by a force so pervasive and so final that it renders language pointless. This silencing of human action and expression was hardly what Wilson had in mind when he called for "Peace without Victory," but as the war of attrition continued, it must have seemed to many as though the war would end by exhaustion rather than by decision. It must also have seemed as though the sinister, silent mud could be the only winner.

Like the prose sketches which make up part 2 of *The Forbidden Zone*, entitled simply "The Somme," these poems, which also appeared in the concluding section of Borden's war memoir in 1929, are based on impressions gleaned during the period in which she ran a hospital of evacuation of three thousand beds at Bray-sur-Somme between August 1916 and February 1917. After a brief period back in Belgium with her own unit, during which the hospital was both shelled and gassed, Borden traveled with Hôpital d'Evacuation 32 to Mont-Notre-Dame behind the Chemin des Dames in time for the Nivelle Offensive in early April. In June, Borden rejoined her original team at Rousbrugge, where she was awarded the Croix de Guerre with palm by General Pétain.[17] She was later also made a chevalier of the French Legion of Honor. As though these constant shifts of location were not enough to unsettle Borden's view of the war, her own personal life was also in turmoil. Sometime during the spring of 1917, she met Edward Spears, an English liaison officer to the French army, with whom she fell passionately in love. From April onward, they exchanged letters almost daily and met in Paris when they could, secretly at first, until Borden's husband was told of the affair and the marriage finally collapsed in September. She was also gravely ill that summer, and for several weeks found herself in a hospital bed, experiencing the weakness and vulnerability that she had observed for so many months in her own patients. Spears later described her ailment as a lung infection developed after nursing a patient with gangrene; however, other letters suggest complications related to an unplanned pregnancy.[18] It was an exhilarating and dangerous time, during which Borden reassessed her own emotional world as well as the course of the war around her. It is perhaps no surprise then that much of *The Forbidden Zone,* especially those sections conceived during the early months of her affair with Spears, should be so concerned with problems of perspective, and with the moral consequences of redirecting one's point of view. Although part 1 of the text, "The North," does not exactly flinch from presenting the sights of war in honest terms, "The Somme" and the poems which follow go even further, not only replicating the external impressions of war, but also probing the processes by which these impressions are gathered and expressed. As noted in Chapter Two, Borden's division of her material in *The Forbidden Zone* was not chronological but geographical, and the fascination with perspectives in the prose and poetry connected to her time at Bray-sur-Somme corresponds to the different quality of the landscape. In the flat coastal plains of Belgium, views are hard to come by, and are quickly interrupted by obstacles. Ellen La Motte describes the compound at Rousbrugge as "surrounded by a thick, high hedge of prickly material. . . . What went on outside the hedge, nobody knew. War presumably."[19] Consequently in "The North," the only points of wide-angle perspective within Borden's narratives are man-made and impersonal: the enemy airplane whirling in the sky above Dunkirk; the observation balloon like "an oyster in the sky, keeping an eye on the Germans," or the disembodied, bird's-eye view of the regiment marching. In contrast, the varied contours of the Somme, with its ridges and valleys (which made it such difficult terrain through which to advance), offered vantage points and vistas from which the panorama of the war was laid out for the observing individual like a theater. To look down from the top of the hill, as in Borden's poem "The Hill," is to assume a position of command, of tactical advantage; it is also to become a spectacle or even a target for others. This uncertainty about who is watching whom is re-created in "The Somme" through the narrative positioning of Borden's sketches, each of which presents a contrasting view of events.

The opening section, "The City in the Desert" reverses the narrative strategy of "Belgium," the opening section of "The North." Instead of playing the role of guide, here the narrator begins with a series of questions: "What is this city that sprawls in the shallow valley between the chalk hills?" Why are there no children?—the narrator would like to know. Where are the cafes? What is the "distant booming" like waves breaking in the distance? Who are the silent old men who walk to and fro with heavy bundles? And, more importantly, what are they carrying?

> You say that these bundles are the citizens of the town? What do you mean? Those heavy brown packages that are carried back and forth, up and down, from shed to shed, those inert lumps cannot be men. They are delivered to this place in closed vans and are unloaded like sacks and are laid out in rows on the ground and are sorted out by the labels pinned to their covers. They lie perfectly still while they are carried back and forth, up and down, shoved into sheds and pulled out again. What do you mean by telling me that they are men?[20]

Here, the use of the second person goes beyond a simple address to the reader. The implied reader ("you") is credited with knowledge which the narrator is unable, or perhaps unwilling to articulate. One outcome of this tactic is an extended moment of dramatic irony, in which the reader understands all too well what is being described, while the narrator is still apparently perplexed. Thus, the recognition of the scene as the site of a military hospital is slowed just long enough for the reader to gain a sense of the incomprehensibility of these images, and to interrogate their own assumptions and complacencies.

No sooner has Borden established this perspective, than she destabilizes the viewpoint of the text again. In "Conspiracy," the narrative voice speaks from a position of knowledge, even authority—though the moral standpoint that is voiced here is not exactly conventional. As though showing a novice or a distinguished visitor around the wards (a role Borden fulfilled countless times throughout the war), the narrator announces: "It is all carefully arranged. Everything is arranged. It is arranged that men should be broken and that they should be mended. . . . Ten kilometres from here along the road is the place where men are wounded. This is the place where they are mended." But this mending of the soldier takes the form of a sinister conspiracy by the military and medical staff: "We conspire against his right to die. We experiment with his bones, his muscles,

his blood," writes Borden. "To the shame of the havoc of his limbs we add
the insult of our curiosity and the curse of our purpose, the purpose to
remake him."[21] This "conspiracy" to keep the man alive while he may be
of use to the army, not only voices Borden's unease at her own collusion
with the machinery of military procedures and regulations; it also drama-
tizes the absurdity of a situation in which men have the status of dispos-
able items, and dares the reader to respond with a refusal to accept this
reality. Six pages further on, in "Paraphernalia," the narrating voice is repositioned once more. Like "The City in the Desert," this section places
the "you" of the narrative in an active role: "you" are the nurse, fetching
blankets and jugs of hot water, handling bottles and syringes, giving injec-
tions in a bustle of futility that cannot hold back the "miracle" of death
that is about to claim the wounded man. The voice of this section, full of
incomprehension at the details of medical care, is nevertheless capable
of interrogation and judgment: "What have you and all your things to do
with the dying of this man? Nothing. Take them away."[22]

As though these contradictory voices have silenced one another, the
section which follows, "In the Operating Room," dispenses with narrative voice altogether. After a brief note describing the scene, there is only
dialogue, as though the text has suddenly become a play. Three surgeons
at work on three different operations—an amputation, a bullet-ridden
lung, and an abdominal shrapnel wound—give orders to the nurses, discuss the day's events, talk over the plans for a new attack, and look forward to their dinner, amid the cries and complaints of the patients, for
whom a trip to the operating room is anything other than routine:

> NURSE: Three knees have come in, two more abdomens, five heads.
> OFFICER (THROUGH THE WINDOW): The Médicin Inspecteur
> will be here in half an hour. The General is coming at two to dec-
> orate all amputés.
> 1ST SURGEON: We'll get no lunch to-day, and I'm hungry. There,
> I call that a very neat amputation.
> 2ND SURGEON: Three holes stopped in this lung in three minutes
> by the clock. Pretty quick, eh?

work of Gertrude Stein and traveled with what she had of it and volumes
of Flaubert to and from the front."²⁶ However, Borden's own response to
Stein was not merely that of an admiring reader, it was also technically
shrewd, comparing her literary method with the distortions of telegraphic
communication and the multiple perspectives of contemporary art. Borden wrote to Stein: "In *Tender Buttons*, you are writing in pure code. I
don't know your cypher—I'm not in the secret—but I would like to have
the key. Oh yes, I've an intense desire to possess the key. It seems to me
that your treatment of subjects is more mysterious than that of painters
such as the so-called cubists—because language is only partly writing,
the rest is talking, and talking and writing upset each other in people's
minds."²⁷ Stein's work relies heavily on the interaction of spoken and written language, often replicating on paper the incoherencies and inconsistencies of talk. Likewise, the format of "In the Operating Room" shows
how written and spoken language "upset each other," allowing the scene
to be conceived as a vivid reality, or as a cynical pastiche—or both at once.
Of course, the word conspicuous by its absence in this section of *The Forbidden Zone* is *theater*, which is both another term for "the operating
room" and a description of the imagined performance—whether a tragedy
or a comedy it is difficult to tell. Either way, there is something uncomfortable about the mix of intimacy and detachment which this form creates.
As in Stein's writing, or in the paintings of Picasso or Gaudier-Brzeska,
Borden is experimenting with a "cubist" kind of literary perspective
which allows simultaneous views of facets of reality that ought to exclude
each other. As Margaret Higonnet points out, this kind of double vision is
common in the work of First World War nurses, because it creates a self-
defensive humor and allows an exploration of conflicting moral perspectives: "Cubist techniques," writes Higonnet, "expose aspects other than
the heroic face of war; they make it possible to show not only the public,
frontal side of medical practice in wartime, but also the back side that is
normally concealed."²⁸ Nevertheless, offering such sights for observation
is also problematic; throughout *The Forbidden Zone*, Borden is evidently
troubled by the way in which the wounded soldiers become spectacles
and curiosities, displayed to generals, medical students, and readers alike.

It is part of the deep humanity of her book that she challenges the reader's glib fascination with dismemberment, deformity, and trauma, and directs our attention to the individual lives and viewpoints behind these. Sooner or later, what she requires of her reader is the imaginative shift of perspective that will create empathy.

Ironically, the section which most effectively achieves this shift of viewpoint is the one which deals most poignantly with the loss of vision, "Blind." This is one of the sections which Borden added to the text in 1929 as she prepared it for publication with Heinemann, and the stable first-person narrative which suddenly appears in this and the following two sections suggests that the distance of time and the commemorative act of writing have given a sense of control, if not yet closure, on the scenes which she describes. However, this impression of control is belied by the sensory and emotional turmoil which is the subject of the piece. "Blind" describes the reception hut of the hospital on a distressingly busy night in November 1916. Four hundred wounded men lie on stretchers, as twelve operating tables work at full tilt, and the orderlies and nurses come and go. Nevertheless, as the narrator admits, she was happy there, fulfilled by a sense of action and agency. Borden's language appeals to all five senses in this extended descriptive passage: the sounds of the guns and the howling wind outside; the smells of blood and mud; the taste one dare not imagine of the amputated knee nearly served up by mistake as a pot roast; the touch of her hand on the pulse of the living patient or on the cold skin of the dying; the continual assault of difficult visual images. Amid this welter of sensory impressions, the narrator's role is that of triage, a newly developed process in which hopeless cases were sorted out from those who had a chance of survival. Triage can also be read as a metaphor of narrative method, as Borden looks back on her disordered memories and images, sorting and selecting this one, but not that one, saving some for commemoration and burying others—but this is not necessarily as detached a process as it may seem. In "Blind," triage is shown as an active, even an intimate, element of medical care: "It was my business to sort out the nearly dying from the dying," the narrator says, describing how she moves among the wounded, feeling for a pulse here and checking a temperature there.[29] However, her visual skills often prove more useful to her in this situation than any of the other senses: "Sometimes there was no time to read the ticket or touch the pulse," she writes, "I could look down over the rough forms that covered the floor and pick out at a distance this one and that one. I had been doing this for two years, and had learned to read the signs."[30] Here the observer's viewpoint, looking down from a height once more as in "The Hill," gives the narrator a sense of command over events, choosing some but not others for the operating room, giving the fatal double dose of morphine to the hopeless case. In the world of the hospital, to see is a powerful form of agency and engagement. In contrast, the title of this chapter, "Blind," highlights the isolation of the single wounded soldier, shot through the eyes, who because of his heavy bandages cannot hear the noisy activity around him and calls out for the nurse, believing that he has been left alone in the dark. At this, the narrator responds with a jolt of emotion, as though it is she who has been blind up to this moment: "I seemed to awake then. I looked around me and began to tremble, as one would tremble if one awoke with one's head over the edge of a precipice." The soldier's question has prompted the narrator to readjust her focus, to shift to a perspective that accommodates the enormity and particularity of what is happening around her. In her distress, she runs to the nurses' cubicle and hides her face in her hands, blotting out all vision, until the orderlies come with kind words and hot coffee, appealing to her through other senses: hearing, touch, smell, taste.

It is a powerful piece, the climactic scene of Borden's book. Its attention to the processes of watching, reading, observing, or absorbing unwelcome sights, shows Borden's intelligent awareness of the power of sight, not just as a means of gathering impressions, but also as an engagement with events, as an element of care, and as an extension of the self into the surrounding reality. In the hospital, as on the page, perspective is never passive, but is continually at work, shaping events and altering judgments. To see is also to feel; even to be blind is to have a perspective. And in a war which was persistently defying resolution or expression, diligence to an individual perspective, or even to a set of contradictory perspectives, was fast becoming the only viable form of intellectual and artistic integrity.

Borden would return to the war as a theme and as a backdrop to her fiction several times in her later work, most notably in *Jericho Sands* (1925) and *Sarah Gay* (1931). She would return to the war in other ways too. Spears, who had struck up a friendship with Winston Churchill in 1915, became a close political ally of Churchill's and served as an MP between the wars. At the outbreak of the Second World War, he was sent to Paris to liaison with the French government, and helped General Charles de Gaulle to escape to London as the Germans invaded in 1940. Borden, unwilling to stay at home in a crisis, set up and served with another mobile field hospital, which operated initially in northern France and then on campaign with the Free French Army in North Africa, before returning to Britain to resume her successful career as a novelist. She was, from any perspective, a remarkable woman.

Initiation

Multiple perspectives came naturally to John Dos Passos. Born to privilege and culture, he yet learned very early to see himself as an outsider to American society. The illegitimate son of a successful New York lawyer of Cuban-Portuguese extraction and an upper-middle-class single mother from Washington, his upbringing was a continual negotiation of shifting identities: as the "adopted" son of his real mother; as a regular "guest" at his own father's house; as a much younger sibling to two half-brothers, one on either side of the parental arrangement; as a second-generation immigrant in America; and for much of his childhood as an American boy in Europe. He even had a different name for the first fourteen years of his life: Jack Madison. When his mother, Lucy Sprigg Madison, finally married John R. Dos Passos in 1910 after the death of his wife, young Jack could finally take on his own father's surname—but for a long time was too shy to use it.[31] It is no wonder that Dos Passos spent so much of his adult life fascinated by or working in the theater; his whole childhood had been one long succession of performances.

On graduating from Harvard in 1916, Dos Passos set about finding a foothold in the treacherous publishing world. As a student he had helped

to edit the *Harvard Monthly,* a role that had brought him into contact with
an ambitious literary set including Edward Nagel, Robert Hillyer, Stewart
Mitchell, and E. E. Cummings. They read T. S. Eliot's early poems and
admired cubist art in Wyndham Lewis's *Blast;* they discovered *The Yellow Book* and D. H. Lawrence. They also printed one another's work, and
in the months following graduation, Mitchell collated an anthology of selected poems from the best contributors, *Eight Harvard Poets,* including
Cummings and "Dos," as he was known to his friends. Dos Passos's now
widowed father put up the money to underwrite its publication. Harvard
friends also found him an opening to write an article for the *New Republic,*
in which he berated the state of American literature as lacking "dramatic
actuality," bound in "the fetters of the 'niceness' of the middle-class out-
look."[32] But Dos Passos was complaining about his own social situation as
much anything else. Like many young men of his age and class, having
behaved responsibly enough through school and university, he was now
eager to for a broader experience of the world. The obvious option was to
see something of the fighting in Europe, primarily as a means of glimpsing
"life"—the politics of the conflict seemed like a secondary consideration.
He would write in later years: "I respected the conscientious objectors,
and occasionally felt I should take that course myself, but hell, I wanted to
see the show."[33] All the same, he deplored the war and the Rooseveltian
ideal of a militarized, "prepared" society. As he wrote to a younger school
friend Rumsey Marvin, who had spent the summer vacation in a training
camp, "When you have an army you immediately want to use it—and a
military population in a government like ours would be absolutely at the
mercy of any corrupt politician who got into the White House, of any millionaire who could buy enough newspapers."[34] Nevertheless, Dos Passos
also recognized the war as a fact of life, as "a human phenomenon which
you can't argue out of existence."[35] Desperate as he was to get a look at it,
there was more curiosity than fervor in his enthusiasm. Initially, he volunteered with Herbert Hoover's Belgian Relief Fund as a translator. His
French was excellent, courtesy of his itinerant upbringing, but he was not
yet twenty-one years old, and the organization turned him away. Next, he
tried to volunteer as an ambulance driver, but he was dangerously short-

sighted and didn't know how to drive. His father talked him out of it; he also put up the money for his son to travel in Spain, studying architecture as a possible future career. Dos Passos came of age during that Spanish trip—in more ways than one. Two weeks after his twenty-first birthday, his father died suddenly of pneumonia. Suddenly, he was no longer John Dos Passos, Junior, and there was no one to stop him heading to the front.

He sailed home mid-February 1917 at the height of the tension of the early days of the German blockade of French ports, reading Henri Barbusse's explosive novel *Le feu* (1916) as he traveled. "The book moved me to frenzy," he wrote, "but already I'd seen enough of wartime France to discover other sides to the story."[36] Other *sides,* plural not singular, were what interested Dos Passos even at this stage, not simply a binary system of allies and enemies, rights and wrongs. He arrived in New York to discover that his father had left him money and debts in about equal measure. By mid-June, with America now fully at war and engaged in the processes of conscription, censorship, and militarization, he headed back to France with the Norton-Harjes Ambulance Corps. It was just in time. Not only did he narrowly avoid conscription, but his outspoken opinions about America's stance on the war, about organized labor and the possibility of revolts in France might well have landed him in prison under the terms of the Espionage Act which came into force five days before he sailed. This act made it an offense to "cause or attempt to cause insubordination, disloyalty, mutiny, refusal of duty, in the military or naval forces of the United States," or to send by mail any items that were covered by this clause.[37] Not many of Dos Passos's letters from 1917 and 1918 would have escaped censure under these terms. More damagingly, he had been keeping what the authorities would have regarded as very poor company. As he wrote to Marvin two weeks before sailing: "My only amusement has been going to anarchist and pacifists meetings and riots—Emma Goldman, etc. Lots of fun I assure you. I am thinking of becoming a revolutionist!"[38] All through his life, Dos Passos would identify with the political underdog—a trait which he ascribed to his own sense of social alienation—though his sense of who the underdogs were in society would shift from decade to decade throughout his life.

At the front, Dos Passos found himself assigned to Section 60, near
the Voie Sacrée, the road to Verdun, in defense of which so many French
lives had been lost the summer before. But at least he had good company:
two friends from Harvard, Robert Hillyer and Frederik van den Arend,
were in the same section. They served twenty-four hours on and twenty-
four hours off, a system that alternated days of stress and occasional carnage with others of recovery, boredom, and the idyllic appreciation of
nature. The three friends found an abandoned garden beside a bombed-
out house, where the smells of honeysuckle and roses mingled with a faint
whiff of poison gas. It offered a contemplative retreat from "the crowded
choking scramble" of the hours of duty. They sat in the arbor, lay on the
grass, or sheltered from passing shells under the concrete fountain. To fill
those hours, Hillyer and Dos Passos started writing a novel about a lad
from Boston, Martin Howe, who would grow up to be an ambulance
driver in France. But the best thing, Dos Passos felt, about the deserted
garden was that the old backhouse was still intact, allowing an escape
from the "slippery planks over stinking pits" of the military latrines. "The
Boche seemed to have an evil intention about them," he recalled, "as soon
as you squatted with your pants down, he would start to shell." The secret
backhouse offered a "halcyon contrast," where one could think and reflect.[39] An old outhouse in the war zone hardly makes a glamorous starting point for a literary imagination, but in many ways it was a suitable
emblem both for Dos Passos's youthful rejection of middle-aged and
middle-class proprieties, and for his subsequent frustrations with literary
and political establishments. He was never afraid to take his writing to
places that many would prefer not to discuss. When Paul Elmer More later
described *Manhattan Transfer* (1925) as "an explosion in a cesspool," he
was unwittingly accurate in locating a key image at the root of Dos Passos's conception of authorship.[40] But the scatological was only one element of a broader confrontation with bodies and their functions and
frailties, which faced the young Harvard graduates in their wartime roles.

In mid-August, Dos Passos and his section saw service in support of
a French offensive near Verdun. He wrote to Marvin that he was in "the
hottest sector an ambulance ever worked."[41] He had been gassed and

shelled, and his ambulance was "simply peppered with *holes*." However, like Borden, he felt a sense of exhilaration and freedom in the midst of the action. He was much happier at the front, he asserted, than "in America, where the air was stinking with lies & hypocritical patriotic gibber." His experiences already suggested to him that the Germans were no worse than the French and that the common soldier on either side was equally capable of atrocities or good humor. "In fact," he wrote, "there is less bitterness about the war—*at the front*—than there is over an ordinary Harvard-Yale baseball game."[42] However, Dos Passos, like so many others, was self-censoring his letters home. His own diary for the same period revealed a much darker set of fragmented impressions:

> The grey crooked fingers of the dead, the dark look of dirty mangled bodies, their groans and joltings in the ambulances, the vast tomtom of the guns, the ripping tear shells make when they explode, the song of shells outgoing, like vast woodcocks— their contented whirr as they near their mark—the twang of fragments like a harp broken in the air—& the rattle of stones & mud on your helmet—
>
> And through everything the vast despair of unavoidable death of lives wrenched out of their channels—of all the ludicrous tomfoolery of governments.[43]

The listed phrases and the dashes all suggest that these were memories too raw to be contained in standard syntax or punctuation—although he was already determined that he would find a literary use for these images. There were other impressions too: gassed horses with blood pouring from their nostrils; truckloads of drunken, desperate French soldiers heading to slaughter at the front; the interminable mud. One day, Dos Passos caught himself calmly eating a tin of sardines while "some poor devil of a *poilu*" was having his leg amputated at the other end of the dressing-station. "God knows I was still morbidly sensitive to other people's pain, but I had learned to live in the world and stand it," he would reflect years later.[44] He was not exactly detaching from events—otherwise he would not have noticed the French soldier's plight or sensed the incongruity of the situation—but the young intellectual had clearly found the means to cope mentally with the intensely physical environment of the front.

In September 1917, the Norton-Harjes Corps, like the American Field Service, was taken over by the Medical Corps of the American Expeditionary Force (AEF). This handover was far from smooth. Richard Norton was unconvinced that the U.S. army understood the terms under which most of his staff had volunteered, or the day-to-day practicalities of running the service. Colonel Jefferson Kean, the officer charged with taking over, retaliated by complaining to General Pershing, head of the AEF that Norton was "underhanded and unpatriotic," and a bitter feud opened up between the two men that dragged on for months.[45] Dos Passos was present at a ceremony at the corps' base at Remicourt, at which Norton handed over command. "Picture the scene," he instructed his friend Arthur McComb,

> Mr. Norton has just finished his very modest speech ending with the wonderful phrase "As gentlemen volunteers you enlisted in this service and as gentlemen volunteers I bid you farewell."
>
> What a wonderful phrase "gentlemen volunteers," particularly if punctuated as it was by a shell bursting thirty yards away which made everyone clap on their tin helmets and crouch like scared puppies under a shower of pebbles and dust. Thereupon, to be truthful, the fat-jowled gentlemen lost their restraint and their expression of tense interest (like that which is often seen in people about to be seasick) and bolted for the *abris*.[46]

Dos Passos's comic sense was clearly intact, despite his recent experiences, although his dislike of military authority had, if anything, intensified—but his grudging admiration for Norton and his values also hinted at the conservative side of his own nature that would become more pronounced in later years. Like the vast majority of Norton's "gentlemen volunteers," number of the places and events which Dos Passos recorded in his letters and diary from the summer of 1917: the hidden garden with the fountain; drinking wine in the school master's garden as truckloads of men head to the front; a five-hour gas attack; reciting poetry under shell fire. There is little that resembles a conventional plot, rather a succession of disjointed occurrences, and an ever-changing stream of minor characters, leading many readers to discount the presence of any organizing principle behind the book's structure, other than "a purposeful approximation of the chaotic nature of the war experience."[48] In the 1940s, Alfred Kazin described the book as "callow" and as "flaky and self-consciously romantic," a judgment that has been repeated many times in different forms. Kazin saw Dos Passos's romanticism as Emersonian in character, the overflow of "a conscientious intellectual self" that is "too much the conscious political citizen."[49] This charge probably did not embarrass Dos Passos overmuch, given his affinity with Emerson and his intellectual legacy in the work of other empirical thinkers such as William James.[50] Nor would Dos Passos have minded being accused of taking an interest in politics and citizens, a position he regarded as a strength not a weakness of his work—though it has won him few admirers in recent decades. Nevertheless, *One Man's Initiation* displays more control of form than many critics allow. There are indeed signs of authorial inexperience, and he overbalances in his handling of the politics of the war—but more importantly there are already in this first published novel traces of the innovative devices that in the 1930s would craft the mass of material of the *U.S.A.* trilogy into such a cathedral of narrative architecture. As in *The Forbidden Zone,* the seemingly randomized impressions of this novel are controlled by the authorial concern with elements of perspective. The novel is narrated by a third-person voice that is generally aligned with Howe's point of view, though at certain times it seems to be outside him, or to simply record visual impressions of shape and color, as when New York recedes into the distance behind the ship, sliding "together into a pyramid above brown smudges of smoke standing out in the water, linked to the land by the dark curves of the bridges."[51] At other times, the narrative is nothing more than a register of sound, notating exchanges of dialogue without descriptions, or barely even interjections to say who is speaking. Like Borden's scene "In the Operating Room," these conversations, often running at cross-purposes, function like small-scale models of the larger text, seemingly disparate, yet constructed to dramatize the difficulties of communicating across the political and ideological barriers which are so much harder to negotiate than those of nationality. These dislocated voices allow Dos Passos to explore the "other sides" of the war, not just to project the contradictory political opinions of the revolutionary French soldiers against the platitudes of the enthusiastic American relief workers, but also to offer nuanced approaches of irony, wit, reverence, disgust, poignancy, enthusiasm, courage, resignation—sometimes within one single character. Character, as an organizing principle of text, breaks down somewhat under this method—though whether this is a sign of Dos Passos's authorial inexperience, or an early indicator of his willingness to deconstruct identity as he would do more blatantly in his later works is a moot point.

One of the reasons Martin Howe seems at times flimsy as a center of narrative consciousness is that he experiences this full range of responses as the book progresses, while at other times he barely responds at all. He careers from one incident to another with little evidence of the kind of maturation or growing sense of agency one might expect from a novel of "initiation." Nevertheless, the reader is inescapably immersed in the viewpoint of Howe—a character whose very name poses a question about the war, although this is significantly a question that is about method rather than motive. Dos Passos is not quite so callow as to structure his book around the question of *why* the war is happening (a tactical error committed by many older, experienced writers who should have known better), rather around the issue of *how* the individual is to survive it. To intensify the reader's experience of identification with Howe's perspective, the novel begins and ends in present tense. This strategy is also used briefly at certain charged moments throughout the text, such as the end of chapter 4, as Martin watches the card game during a bombardment, or at the end of chapter 6, as he cradles an injured man in the back of the ambulance: "Pitch dark in the car. Martin, his every muscle taut with the agony of the man's pain, is on his knees, pressing his chest on the man's chest, trying with an arm stretched along the man's leg to keep him from bouncing in the broken stretcher." The immediacy of this physical encounter is brutally snapped by the sudden return to past tense, as the empathy of hope is broken on arrival at the hospital in the very next lines: "'Needn't have troubled to have brought him,' said the hospital orderly, as blood dripped fast from the stretcher, black in the light of the lantern. 'He's pretty near dead now. He won't last long.'"[52] The tactile emphasis on the pressure of body on body provides an echo perhaps of the author's reading of Barbusse in early 1917, but the self-conscious manipulation of the narrative perspective is Dos Passos's own. His handling of voice in this short novel clearly figures forward to his later, more accomplished works such as *Manhattan Transfer* and *U.S.A.*, where "The Camera Eye" sections juxtapose multiple perspectives and deliberately blur the boundary between fiction and fact. If Howe's experiences represent any kind of initiation, it is as an observing consciousness, as one who sees that his role is not to intervene or influence events—an attempt which would be futile given the scale of the war—but to function as a register of impressions. Kazin was probably right to sense an Emersonian strand within this work, as Howe's development in the book is toward that of the all-seeing "transparent eye-ball," a narrative position which in Dos Passos's later work will evolve further into the modernized and mechanized eye of the camera.[53] The novel's attention to matters of light and dark, of shadows and reflections, suggests that Dos Passos is already thinking in these cinematic terms. His technical decisions about the format of the text are partnered by the content of its closing scenes. Howe's encounter, in the penultimate chapter, with the man who by candlelight cuts shoelaces from the leather boots of dead men is both macabre and redemptive, the cobbler's task both grisly and creative. Howe offers no judgment, and pays his six sous for the laces. Meanwhile, the revolutionists Merrier, Lully, Dubois, and Chenier, who had seemed to offer the hope that one "needn't despair of civilization," are wiped out in a single shell attack. "Everybody's dead. You're dead, aren't you?" says the mortally wounded soldier in the closing scene. "No, I'm alive," replies Howe, though the present-tense narrative and the surrounding context offer no guarantee that this will last for long.[54]

One Man's Initiation is an apprenticeship piece, though one which clearly bears the hallmarks of the craftsman's later skill. Its lack of formal or philosophical resolution, a trait it shares with both La Motte's *The Backwash of War* and Barbusse's *Le feu,* is no doubt a symptom of the fact that, like these other texts, it was written while the war itself seemed like it might never end. Strategies for creating closure in such narratives had not yet evolved, and would remain troublesome even for much later writers who had the advantage of hindsight. Hemingway once admitted that he drafted thirty-nine alternative endings for *A Farewell to Arms* (1929).[55] Many readers still find his final choice problematic. That Dos Passos, in the thick of events, should have produced a text which, despite its flaws and immaturities, still strikes a plausible and perceptive tone suggests that here was a formidably shrewd observer in the making, one who understood that twentieth-century culture both artistic and political would be governed by the use and the analysis of perspective. In 1919, the London publisher Allen and Unwin agreed to publish the text on the condition that Dos Passos tone down the strong language and underwrite the publication costs out of his own pocket. The book appeared in October 1920. After six months, the firm reported sales of sixty-three copies.[56] Obviously, this was not how the reading public wished to remember the war. By this stage, however, Dos Passos was already at work on another novel.

The Windows of Nowhere

On 7 April 1917, the day after America declared war against Germany, the young Harvard graduate E. E. Cummings wrote to his mother that he was hoping to avoid conscription. He added, "I don't know why I talk of this pseudo 'war' as I have no interest in it—and am painting and scribbling as ever." Within two weeks, however, he had abandoned his bohemian life as a writer and painter in New York, and signed up with the Norton-Harjes Ambulance Corps. Like his friend Dos Passos, he was determined to stay out of the army, but also wanted to see the show: "Hope the war isn't over before I get there," he wrote. It wasn't—although as things turned out, he would see it from a very strange angle.[57] On the boat to France in

May, Cummings struck up a friendship with another young volunteer, William Slater Brown, and by a series of mix-ups, the pair found themselves separated from the rest of their contingent on arrival in Paris. In the end, they spent five weeks in the city, ostensibly waiting for uniforms, but in reality living as only young Americans in Paris could live—eating, drinking, sightseeing, and flirting with two streetwalkers whom they befriended. Whether, for Cummings, this liaison ever went further than a boyish holiday romance is unclear, but it certainly fired his passionate imagination, and prompted him to see French life and culture from a point of view unsanctioned by Ambulance Corps management.[58] Cummings and Brown were eventually posted to a quiet section near Noyons. They transported injured soldiers from hospital to hospital, and were occasionally sent up toward the front, but the endless inspections and washing of ambulances were hardly what they had signed up for, and the military-style discipline sat uneasily with these self-assured college men. They developed a particular dislike for their *chef de section,* Mr. Anderson, who frankly did not think much of them either. Mostly, they preferred the company of the French cooks and mechanics, and through these contacts they got wind of the rumors of revolt spreading through the French army like wildfire in the summer of 1917. Brown's letters home on this subject caught the eye of the military censor, and both young men were arrested in mid-September on suspicion of sedition. After a series of cells and railway carriages, Cummings asked where he was being taken, and he heard the response "Mah-say."[59] But he wasn't going to Marseilles as he imagined; he was bound for La Ferté-Macé, a small town in Normandy, where he would be held at a detention center until December, when intense diplomatic pressure from the U.S. embassy would eventually secure his release. Brown, who was latterly transferred to a prison, would likewise be freed a few weeks later.[60]

In La Motte's turn of phrase, therefore, what Cummings saw in France was not the front but the "backwash" of the war, and this, in part, determined the viewpoint from which he would write about it. However, as Cummings's letters home show, even before his arrest he was already predisposed to take a sardonic and truculent approach to the whole conflict.

expectations of the state—or face punishment as an enemy. Given this
stark choice, Cummings would much rather be on the side of those who
value their individuality and assert their freedom of consciousness, even if
this means going to jail. This position governs the apparently inverted
logic of the book, in which Cummings experiences his imprisonment as a
release from the constraints of conformity. On his first night in the cells at
Noyons, he rejoices in having been set outside of the disciplinary system
of the ambulance unit and having thereby regained his own perspective:
"An uncontrollable joy gutted me after three months of humiliation ,of being bossed and herded and bullied and insulted . I was myself and my own
master ."[63] This defiant refusal to endorse the values of "*le gouvernement
français*" (or even to give it capital letters) also extends to how Brown and
Cummings feel about their incarceration at La Ferté-Macé. On arrival,
Cummings asks his friend if they both have been arrested as *espions:* "'Of
course !' B said enthusiastically . 'Thank God ! And in to stay . Every time
I think of the section sanitaire ,and A. and his thugs ,and the whole rotten
red-taped Croix Rouge ,I have to laugh . Cummings ,I tell you this is the
finest place on earth !' "[64] This clash of perspectives between the individual and the system—including those at home whose complicity fuels the
ideology of war—affects how the inmates view not just their own situation
within the walls of the Enormous Room, but also the abstract values of
society outside it. When the German prostitute Lena has been put in solitary confinement in the *cabinot* for sixteen days, defiant despite the cold
and the damp and the lack of proper rations and the worsening cough
which racks her body, Cummings questions more than just the running of
the war: "I realized fully and irrevocably and for perhaps the first time the
meaning of civilization . And I realized that it was true—as I had previously only suspected it to be true—that in finding us unworthy of helping
to carry forward the banner of progress ,alias the tricolour ,the inimitable
and excellent French government was conferring upon B and myself—
albeit with other intent—the ultimate compliment ."[65] "Civilization," from
the perspective of "Nowhere," is nothing to celebrate. Inside the *camp de
triage,* the rhetoric of war is exposed as a shabby thing indeed; ideals and
governments are merely vacuous expressions, and only the experience of

patterns of verse, the breaking up of individual words across lines, and the playing with white space on the page as though the poem were an abstract painting. Indeed, Cummings was skilled with both pencil and paint-brush, and for most of his life described himself as an artist rather than an author. As with Stein's "cubist" writing, Cummings's work regularly ex-ploits the interplay between aural and visual language, inviting the reader to see the text anew, as well as to hear it in some inner ear. Much of the comedy of *The Enormous Room*—and some of its pathos—is created in the movement between these two modes of language, and the new, unconven-tional conceptual space which this movement opens up. Or to put it an-other way, the visual strangeness of the text forces an adjustment of focus in line with the moral and political adjustment that Cummings requires of his reader. Commas and periods are displaced, with a space before them rather than after; dialogue is denoted sometimes by dashes, sometimes by quotation marks, sometimes by neither or both. Capital letters mark out noises, emphases, objects of sarcasm or ridicule—but there is often a method within this typographical madness. Mr. Anderson is always des-ignated as "A." with a period, because he is bound by convention; Brown is designated as "B" without punctuation, because he is not. The definite article for the nicknames of Cummings's fellow prisoners is usually given a capital *T* because they have definite personalities; the names of the guards are presented with a lowercase *t* because they do not. Foreign words are not italicized, but run into the English of the text and out again, not always very correctly—nor is Cummings's French always very polite. Phonetic spellings exaggerate the sense of dislocation and incom-prehension. On arrival at La Ferté-Macé, an official repeats the word "KEW-MANGZ," an "extraordinary dissyllable" which is baffling to Cum-mings, until he realizes it is his own name. "MAY-RRR-DE à la France !" shouts Jean Le Nègre for one entire afternoon.[68] In his later poems, the inventive layout of text is used to generate newness of perception; words are fractured, interrupted, conjoined, relocated into margins or to the bottom of the page, startling the reader into seeing them, or hearing them, as though for the first time. The enduring popularity of Cummings's work would eventually make this kind of playfulness with text a very familiar feature of twentieth-century poetic expression.[69] However, the startling thing, or one of the startling things, about *The Enormous Room* is how quickly one gets used to Cummings's idiosyncratic system; after a chapter or two, the displaced commas, periods, and colons seem standard, the capital letters comic rather than unsettling, the French interjections—which one may or may not understand—simply part of the verbal landscape. All that is required from the reader is a shift of perspective, a willingness to accept a new system that runs counter to expectation. Consider the irony, therefore, of the fate of the first edition of the text, in which all Cummings's punctuation had been "corrected" by a helpful typesetter, the French phrases translated, and the strong language expurgated—changes hastily approved in proof by Cummings's father, to the exasperation of the author, who was traveling in Europe with Dos Passos when the book came out.[70] The original layout of the manuscript was partially repaired in later editions, but not fully restored until the 1970s. Typographical conventions, it seems, die as hard as social and political ones.

Cummings not only messes with the rules of verbal expression in *The Enormous Room;* he also disrupts the progression of narrative time. The narrator describes his time in the detention center as "like a vast grey box in which are laid helter-skelter a great many toys ,each of which is itself completely significant apart from the always unchanging temporal dimension which merely contains it along with the rest ." He explains this phenomenon for the benefit of those "who have not had the distinguished privilege of being in jail ." To the prisoner, especially to one whose sentence is indefinite, events can no longer succeed each other, as he or she must give up thinking about the past and the future in order to retain the ability to cope with the present: "whatever happens ,while it may happen in connection with some other perfectly distinct happening ," he writes, "does not happen in a scale of temporal priorities—each happening is self-sufficient , irrespective of minutes months and the other treasures of freedom ."[71] Obviously, this collapse of time creates a difficulty about how to tell a story in a setting without sequence. One solution to this problem is the temporal play that Cummings creates within the text by his use of a double narrative perspective. Not only does he recount what happened, he also voices the moment of writing, thus creating two narrative selves for the reader to deal with. "If he ever reads this history," he says of Mexique, "I hope he will not be too angry with me ." Or of Surplice: "His eyes opened . I have never seen eyes since ."[72] In both instances the reader is reminded that what is being experienced is a highly manufactured and subjective text. Cummings the narrator also creates moments of dramatic irony by jumping forward in time to relate information out of sequence. The reader, for example, knows that Brown will be going to Précigné, the permanent prison, several chapters before he knows himself, casting a poignant shadow over all the comedy of the later sections of the book. Time may not be moving neatly forward in this text. However, it is carefully manipulated to control the reader's perspective and to open it up to new experience.

In order to navigate around this lack of narrative linearity, the bulk of Cummings's text is made up of a sequence of character sketches, verbal parallels of the pencil sketches with which he filled his notebooks during his weeks in captivity.[73] To give his text cohesion and direction, Cummings places his figures within the landscape of John Bunyan's religious allegory *The Pilgrim's Progress*. Six of the novel's thirteen chapters carry titles that refer to Bunyan's text, and throughout the book there are multiple references to the journey of Christian from the City of Destruction, through the Slough of Despond and Vanity Fair, via Doubting Castle to the Celestial City. Cummings's midnight moment at the foot of the cross also acquires an extra resonance in this context. The dapper, yet fearsome *directeur* of the camp is "Apollyon," and the commission of "Three Wise Men" who decide the fate of Brown and Cummings are mocked not just for their disparity to the Magi of the Christmas story, but also for their similarity to "Mr Worldly-Wiseman" in Bunyan's fable. Since it was published, readers of *The Enormous Room* have disagreed about whether Cummings's use of Bunyan's text was pragmatic or redemptive.[74] Either way, it seems clear that Cummings, like Norton, recognized the status of *The Pilgrim's Progress* as a text with powerful cultural and moral capital in post-Puritan America, but also as a text subject to a diversity of applications and interpretations. This was a disruptive strategy. Cummings's use of the language of *The Pilgrim's Progress* destabilized sentimental readings of Bunyan's text, by emphasizing its brutality and rediscovering its relevance to modern-day injustices, but also unsettled any single reading of his own narrative by introducing multiple (and often contradictory) levels of association and symbolism. Like Cummings's disruptive use of language, this use of textual allusion deliberately refracts the text, forcing the reader to do the work of rationalizing the conflicting surfaces displayed. Here is another verbal cubist at work. Naturally, this also opens the text up to misinterpretation. As Marilyn Gaull has pointed out, the problem of how to read *The Enormous Room* is nowhere more evident than in Edward Cummings Senior's introduction to the first edition, which demonstrates his determination to read his son's book as a text about the sanctity of liberty, patriotism and the cause of France, apparently unaware that these "habitually conditioned attitudes" are pilloried and rejected at every opportunity throughout the text which follows.[75]

But just because a text has been misunderstood, this does not mean that it is incomprehensible. Baffling as it was to early readers, complex and multi-layered as it still seems today, *The Enormous Room* is far from being a solipsistic text, which has nothing to express except its own mode of expression. The overwhelming tendency in criticism of technically innovative poetry and prose over the past century has been to focus on the play of signification, in preference to that which is signified; to approach the modernist text as a "speech-act" which creates its own meaning, rather than as a purposeful medium of communication between author and reader. Texts which invite this "locutionary" approach, or which stand scrutiny under these terms have long enjoyed a cultural ascendency over those which betray evidence of any utility or social sympathy.[76] "All art," as Oscar Wilde said, "is quite useless"—a statement which has often been taken to mean that anything useful cannot truly be art.[77] This critical tendency, of course, tells us more about recent modes of reading than about original modes of writing. It also goes some way to explain why certain experimental texts about the First World War found themselves so consistently disregarded within literary canons, both formalist and historical-cultural, in the decades following the war. How, for example, would one apply the common theoretical distinction between texts whose composition is worthy of structural and linguistic approaches and those whose content is suited to historical interpretation, to works such as Borden's *The Forbidden Zone* or Dos Passos's *Three Soldiers,* which stubbornly insist on keeping a foot in either camp? It is much easier to look past these texts to something like Eliot's *The Waste Land,* or H.D.'s *Sea Garden,* for confirmation of learned orthodoxies about the division of aesthetic merit from political intent, innovation from conscience, lyrical individualism from community—although even here such divisions are not nearly as clear-cut as one might expect.[78]

As earlier chapters of this book demonstrate, strict battle lines between modernists and genteel writers, between art and propaganda, between formal analysis and cultural history, between idealism and disillusionment, between style and politics, are both artificial and anachronistic, and are inadequate to illuminate or understand many of the war's most powerful literary products. Cummings's war writing is particularly resistant to such categorizations—partly because he was so mercurial in his allegiances and opinions. Nevertheless, despite his technical virtuosity and the intensity of his individualistic lyricism, there is yet an appeal in his work to a set of values beyond art and beyond the self. These are by no means the normative social values of his nation and class, although they do have a Transcendentalist and Emersonian quality, like those of Dos Passos. Cummings's ideals are original—in the sense of being old and atavistic, as well as new and uniquely personal, carved from his own experience. But this does not mean that they had little to contribute to the context of the era in which they were crafted, or that they have nothing to say today. As Tim Dayton argues, the lyric subjectivity of Cummings's war poetry, so often cast as a withdrawal from the collective struggles of society, makes more sense when read in the light of Theodor W. Adorno's defense of the lyric voice as a dynamic element in the relationship between individual and society. Dayton interprets both Cummings's "satirical negation" of the clichés of wartime society, and his "lyrical affirmation" of the individual's right to speak as "moments in a vital discursive struggle, in which he contests the meaning of the Great War, very much a matter of public concern."[79] Thus "my sweet old etcetera" and "next to of course god america i" derive their caustic humor and their impact from the political and poetic culture in which they are embedded. This can also be said of *The Enormous Room*, which takes evident delight in exploding the conventions of the newly emerging genre of the war memoir, and which presents the struggle for self-expression and freedom of conscience—perhaps the most compelling parallel that Cummings invokes with the imprisoned figure of John Bunyan—as the real war within the war. This struggle is not political in that, almost by definition, it cannot be conducted on behalf of the individual by any organization or proxy. Conversely, it is profoundly political in the broadest sense, because the outcome of this never-ending struggle has far-reaching implications for the kind of society in which we live.

This focus on freedom of thought and expression explains Cummings's admiration for the four fellow inmates whom he designates "The Delectable Mountains." Named after the uplands in *The Pilgrim's Progress*, from which Christian and Hopeful catch their first glimpse of the Celestial City through a "perspective glass," these figures allow the narrator of *The Enormous Room* to shift his perspective sufficiently to glimpse something worth struggling to reach.[80] Foremost among this group is Zulu or Zoo-loo, who prompts one of Cummings' earliest articulations of a concept that would govern much of his artistic vision throughout his writing life: "IS." "There are certain things in which one is unable to believe for the simple reason that he never ceases to feel them . Things of this sort—things which are always inside of us and in fact are us and which consequently will not be pushed off or away where we can begin thinking about them—are no longer things ; they ,and the us which they are ,equals A Verb ° IS ."[81] For all his careful and playful proliferation of voices and perspectives in *The Enormous Room,* Cummings articulates here an Emersonian reliance on the self, and on a felt state of individual being. "Modernist" though this passage is, both in its linguistic expression and in its essential subjectivity, there is none of the distancing that Cowley saw as the outcome of the "*spectatorial*" attitude of the eyewitness to war. Zulu does not speak any language that Cummings can understand, but must communicate through signal and expression, thus allowing a level of intimacy not possible through the conventions of language. Here, as in Borden's "Blind," watching is about much more than simply spectating, and perspective collapses into immediacy, as the universal "is" becomes visible in the eloquent gestures of this unlikely existential hero.

The tension between the lyric voice of the individual and the social network within which this voice must speak comes to the fore in the closing stages of the narrative, in which Cummings suddenly finds himself, ejected from the *camp de triage,* briefly accommodated in a Paris hotel, and then shipped home on a comfortable liner. As his father's notes make clear, Cummings's survival of and escape from the French penitentiary system was only partly due to his philosophical resistance to injustice, but also owed much to interventions by family, friends and officials, including Richard Norton.[82] Edward Cummings Senior wrote directly to President Wilson, invoking the rights of "American citizenship" and the anguish of Mrs. Cummings as causes for intervention. That the U.S. embassy in Paris subsequently took measures to secure the release of both Cummings and Brown suggests that this letter played its part to some purpose. However, these external views, even where they cut across the apparent cynicism of the text, only serve to affirm Cummings's fundamental commitment to a multiplicity of perspectives. Like the dysfunctional community of the *camp de triage* at La Ferté-Macé, society at large is composed of the diverse and the particular, people who, however insignificant, gifted, or disruptive, nevertheless may contain the "spark of God"—as Dos Passos termed Cummings's test of human worth. Thus the final image of *The Enormous Room,* in which the returning consciousness is absorbed into the disjointed landscape of New York, provides a destination—though emphatically not a conclusion—in which the self-aware individual must return and be repositioned as but one perspective among the multiplicity of standpoints within a city so complex that it cannot be reduced to simple syntax: "The tall, impossibly tall, incomparably tall, city shoulderingly upward into hard sunlight leaned a little through the octaves of its parallel edges ,leaningly strode upward into firm hard snowy sunlight ; the noises of America nearingly throbbed with smokes and hurrying dots which are men and which are women and which are things new and curious and hard and strange and vibrant and immense ,lifting with a great undulous stride firmly into immortal sunlight . . ."[83] For all his cynicism, Cummings carefully closes his text with a statement redolent with the lively potential of humanity. The "hurrying dots" of the men and women on the quayside, whose lives are so "new and curious and hard and strange and vibrant and immense," are doubled and reflected in the hurrying dots of the ellipses placed at the end of the passage, both words and punctuation powerfully suggest that this experience of war has been for Cummings but the beginning of perception.

1918—Compromises

GERTRUDE STEIN, AS MANY READERS know, called them the "lost generation." A phrase redolent with pathos and quasi-biblical gravitas, it has become a familiar term for the thwarted promise of so many young lives scarred by war, or for the many millions killed in the conflict. Yet, not everyone knows that Stein coined the phrase in frustration at the ineptitude of a young veteran mechanic at her local garage, who had failed to fix her car. Technically, in fact, she did not coin the phrase at all, but borrowed it wholesale from the *patron* of the garage, who had used it against his assistant. Stein then turned both the phrase and her frustration about the unrepaired Ford onto Ernest Hemingway, who happened to be hearing the anecdote. At least, that is how Hemingway tells the story. *Une génération perdue,* the romance of the phrase lingers, but is oddly misplaced. Stein meant nothing poetic by it; and Hemingway went away cross. "The hell with her lost-generation talk and all the dirty, easy labels," he said to himself as he walked home.[1] To each of them, this was a phrase that signaled, not regret or commemoration, but a clash of generational values: the fault-finding of the middle-aged versus the fecklessness of the young. All the same, in 1926, Hemingway placed the phrase as an epigraph at the opening of his postwar novel *The Sun Also Rises.* Apparently, on reflection, he was rather proud of being "lost" to the values of the prewar years. Like many among the new tranche of American writers who had had a brush with militarism, he was determined to find his own way without advice from his elders. "Down with the middleaged!" Dos Passos had cried in 1917 in his fury at the mismanagement and pettifogging of the war—although in later years he would reflect that this cry was probably repeated "by every new generation since Man came out of the caves."[2]

Nevertheless, the "middleaged" still had plenty to say. The moment of James, Howells, and Twain was passing, but many established writers of the era such as Stein, Dreiser, Wharton, and Cather, were just about to come into their most productive and successful periods. Wharton would receive the Pulitzer Prize in 1921 for *The Age of Innocence.* Cather's war novel *One of Ours* would win it in 1923. Their work was by no means as vitriolic or as politically radical as that of the younger writers, but these writers had strong opinions about the war, and about the moral and personal compromises it had entailed. Some, like Wharton, were physically and emotionally exhausted by the work it had demanded. Others, like Cather, were weary of the imaginative strain of spectating from afar on a set of events in which they felt somehow complicit but could take no active part. In contrast, the youth of America were signing up to the military in their droves, some enthusiastically, some with marked reluctance. By the time of the Armistice, 4 million Americans had enlisted, twice the number of troops who served on both sides of the Civil War combined. Adding in those employed in government agencies and munitions industries, almost 5 percent of the American population were in war service in some capacity. Nearly four thousand men refused to join up. While most of these accepted noncombatant service, five hundred went to prison instead.[3] At the start of 1918, around 175,000 U.S. troops were already in France. By its end, 2 million military personnel had been shipped across the Atlantic, among them two hundred thousand African-American servicemen, including the celebrated "Harlem Hellfighters" of the 369th Infantry.[4] At the height of the mobilization, in the summer of 1918, the U.S. army was embarking ten thousand troops a day. The absence of a strong cultural legacy in America from the First World War has many causes, but the arithmetic of the event is surely not one of them. By the end of the fighting, 1.4 million troops had been in action at the front, most notably as replacements for French battalions worn out by long fighting and internal rebellion in the Meuse-Argonne region north of Verdun—that same heavily wooded and once-stable sector near the French-German border which

Wharton had toured in 1915. Historians still dispute whether the value of the American troops to the Allies was strategic or symbolic.[5] Either way, their arrival in Europe probably did hasten the end of the fighting—though some commentators, like Dos Passos, never lost their conviction that it would have been better for America, and the world at large, if Wilson had stuck to neutrality. More than a hundred thousand American troops would not survive military service. Of these, less than half would die in battle. Accidents and illnesses, especially Spanish flu, would claim the rest. Many of these fatalities never even reached France, but fell victim to the flu as it swept through the training camps at home or the transatlantic troop ships, where the men were packed in like livestock. For all the talk of freedom and democracy, the organization of the war was not exactly designed around the needs and rights of the individual soldier.

Disillusionment, irony, fragmentation of viewpoint and of language, alongside a keen sense of the futility of human endeavor, have long been seen as distinctive traits of the cultural legacy of the war. As preceding chapters have shown, the personal encounter with the effects of war, whether in hospital or prison or through aid-relief to refugees, prompted writers to search out words and forms to express the chaos of their experiences and reassert the dignity of humanity. However, army life, as experienced in training camps up and down America between 1917 and 1919, went even further in exposing a whole generation of young men to situations of absurdity and futility, a situation which could only fuel responses of cynicism and dark comedy. Humanity seemed suddenly to have very little to do with it. Army training also billeted a sheltered and privileged, but highly educated, class of aspiring writers alongside other social strata and ethnic groups, with whom they would have been unlikely to rub shoulders under any other circumstances. This was no longer the world of Richard Norton's "gentlemen volunteers"—which may have been no bad thing. The conversations, dialects, anecdotes, and songs of the "doughboys," juxtaposed with the incongruities of military regulations and commands, disrupt and enliven the neat patterns of college-learned language in ways that are notably absent from the work of certain writers, such as Eliot and Pound, who missed the experience. The ambulance units may have provided a "finishing school" for the next generation of writers, but the robust, resentful, even bruising, encounters with the armed services soon made sure that some of that "finish" was rubbed off, often revealing a tougher and richer texture beneath.

The list of literary names soon to be reckoned with among the enlisted of 1918 is formidable. The conscription board caught up with Cummings in July 1918 and enrolled him as a private for training at Camp Devens. He was encouraged to apply for officer training but refused, bullishly preferring to see the war from the common man's perspective—though he found that perspective limited and frustrating, and came to despise the patriotism and narrow-mindedness of his fellow conscripts. After the easy camaraderie and hilarity among the dispossessed of La Ferté-Macé, army camp talk seemed mundane and parochial, although he did relish the outdoor living and the physical fitness which he acquired. It was an uneasy compromise for a man to whom compromise did not come naturally. Cummings's unit had not completed training when the Armistice was announced, and he was never sent back to France. After repeated applications, he was eventually discharged from the army in 1919. However, as his biographer Richard Kennedy points out, Camps Devens had provided the "time and the psychic challenge" for him to identify principles that would govern his artistic and personal life in years to come: experience, creativity, uniqueness, primitiveness, freedom, independence.[6] Just as importantly, the patterns of common speech Cummings learned in the army would inflect his poetry for the rest of his life. Meanwhile, Dos Passos, having been determined to get out of the American Expeditionary Force, now could not do enough to get back in. Determined to rejoin as an ambulance driver, he asked family contacts to pull what strings they could to have him accepted for duty, although his eyesight was so poor that the recruiting sergeant had to let him memorize the letters on the eye-test board. In June 1918, after failing to get into the U.S. armed services, William Falkner of Oxford, Mississippi, added a *u* to his name, and as William Faulkner joined the Canadian Royal Air Force, using forged papers and faking an English accent. The war was over before he had completed his training, and there is considerable doubt as to whether he ever actually flew an airplane, although he did claim to have crashed one during a drunken celebration of the Armistice. He certainly did little to discourage his subsequent reputation as a wounded war hero in the years after the war.[7] T. S. Eliot applied to join the American Naval Intelligence unit in London, until Lloyds arranged with the U.S. embassy to have him exempted from military service, because they valued his services as an international banker. In a war that was increasingly about economics—as was the following peace—it could be argued that he did as much for the war effort as many of those in uniform.[8] F. Scott Fitzgerald was drafted into the army and sent for training to Camp Leavenworth, where his training captain was a promising young man named Dwight D. Eisenhower.[9] Fitzgerald was a reluctant soldier, to say the least, although when he was relocated to Camp Sheridan at Montgomery, Alabama, he was glad to make the acquaintance of one of the local girls, Zelda Sayre, whom he would marry in 1920. Fitzgerald's unit was getting ready to sail from New York when the Armistice took place. Likewise, the poet John Peal Bishop was in training in 1918, but never got as far as France.

Others did. John W. Thomason, a young Texas journalist working in New York, enlisted in the Marines on 6 April 1917, the day America declared war. He was awarded the Navy Cross for his service with the 1st Battalion, 5th Marine Regiment. In 1925, he published *Fix Bayonets* with Scribner's, a vivid collection of short stories based on episodes experienced in France. William March from Alabama enlisted in the marines, and in the Meuse-Argonne would earn himself the Distinguished Service Cross, the Navy Cross, and the Croix de Guerre—though all his medals would not prevent him from posting one of the most bitter indictments of U.S. military life, in his novel *Company K*. Thomas Boyd also served in the marines with the 6th Battalion, seeing action in the infamous Belleau Wood, Soisson, and Blanc Mont, where he was badly gassed. Archibald MacLeish, poet, scholar, and later president of Harvard University, initially volunteered as an ambulance driver in the Yale Mobile Hospital Unit, but after America declared war he enlisted and served as an officer in the field artillery in the Second Battle of the Marne. Edmund Wilson, who would be one of the finest literary critics of his generation, joined the

army as a nurse and in October 1917 was posted to a military hospital in
Vittel in the Vosges region of northeast France, where, like Borden and La
Motte, he dealt with the horrific consequences of the fighting.

The mobilized soldier of 1918, therefore, as both writer and subject,
is a key figure in the emergence of (and at times the resistance against) the
new literary culture of postwar America. Whether he represents the random victimization of the individual by the grotesque forces of society, government, and circumstance, the primitive brutality under the surface of
normality, or the creative defiance of the imaginative mind against conformity, the soldier provides the model for a new kind of antihero in American discourse, both fictional and poetic. His existential conundrum as an
individual who has signed away his individuality opens up new, and often
disturbing, angles from which to explore the nature of consciousness or
the position of the self in society, angles which are exploited in the work
of later writers. Joseph Heller's *Catch 22* (1961) and Kurt Vonnegut's
Slaughterhouse Five (1969) offer vivid examples. For combatant writers of
the First World War, such as Thomason, Boyd, and March—the fictional
soldier offers an accessible figure of identification, onto which personal
memories and opinions can be directly projected in a form of displaced
autobiography. Noncombatant writers, however, have a more problematic
relationship with the figure of the soldier, whose experience—especially
in battle—lies at the extreme of human endurance, and does not easily offer up its secrets to even the most imaginative of authors. Nevertheless,
as Keith Gandal notes, this gap between experience and imagination is
not without creative potential. In *The Gun and the Pen,* he argues that
Hemingway, Fitzgerald, and Faulkner, often seen as "the 'quintessential'
male American modernist novelists," were motivated in their postwar
writing "not so much, as the usual story goes, by their experiences of the
horrors of World War I but rather by their inability to have those experiences." The "loss" felt and dramatized by these writers is not "the disillusionment or the alienation from traditional values brought on by the crisis
of the Great War," but is instead a sense of emasculation brought about by
their "personal rejection from the U.S. Army."[10] Postwar narratives by
these writers, says Gandal, are not so much about the physical wounds of

war or even the psychological effects of witnessing trauma; they are about
the sense of inadequacy and resentment on finding themselves outplayed
by ethnic Americans in an intranational battle about jobs, position, and
sexual conquest. Thus, Hemingway, Faulkner, and Fitzgerald were not
"lost" in the war, but rather "lost out" by failing to succeed in military action, and felt driven to write in an assertively masculine style to compen-
sate.[11] Even Hemingway's celebrated wounding at the Italian Front, for
which he was decorated by the Italian army, was not nearly as heroic as
many readers believe. The nineteen-year-old Hemingway had swiftly
given up ambulance work, and was delivering chocolate and cigarettes to
the Italian trenches as a canteen runner when he was caught in a shell
burst, collapsed, and was carried away by stretcher bearers.[12] His own account of his conduct under fire and the extent of his wounds has never
been fully corroborated and remains a question of some debate.

Gandal's suggestion that many key literary responses to the war
were prompted not by military combat but by the changes in attitude to
class, race, and sexuality brought about by the process of mass mobilization, undermines not just the authority of certain texts, but also the very
idea that combat is the element that generates authority in texts about the
war. As Cummings and Dos Passos both knew, one could be a soldier and
see little fighting, whereas one could be an ambulance driver or nurse
and be intimately involved with frontline practices. One could be in prison
and witness more of the effects of the war than one might do in a trench.
One could also be a war hero and write about it very poorly. Once this hierarchy of experience unravels, other categories and polarities also lose
their currency, and it becomes possible to approach war literature across
lines of gender, class, and genre. New patterns of reading emerge which
may have more to say to the twenty-first century about the impact of war
on society. Such patterns often entail compromises between conflicting
agendas: male and female, soldier and civilian, old and young, art and reality. Compromise in art, as in life, is a much underrated virtue, often perceived as a weakness or an inability to hold a position. However, it can
also be understood as adaptability, as a method for accommodating multiple points of view, as a strategy for effecting change, as an antidote to

excessive idealism. The following pages look at two novels begun as the war drew to its end and completed in its immediate aftermath: Wharton's *Son at the Front* (1923) and Dos Passos's *Three Soldiers* (1921). At first glance, they appear to occupy polarized positions on the spectrum of war literature. Wharton's book is a study of a middle-aged civilian; Dos Passos's book conveys the experiences of young recruits. However, these novels share a note of compromise and disillusionment that is distinctive of the war-weary months at the close of the war. The satiric instinct that prompts Wharton to burst the champagne bubbles of the expatriot community in Paris is not so far from that which governs Dos Passos's dark portrayal of military service. As Arthur Mizener says, here is a novel which shows "how greed and lust in their various local American forms operate to destroy the virtues American society is supposed to live by."[13] He is talking about *Three Soldiers,* but he might just as easily mean Wharton's book. In both novels, there is an exploration of the personal compromises demanded of the individual, especially of the soldier and the artist, in wartime. Neither book offers a neat or comfortable resolution to the problems created by conflict. Rather, these narratives show how the First World War led to a dark end point which failed to justify the means by which it had been fought.

Evaporating Words

"It is one of the things most detestable about war that everything connected with it, except the death and ruin that result, is such a heightening of life, so visually stimulating and absorbing."[14] As earlier chapters show, Edith Wharton experienced the First World War as a powerful paradox, one which not only drew from her the polarized responses of grief and elation, but which also highlighted the very best and the very worst of her personal and literary qualities. They are all here in this sentence from 1915: her passion for experience, the desire to observe and to understand, the ability to bind together the bitter and the beautiful, but also a chilly sententiousness, and an intellectual confidence so assured as to chase the death and ruin of war into parenthesis. But Wharton herself was a mass of contradictions, and if she responded to the events of 1914–18 with an odd mix of incision and embroidery, this was probably because it was how she responded to life in general. Born into the aristocratic clan of the New York Joneses—those very same Joneses with whom ranks of social climbers have tried to keep up ever since—Wharton had spent much of her adult life pulling against the proprieties and material excesses of the tightly knit society that had cramped her early intellectual growth and corralled her into a glamorous but unhappy marriage. But she could never escape entirely; the standards of Old New York were too deeply engrained. Wharton valued emotional and sexual freedom, but disliked vulgarity and promiscuity. She was uncomfortable with the prevalent female roles of wife, mother, or object of illicit desire, but could imagine little else for women to do in society. She scorned social snobbery, but valorized good breeding. She was intense to the point of earnestness, but possessed a mischievous and sharply ironic sense of humor. She felt the importance of art to the lives of the masses, but believed education and taste were required to really appreciate it. Her first book, *The Decoration of Houses* (1902), a handbook of interior design, had recommended the virtues of "simplicity and common sense"—by which she meant architectural proportion, uncluttered surfaces, clean lines, and good craft. However, she seemed not to notice that this was the kind of simplicity which only money could buy, and capable servants could keep tidy.[15] It was the same in her fiction. Again and again in early novels and short stories, she satirized the obsession of her own class with those rituals and luxuries which she herself could not live without. Wharton's early work is at its finest when these contradictions come to the surface and expose themselves as the unsustainable values of Gilded Age America. Lily Bart's tragic downfall in *The House of Mirth* (1905) is both a poignant movement of self-sacrifice and a damning indictment of a fatuous society which produces an upper-class heroine so helpless that she cannot decorate a hat to save her life. The war, however, taught Wharton that some contradictions could not be sustained through nervous energy, verbal virtuosity, or enthusiasm. Sometimes one had to learn to compromise.

In April 1916, as *The Book of the Homeless* was selling in the fashionable drawing rooms of New York, Wharton was made a chevalier of the

French Legion of Honor in recognition of her ongoing charity work. It was an exceptional accolade, as the French government had just announced that it would not make the award to any foreigners during the war. This was the emotional high point of Wharton's wartime experiences. Only a few days later, as congratulations poured in, her life-long friend and mentor Egerton Winthrop died, closely followed by her old tutor and secretary Anna Bahlmann. Coming so soon after the death of Henry James that February, these losses hit Wharton powerfully. They also seemed to signal the start of a decline into sorrow and disillusionment. That is not to say that Wharton flagged in her activities. Much of 1916 was taken up with setting up her tuberculosis convalescence homes at Groslay, near Montmorency, work which was done while Elisina Tyler was mourning the death of one of her children. Wharton soldiered on, but the sense of the war as an epic adventure was waning, and she was clearly beginning to feel the strain of her relentless activities. She was short-tempered with her coworkers, and was continually being ordered away to rest by her doctors—though she was usually back in Paris as busy as ever after a couple of days. In November, she collapsed, worn-out with the incipient anemia and heart trouble that would dog her for the rest of her days. All through 1917, she continued to have bouts of ill health. She was delighted at the news of America's entry to the war. However, like Richard Norton, she was soon horrified by the incompetence and high-handedness of the American Red Cross, which took over the running of the American Hostels for Refugees in Paris and her tuberculosis clinics, and she spent much of 1917 and 1918 trying to mitigate the consequences of the handover— though she retained control of her convalescence homes for mothers and children at Groslay.[16]

Throughout all of this, Wharton never stopped writing; it appears to have been the way that she organized her inner world while everything around her was in turmoil. In 1916, she published a book of short fiction, *Xingu and Other Stories,* which included the war story "Coming Home," about a young woman in occupied northern France, who sleeps with a German officer to save the home of her fiancé's family from destruction. The same year, Wharton produced *Summer,* a dark and troubling novel about poverty and sexuality set in rural Massachusetts. The setting was distant, but the story was infused with the violence and anxiety of war nevertheless. They were both stories of women driven to sexual compromise by circumstance, women whose ideals have to give way to survival. After the handover of the hostels to the Red Cross in September 1917, Wharton traveled to Morocco with Berry and General Lyautey, and produced a set of travel essays for *Scribner's Magazine,* later published as *In Morocco* (1920). In 1918, as American troops began to arrive in France, she wrote two further war stories: "Writing a War Story" which satirized the whole process of engaging with public opinion about the war; and "The Refugees," which did exactly that. She "was asked," probably by the CPI, to produce a series of articles for several journals designed to educate the American public about the social mores and manners of France—a task that seemed worthwhile to Wharton in the wake of her outrage at the lack of sensitivity and understanding shown by the Red Cross in its interactions with refugees and French volunteers.[17] She also gave a talk to American soldiers on the same theme.[18] These essays were later collected as *French Ways and Their Meaning* (1919). Like much of Wharton's war writing, they are routinely dismissed as patronizing or as propaganda, but they reveal an underlying sense of frustration at the overconfidence and short-sightedness of her compatriots, not dissimilar to the irritation and disgust felt by Cummings and Dos Passos.

In the spring of 1918, while recovering from one of her bouts of ill health, Wharton began work on a longer piece of fiction about the war. Taking Paris as its backdrop, this book was to focus on the American community in exile. With her sharp eye for social comedy, Wharton had seen how easily she could expose the hypocrisies and pretensions of those who fed off the war as a means to excitement and entertainment. She was even, if it came to that, prepared to ironize her own activities, such as the benefit concerts and the charity auctions. However, with ten thousand American troops arriving daily in France and the war entering its desperate, final stages, nobody was much in the mood for comedy. After completing only a few chapters, she broke off work on this novel to write a much shorter, serialized story, *The Marne,* which would be published as a book in December by her new publisher, Appleton.

This was the tale of an upper-class American youth, Troy Belknap, partly raised in France, whose French tutor M. Gantier was killed in the First Battle of the Marne in 1914. Although he is outraged and impassioned about the cause of France, Troy is too young to sign up and is taken back to America by his parents, where he witnesses the condescension and sentimentality of attitudes toward France with distaste, and he fumes at the delays and hesitations of Wilson's neutrality. After his nineteenth birthday, Troy volunteers as an ambulance driver, only to be wounded attempting to rescue an injured soldier in the Second Battle of the Marne, which was raging in August and September of 1918 as Wharton worked on the story. Troy is brought back to the safety of a dressing station by a mysterious unknown soldier, but he is convinced that this figure in the uniform of the *chausseurs à pied* who carries him from the field is the ghost of M. Gantier. *The Marne* was a slight story, written to raise some much-needed income, and to help Wharton feel that she was involved in the national mobilization. Down the years, critics have savaged its didactic tone and stagey conclusion. Stanley Cooperman complained that "Miss Wharton saw American troops as Boy Scouts out on a field trip, serious about killing Germans, gay among themselves, polite to women, and giving their lives as a sort of good deed for the day."[19] Troy's experience of battle, however, does not quite answer to Cooperman's description. Deserting his ambulance for the chance of fighting, Troy finds himself crawling through a wheat field with little idea of what is going on before he is shot in the half-light of dawn. His attempt to rescue the wounded soldier is prompted by his guilt at abandoning his ambulance and his patients in search of the thrill of action—and is probably a futile gesture as the man he tries to save is never heard of again. France in the supernatural form of M. Gantier comes to rescue Troy, but clearly the young idealistic American is not much practical use in the battle to rescue France. Nevertheless, *The Marne* is a difficult novel to admire, largely because one cannot shake off the feeling that Wharton should be able to come up with something more subtle. As Cooperman writes: "It would be simple to dismiss such fiction as unimportant. The significance of *The Marne,* however, is that a novelist of Miss Wharton's stature cannot be dismissed. If she exhibited provincialism and sentimentality toward the war, it was because provincialism and sentimentality were basic characteristics of the American journey into battle. This journey, furthermore, was shaped by a pre-existing national attitude toward the glories of war."[20] It takes a brave man to accuse the cosmopolitan Wharton of provincialism, though the sentimentality, in this case, is probably a fair charge. But, despite its militarist tone, there are flashes of Wharton's characteristic skepticism in *The Marne:* in her mockery of Mrs. Belknap talking up her minimal experiences in France as though she has seen the horrors of the front (mockery which perhaps betrayed a nagging doubt about the limitations of Wharton's own frontline tour in 1915); in the narrow-mindedness of the American troops; and in the description of the nurses in the hospital as a set of "benevolent-looking hypocrites."[21] The project had also taken on an elegiac quality for Wharton after the death of her young friend Ronald Simmons in August. Simmons had been an aspiring artist, who had aligned himself with Wharton's charity work, but on America's declaration of war, he enlisted, and was sent to Marseilles on an intelligence job, where he died of double pneumonia. The deaths of old friends had been hard enough; the death of the young was unbearable. "This breaks me down to the depths," Wharton wrote to Bernard Berenson.[22] She also published a poem, "On Active Service—for R.S." in memory of Simmons.[23] It is perhaps her best poem, and is certainly the most resentful she wrote about the war, refusing spiritual consolation in the assertion that "his great gift was to be man." To compound Wharton's grief, Simmons's death was swiftly followed by that of her young cousin Newbold Rhinelander, an aviator shot down behind German lines in the final weeks of the war. Wharton dedicated *The Marne* to Simmons, as later she would also *A Son at the Front,* in which the capable, good-natured character Boylston would show many of Simmons's characteristics.

   A Son at the Front was mostly drafted during the winter of 1918–19 and the following spring. Wharton sent the manuscript to Appleton at once, hoping to follow up on the commercial success of *The Marne.* How-

ever, the public appetite for fiction was changing, and sales of *The Marne*
had tailed off dramatically. Perhaps it was the growing cultural awareness
of the mistakes and mismanagement of mobilization, or the flu epidemic—
which also devastated the civilian population—or a growing sense of disbelief and revulsion at the culture of hatred, fear, and hysteria which large
sections of the public had endorsed during the conflict. Whatever the
reason, attitudes were shifting, and the war was beginning to be an un-
pleasant and embarrassing topic. Appleton shelved the manuscript, quite
literally, in the company vault—but it was later offered to Charles Scribner, who published it in 1923 after some revisions by Wharton. It was a
study, not of the war itself, but of "the world at the rear," the environment
of Paris with its charity organizations, celebrity hospitals, and anxious
reading of newspapers. It was also an attempt to come to terms with the
personal cost of the war. In her autobiography, Wharton would write:
"My spirit was heavy with these losses, but I could not sit still and
brood over them. I wanted to put them into words." This process of self-
expression allowed her to see the years of the war "with a new intensity of
vision, in all their fantastic heights and depths of self-devotion and ardour,
of pessimism, triviality and selfishness."[24] It was a damning turn of
phrase. This "pessimism, triviality and selfishness" were what had become of the civilization which the war had been waged to protect. Wharton's critics often accuse her of remaining blind to the real consequences
of the war; one reviewer famously described *A Son at the Front* as "a belated essay in propaganda."[25] Even Wharton's staunchest defenders tend
to read her fiction as "preserving a belief in the war's transformative
power."[26] However, there are passages where Wharton is acutely aware of
the "long-drawn useless horror" of the trenches, of the "cold and filth and
hunger, of ineffectual effort, of hideous mutilation," and, worse still, of the
"military blunders, medical neglect, carelessness in high places."[27] There
are certainly moments of fervor for the Allied cause, but the ending of *A
Son at the Front* resolutely refuses to offer us a vision of anyone or anything transformed for the better by the years of fighting. It is an exasperat-
ing book. At times it appears to be mawkish and heavily romanticized,
while at others it appears to be a sharply drawn study of the mawkish and

tions to Mr. Brant the banker, who is clearly a well-intentioned, if emotionally stilted, sort of person, are erratic and self-centered, possessive to
the point of irrationality in his affection for his estranged son, whom he
only really comes to know through the traumas and contingencies of the
conflict. While he insists, sometimes to the point of petulance, on his devotion to George, in truth he has a much closer and more plausible relationship with Boylston, the genial art student and charity volunteer based on
Simmons. Campton is not a sturdy or sensitive father. He is too indulgent and emotionally needy. He repeatedly thinks of George as a small
boy, "*his* boy," countermands his decisions, and meddles in his personal affairs.[29] Campton has trouble accepting his son's adulthood and
his relationships with others, especially Madge Talkett. Likewise, Campton's reactions to the war are neither well-considered nor consistent—
though they are often taken to be Wharton's own. At the outbreak of the
war, his immediate reaction is resentment at missing his planned holiday
with George. After that, his emotions are swayed, not so much by the
progress of the fighting or the politics which govern it, but by his perceptions of George's safety or danger. Depending on how George is faring,
the war is variously a fight for civilization, a testing ground of youth, a
horrid hellhole "Out there," an opportunity for community, or a senseless
butchery of the young and promising.[30] Some of Campton's statements on
the war are overly idealistic. When the nephew of his old friend Dastrey is
killed, the two men agree that with the young men gone, France has become only "an Idea." For Dastrey this seems a last resort, an emotional
dead end. For Campton, however, this idea is "a luminous point about
which striving visions and purposes could rally." It is the unreliable painter
who believes that "if France went, western civilization went with her."[31] A
few pages later, his own son dead, Campton is able to feel no such tran-
scendence. His responses in the final pages of the novel are wooden, tetchy,
and introspective, not ennobled by national fervor or the joy of sacrifice in
a higher cause. He is fearful for the young American soldiers he sees off to
the front, and it is mostly his softening toward the harmless but long-hated
Mr. Brant which offers the suggestion that he has not been completely em-
bittered by his loss. The consoling emotion in the closing pages is the

sense of closeness that he finally achieves with his son through creating a sculpted memorial for him.

Thus the internal structure of the book is predicated upon emotional instability, and the text's judgments about the war are always delivered in the context of Campton's constantly shifting response. This was not always very successfully done. Campton's changes of mood sometimes seem arbitrary and unsupported. The "shock" of discovering that George has been in action at the front all along is clumsily undermined by the many hints to this effect offered to the reader in the first half of the novel— not least by its title. The scope of the book, from August 1914 to somewhere in the fall of 1917, was probably too ambitious for a subtle analysis of human feelings at a time when social and political geography was changing so fast. Nevertheless, the use of the focalized narrative perspective provided Wharton with a means to dramatize a range of contentious views through Campton's perspective without providing any external moral judgment on that perspective. It was a technique she would employ more adeptly in her next novel, *The Age of Innocence,* in which the world of old New York is examined through the engaging yet unreliable perspective of Newland Archer. However, that book would appear in print almost three years before *A Son at the Front,* thus giving the impression to many readers that the earlier novel was stylistically a poor copy of the later, whereas much of the technical groundwork for *The Age of Innocence* was laid here.

The disjunct between idealism and disillusionment within Wharton's war novel is also a product of external factors. The political and nationalistic fervor of *The Marne* has certainly been diluted in this book, but Wharton seems uncertain what to put in its place, other than a sullen, resentful grief. Those critics who read the novel as a justification of militarism rarely notice that the final stages of the war do not appear in the story. After George's death, the progress of the fighting loses what little meaning it ever had for Campton, and his attention returns to his art. The closing months of conflict and the triumph of the Allies do not even feature, suggesting that for Wharton, too, the outcome of the war had by that stage been overtaken by the emotional impact of personal loss. She was not alone in this. Indeed, though its action is set earlier, the novel articulates the moods of the post-Armistice months: angry, elegiac, cynical, resigned, exhausted, yet not completely disillusioned. It was only after the Treaty of Versailles and Wilson's subsequent failure to establish an effective League of Nations that the American public—and Wilson himself—really began to ask what it had all been about. Wharton was probably somewhat ahead of the American public in her questioning of the motives and methods of the war, and in her caustic distaste at the merry-go-round it had become. Reflecting on the internal wranglings of the "Friends of French Art," Campton finds himself sickened by "everything connected with this hideous world that was dancing and flirting and money-making on the great red mounds of dead." He can hardly believe "that he had once believed in the regenerative power of war—the salutary shock of great moral and social upheavals," and he grieves for "the millions giving their lives for this handful of trivial puppets."[32] If Appleton had rushed the book to press in the spring of 1919, it might have been seen, both then and now, as an early example of the postwar reappraisal of cultural values that would intensify toward the outright rejection of militarism in the writings of Wharton's younger compatriots. The novel's apparent ideological confusion, which makes it such an unsatisfying read for present-day readers, can be understood as the beginning of the processes of distancing and disavowal which would become commonplace in the aftermath of the war. But by 1923, when the book at last emerged, it was already out of date. With the benefit of hindsight, its criticism of certain elements of the war was too tentative, and its acceptance of others seemed facile. According to one review, "many critics cannot conceal their surprise that Mrs Wharton should have attempted to revive details of the war at this late date." Reverting to the subject was like "lugging in an old nightmare or else carrying on a rather futile bit of propaganda for France."[33] Ferris Greenslet's rule that the best time to publish a war book was the day it was accepted by the publisher clearly held good for postwar texts as well. Besides, Wharton never did move on from her faith in the cause of France, or accept that the war may have been avoidable. As she said in her "Talk to American Soldiers," in 1918, "I believe if I were dead, and anybody asked me to come back and witness for France, I should get back up out of my grave to do it."[34]

A Son at the Front, however, had a more specialist agenda than many other "home front" novels. While it was concerned with the world at the rear of the action, Wharton's book was particularly focused on the effect of the war on the artist. Initially it seems strange that Wharton, with her close involvement with refugee charities, should not have chosen to deal imaginatively with the impact of large-scale events on these civilian lives, rich as so many of them were with dramatic incident, pathos, and significance. Nor did she turn her satiric gaze on the activities of the American Red Cross in 1917–18, a subject which was clearly a source of personal interest and frustration—though she may have wisely realized that the reading public would have been unwilling to hear the kinds of things that she wanted to say on that issue. One reviewer complained that it was a mistake by Wharton to make the figure of Campton an artist: "The artistic temperament and all the vagaries of a somewhat jealous, hot-headed and wrong-headed man do not help to develop the central theme; they merely complicate the situation to no particular purpose."[35] However, there are many ways in which art, as much as war, is the central theme of the book. Campton may be a fallible parent (and Wharton herself was not best placed to explore the theme of parenthood), but he is clearly a fine painter, and through him Wharton is able to explore her troubled feelings about her own activities throughout the war years.

Although young George Campton is the title figure of *A Son at the Front,* in this book the soldier appears not as an active agent but as a passive, often helpless, subject of art. For all that we are told about his manly physicality and his many abilities, George is rarely seen in the novel unless he is injured or asleep. Mostly he is present through his father's pictures, initially through the masterpiece portrait that hangs in the Museum of the Luxembourg, and which his stepfather Anderson Brant would so love to buy. This finished and admired image, however, is quickly replaced with another, the sketch which Campton makes of the young man as he lies sleeping on the night before his mobilization, "as if he were posing for a tombstone."[36] This picture is not completed; Campton throws down his sketchbook in frustration, but it is the image of George that returns most frequently throughout the narrative. There are also other iterations of the young soldier, we learn as the book progresses—an entire folder of Georges in different media, that Campton has stored up over the years. There is the study for the Luxembourg portrait, which he tries to give to the wounded artist René Davril, but after his death, it is sold through a dealer, partly to keep it out of the hands of Brant—though it then falls into those of Madge Talkett. To compound the futility of Campton's efforts off-canvas, Davril's family refuse the money raised by this sale. Later in the novel, after he has painted the portraits of Mrs. Talkett and the grieving concièrge Madame Lebel (this latter, one suspects, is his best work from the war), Campton attempts to catch on canvas his last sight of George as he leans from the train which will take him back to the front, "the good-bye look of the boy George going back to school after the holidays."[37] No doubt, this is the kind of passage Cooperman objected to, in his jibe at Wharton's perception of troops as "Boy Scouts out on a field trip," but this illusion is Campton's, not Wharton's, and despite his attempts to capture this look in paint, it will not materialize. A few pages later, Campton suspects that "the vision of the boy George, the careless happy George who had ridiculed the thought of war and pursued the millennial dreams of an enlightened world—that vision was gone."[38] The next day, just as Campton begins to feel he is recapturing that happy look, Brant arrives with the news of George's mortal wounding. We never hear about the picture again. Thus the portrait that attempts to interpret the war as a positive, "transformative" event is replaced once more by the early un-finished sketch of George sleeping like a dead knight, which will form the basis for Campton's sculpted memorial for his son—a memorial which, in a rare gesture of generosity, he will allow Brant to finance. So, the book closes where it opened, with Campton reworking his old subject (and his old resentments) over again, but this time in a new medium, the modeling clay out of which a creative God fashions life. The final word of the book is "began." Yet this creativity must come to terms with the fact that it is set in motion by death—and we never do see it brought to completion.

passages about meaning are steeped in the tropes of the past: France's Napoleonic history, its artistic legacy, and the image of language as a wine cellar in which quality comes to maturity. As Olin-Ammentorp notes, *A Son at the Front* was not just about Wharton's personal experience of the war, it was also a deeply historical work, one which was embedded in real events and significant dates and places.[41] Meaning, for Wharton, relied on continuity, on a shared register, which was why war threatened the very basis of civilization by rupturing cultural and social links with the past. It was no coincidence that her next work, *The Age of Innocence,* would look back to the 1870s in an attempt to restore the connection to the world of her own childhood, a connection which had been so sharply threatened by the turmoil of the war years. She rarely dealt with the war in later works, though it does form a backdrop for the postwar setting of *The Mother's Recompense* (1925), but the themes of repressed violence and the fragility of society are also explored in less overt ways in her postwar fiction.[42] Through Campton, however, Wharton offers a parody—perhaps even a self-parody—of the conception of art as a means of capturing history. In *The Great Gatsby* (1926), which is also in many ways a novel about the First World War, Nick Carraway cautions Gatsby, "You can't repeat the past," to which Gatsby, still absorbed in his extended infatuation with Daisy Buchanan, replies, "Why of course you can!"[43] Campton might well have given the same reply; repeating the past is in many ways his job. The artist (and Gatsby too is a kind of artist) continually attempts to stop time for the benefit of futurity, to catch a particular look or scene which has already evaporated. At its best, Campton's artwork provides a record of the effects of the war on the women whose anxiety and grief is etched into their faces; at its worst it is fixated on the lost childhood of the son from whom he walked away. Either way, it affirms an intensely historic conception of the role of art in society, which is not out of step with Wharton's sense of her own fiction as a medium for charting the impact of the past on the future. Like Campton, even like Gatsby, Wharton felt the loss of the prewar world keenly, but she also knew that there was no putting the spilled wine back in its bottles.

A Hall of Mirrors

By October 1918, after his adventures with Red Cross authorities, recruiting panels, and military doctors, Dos Passos was back in the army. Like Cummings, and like Wharton's character George Campton, he accepted that if mobilization was the general experience of the moment, he was not going to miss it. However, the experience was hardly what he had hoped for. Optimistically, he had assumed that his previous experience of frontline service would ensure a fast track through basic training and a swift dispatch back to France to rejoin an ambulance unit. Instead, he found himself washing windows in Camp Crane, near Allentown, a county fairground commandeered by the army, where the buildings were still labeled according to the animals once shown there: "POULTRY AND RABBITS, FAT STEERS or just HOGS."[44] If Dos Passos had been looking for a metaphor for the dehumanizing processes of mass militarization, he could hardly have found one more apt. He spent a lot of time in the YMCA library, and he took a lot of notes. He wrote down conversations verbatim and noticed in particular a young farm boy from Indiana and an Italian-American from out west. Over the summer of 1918, he had revised and completed the story of Martin Howe's adventures that would become *One Man's Initiation,* aware that enlisting in the army would probably shift his perspective away from the view of the uninitiated ambulance volunteer. Now, in the surreal surroundings of Camp Crane, faced with a class of ordinary working Americans from whom his moneyed upbringing had carefully separated him, he began to think about another novel. He planned to call it *The Sack of Corinth,* but it would eventually be published as *Three Soldiers.* However, writing in the army in 1918 was not a sanctioned activity. On 2 January, the War Department had announced that those in military service were forbidden to write for publication or to accept pay for their writing. On 4 October, this was mitigated somewhat and soldiers permitted to write fiction and letters for paid publication, but more political and analytical forms of expression, including journalism and literary criticism remained off-limits.[45]

Despite the opportunities to observe, Dos Passos could not get out of Camp Crane fast enough. Through a family friend, he was appointed a

quartermaster sergeant to Ambulance Section 541, largely on the strength
of the fact that he could type with two fingers, a rare skill that made up for
his short-sightedness. The unit was to sail for France at once; they left on
11 November 1918, the day the Armistice was signed. Dos Passos was put
in charge of running the mess hall, and spent the voyage serving up rations in the bowels of the ship. There was flu on the boat, and men died
every day; Dos Passos contracted the disease as it swept through his company after they landed in England. It was his job to make out the hospital-
ization orders for his sick men, but those who went to hospital never came
back. So, he determined not to send himself there, but instead rode out
the illness drinking quantities of rum.[46] Once in France, the unit had little
to do now that the fighting was over. The U.S. army had 2 million troops
on the ground, and it would take months to get them all home. There was
a great deal of drilling and cleaning and boredom. Dos Passos's idea of
drilling his company was to march them all to a nearby orchard, where
they would sit around under the apple trees and smoke. Once, when a colonel showed up at the base demanding to see a close drill, Dos Passos lost
concentration and marched his men straight into a wall; he was demoted
to private on the spot. The pointlessness of sitting around waiting to take
part in a war that was over was at times comic, at others overwhelming. He
wrote in his diary: "The days succeed one another sordid, without a jot of
variety. O the unexpressible sordidness of army life—the filth and greasi-
ness of it."[47] But he had time in which he could write, and the material he
needed was close at hand. Daily scenes went into notes, or straight into
the new novel, "a monumental work on America Militant," as he called it.[48]
He tidied up the manuscript of *One Man's Initiation* for publication, and
on days off, he traveled up to Paris to see friends and talk about books,
both his own and other people's. His head was full of plans and outlines for
books and plays. He was already thinking ahead to another even more ambitious novel, that would eventually become *The 42nd Parallel* (1930), the
first volume of *U.S.A.* Meanwhile, he signed up for a program that allowed
him to study at the Sorbonne while waiting for a discharge. He was not his
own master, and that made him impatient; impatience made him ambitious,
and ambition made him work.

When John Andrews is injured at the opening of part 4 of *Three Soldiers*, the section entitled "Rust," he has fallen behind his company to look at his own reflection in a puddle where tiny green frogs swim under the surface: "He looked at it curiously. He could barely see the outlines of a stained grimacing mask, and the silhouette of the gun barrel slanting behind it. So this was what they had made of him."[49] It is a quiet moment of narcissistic self-regard, but also a moment of luck; had he walked on with his line to where the shrapnel shell exploded, he probably would not have lived. Of the novel's three eponymous soldiers, only Andrews the aspiring composer has this reflective quality that makes him wonder about the effect of the war on his identity. Fusselli worries more about what other people think of him, and Chrisfield doesn't care. As the three friends from training camp move through the routines and rigors of war, Fusselli reveals himself to be bound by expectations, eager to please superiors, more frightened of being singled out for reproof than he is of actually coming to harm. He has flickers of perception and inquiry, but hastily sweeps these under the rugs of compliance and ambition. Chrisfield, conversely, is not cowed by military protocols; indeed he can barely contain his instinctive rage, which renders him equally willing to kill the young German soldier he finds hiding in a farmhouse and the American officer, Anderson, who once slighted him. The hand grenade is, aptly enough, the weapon of choice for this explosive, brutalized figure, who yet has qualities which beyond the arena of war could have made him a decent man. Andrews, however, whom we never see fighting, is thoroughly unable to adapt to army life. He is continually coming up against reflective surfaces that remind him who he is, or perhaps more accurately who he is not: for example the windows which he is interminably washing in camp, both in America and in France.

Andrews is surrounded by the imagery of water and fluidity. To start with, "Rust" is the effect of water on the metal from which Andrews and his fellow soldiers are supposedly formed in the other section headings: "Making the Mold," "The Metal Cools," and "Machines." Early on, Andrews fantasizes that he will escape from the army by swimming across a river in a ritual of baptism and rebirth—which prefigures his actual escape from military prison camp later in the novel. In hospital recovering from his shrapnel wound, as he realizes that he is free from the routines of active service, he feels the "strange fluid harmonies that permeated his whole body," but when he attempts to catch hold of his thoughts and give them musical form, they vanish "the way a sandy inlet that has been full of shoals of silver fishes, becomes suddenly empty when a shadow crosses the water, and the man who is watching sees wanly his own reflection instead of the flickering of thousands of tiny silver bodies."[50] Later in Paris, when Andrews requests a discharge from a major seated in "a large white-painted room, with elaborate mouldings and mirrors in all four walls," both the major and Andrews are "reflected to infinity in two directions in the grey brilliance of the mirrors." That evening, as he thinks about (or reflects on) this scene, it seems to him that the selves in the mirrors represent the fracturing of his own identity that life in the army has required of him: "This sentient body of his, full of possibilities and hopes and desires, was only a pale ghost that depended on the other self, that suffered for it and cringed for it. He could not drive out of his head the picture of himself, skinny, in an ill-fitting uniform, repeated endlessly in the two mirrors of the major's white-painted office."[51] John Andrews, originally a character rescued and extended from Dos Passos's earlier collaborative tale *Seven Times Round the Walls of Jericho,* begun with Robert Hillyer in August 1917, becomes in this novel an outlet for many of Dos Passos's own opinions and frustrations about the war—and is in that sense also another kind of reflective double.[52] However, that this authorial surrogate should be so concerned with depths and surfaces suggests that this novel is wrestling with questions about the nature of internal and external experience as well as with the more obvious politics of war—vital though these are to the book. As Michael Clark points out, the novel contains a whole series of doubles and parallels, as though Andrews's divided consciousness is externalized in many of the reciprocal characters and images around him: Fusselli and Chrisfeld; Jeanne and Genevieve; the lame boy and his girl; city and country; military and civilian life.[53]

These built-in dichotomies may have in some measure invited the polarized reception which the novel was given. When it emerged in 1921, in those uncertain months when the war still seemed too raw to read about, critical reviews of the book were divided between viewing it as a work of "genius" and an outrage against the integrity of the army.[54] Norman Shannon Hall accused Dos Passos of "distorting the truth," and said it was a shame that the author of the book was currently overseas because he "should be locked up" for suggesting that American soldiers would ever "whine" or "boot-lick."[55] One *New York Times* reviewer noted rather pointedly that the dust jacket of the book was "yellow."[56] However, Henry Seidel Canby in the *New York Evening Post* claimed it was the first American book about the war "written with sufficient passion and vividness of detail to count as literature." It was, he said, "a passionate study of human nature under fire," which may have been more of a metaphoric than a literal assessment, given how little fighting there actually is in the novel—though the reference to Barbusse's novel, translated with the English title *Under Fire,* was probably not accidental.[57] In contrast, Coningsby Dawson complained of the novel's "unmanly intemperance both in language and in plot." He illustrated his point with a statement from a Russian friend with whom he had been discussing the question of how so many men could have experienced the same war but come out with such different responses: "My Russian gave an answer that was very true. 'Men got out of the war,' he said, 'what they brought to it. The hero found heroism: the coward found cowardice. Except in rare instances the war did not recreate men; it only made more emphatic in them tendencies that had been latent.'"[58] Dawson apparently saw this explanation as a means of undermining Dos Passos's interpretation of the war as a degrading and dehumanizing experience. However, he rather missed the irony that this statement about the reflective force of the war was very much in line with the central theme of *Three Soldiers.* Dawson, who had written his own patriotic war novel, *The Glory of the Trenches* (1918), while serving with the Canadian Expeditionary Forces, presumably had never possessed a latent sense of irony for the war to emphasize.

In *Three Soldiers,* then, Dos Passos presents the war as an event that mirrors humanity on a number of levels. The development of the plot suggests that he would have agreed with Dawson's Russian, that military life doubles and intensifies the traits and characteristics of recruits, repeating them endlessly in a series of opposing mirrors. Thus, Fusselli's natural eagerness to please becomes a slavish regard for authority. Chrisfield's hot-headed aggression makes him a reckless killer. Andrews's sensitivity and creativity drive him to solipsism and irrationality, leading him to take ever more extravagant and self-destructive risks. For Dos Passos, this intensification of character shows the fundamental ineffectiveness of army training, which is supposed to efface not foster such individuality. The war reveals these men for what they are; and not one of them is either a "hero" or a "coward." As Hemingway might say: "The hell with all the dirty, easy labels." Dos Passos's war, however, does not simply provide a mirror for the individual characters; it is also reflective as a philosophical subject. The meaning of the conflict as a human event cannot be revealed—no amount of window washing will ever open up a perspective that shows what it is all about. Rather, the war presents only a hard, shiny surface in which characters and readers find their own moral and political views repeated and intensified—as ably demonstrated by Dos Passos's reviewers. It seems significant that the sharpest vitriol in the novel is reserved for the "Y" men, who purport to see teleological purposes in the conflict, where for Dos Passos none exist. Meaning cannot be uncovered within the war, even by the most sensitive observer; it can only be supplied. And the many viewpoints about the war expressed by his characters, both major and minor, testify to the impossibility of regularizing and codifying the many individual readings imposed upon it. The utterly incomprehensible First World War thus provides Dos Passos with the largest and most effective mirror for the reflection of American society in all its multiplicity—which is, no doubt, why he returned to it again and again as a subject for his fiction throughout his career.

Just in case the reader misses the idea that the reflexivity of the characters is also a metaphor for war's ability to reflect society as a whole, the major's office of mirrors functions as a miniature model of the "Hall of Mirrors" at Versailles, where Wilson arrived in January 1919 to argue his Fourteen Points in the postwar tussle between the victorious nations about sovereignty and economics—another kind of rationality that was imposed on the four years of conflict. Early in *Three Soldiers,* Fusselli's company look out from their railcar at "a foreign-looking station where the walls were plastered with unfamiliar advertisements." Fusselli spells out the name of the station "v-e-r-s-a-i-l-l-e-s," and Eisenstein the radical offers a pronunciation "Versales."[59] In the phonetic, anglicized French which the soldiers talk, it sounds exactly like "for sales," and certainly the economics of war both micro and macro, are never far from Dos Passos's mind. In his later dramatization of the background to the Paris Peace Conference in *1919* (1932), Dos Passos depicts J. Pierpoint Morgan, not "Meester Veelson," as the central power at the negotiating table: "by the end of the Peace Conference," he writes, "the phrase *J. P. Morgan suggests* had compulsion over a power of seventyfour billion dollars."[60] In *Three Soldiers,* the helplessness of the soldiers, and the general breakdown of French society are compounded by the gestures and failures of financial exchange. Sometimes the soldiers have no money and find themselves dispossessed and emasculated; when they do, there is nothing to spend it on except the transient pleasures of sex and alcohol. The major in the mirrored hall refuses to discharge Andrews until he produces an affidavit that he can support himself financially, thus delaying his discharge just long enough for him to get himself arrested for not carrying his papers. At the end of the novel, Madame Boncour turns him in to the military police when he no longer has money to pay his bill.

In later works, especially in *The Big Money* (1936), Dos Passos would develop this theme of the transactional nature of human life to a central motif—a trait within his writing that would be interpreted by some as a fundamentally Marxist conception of society, even after he had lost his youthful enthusiasm for socialist politics, as many of his generation did.[61] But Dos Passos's fascination with different kinds of currency can also be understood as part of a wider exploration of the ways in which values are ascribed by social groups. Thus, in the novel, military rules and hierarchies are exposed as arbitrary systems of exchange which bear scant relationship to anything beyond their own continuation—and certainly have little to do with the business of battle, as Chrisfield so forcefully demonstrates. Language also, as the many transactions across the French-English boundary show, is devoid of intrinsic value but operates by a system of warped conventions and agreements. The soldiers bastardize French phrases, and then complain that the locals cannot even understand their own language. They refer to the "Oregon Forest" instead of the "Argonne," thus confusing the geography of the setting as well as its name, blurring an entire continental divide in the process.

Wharton's *Son at the Front* raised the question of the subjectivity of viewpoint through her use of Campton's perspective as the filter through which the story was told. In *Three Soldiers,* Dos Passos dispersed meaning and significance through three contrasting, sometimes conflicting, narrative perspectives. In later works, even this would seem too narrow a framework for Dos Passos, and from *Manhattan Transfer* onward his works would explore multiple narrative viewpoints. In the 1950s, Blanche Gelfant described Dos Passos's works as "synoptic" novels, borrowing a term more usually applied in biblical criticism to the overlapping and yet contrasting Gospels of Matthew, Mark, and Luke.[62] Dos Passos, no doubt, appreciated the irony. However, in *Three Soldiers,* he had not yet fully developed this narrative process into the powerful, clinical method it would become for probing the individual experiences of the interconnected lives of his characters within the wider community. Socially and psychologically, the author is perhaps too close to John Andrews to allow for the dispassionate treatment this method requires. Thus as Robert Rosen points out, Dos Passos's attempt to "declass" himself and write a novel that would "embody more than one social perspective" is only "partially successful;" the novel of social record which it could have become is continually conflicting with the demands of another kind of modernist genre, the "Art Novel" which charts Andrews's journey to self-awareness.[63] But, to other readers, the admission of the "sensitive, suffering, aspiring young hero" into the plot is a welcome and humanizing gesture, in contrast with Dos Passos's later novels, where this sort of character is ruthlessly "annihilated."[64]

Whether there is too much or too little of it, the theme of artistic creativity is more than just a distraction from the gritty details of the other elements of the story. Indeed, Dos Passos's decision to put an artist figure at the heart of the novel, as Wharton also does, highlights the very problem of representation that the novel is trying to address through its own experimental structures and forms of language. Given Dos Passos's experimentation here with a "synoptic" model, it seems important that Fusselli's main use to the army (that is, before he is court-martialed for contracting venereal disease and condemned to permanent kitchen duty) is as someone skilled in handling "optical goods." This is also his main use to the reader, as someone who, like the impersonal "camera eye" of Dos Passos's later novels registers impressions of what is going on around him—with little analysis or insight into their causes or effects. But it also seems important that, despite this reminder to the reader to pay attention to visual images (such as the many reflected scenes or impressions framed by windows and doors), Dos Passos chooses neither painting nor writing as the medium in which Andrews attempts to express himself. Instead, the young artist is engaged in an aesthetic form which is less representational: music.

La Motte, Cummings, and Borden can all be said to be exploring cubist narratives in their portrayals of the war, juxtaposing jarring perspectives and exploring strange angles and approaches in their view of the subject of war. *One Man's Initiation* also works as a kind of cubist narrative, juxtaposing disjointed scenes and voices. However, in his selection of the musical composer as the sentient figure within his narrative, Dos Passos suggests a different kind of relationship between reality and art, although one which also questions the comprehensibility of war. In many ways music is an odd choice of theme, as Dos Passos, unlike Cummings, was not especially skilled as a musician, and it has to be said that the text is rather scanty on the technical details of what Andrews is doing much of the time. As with Wharton's presentation of the artist Campton in *A Son at the Front,* Dos Passos here uses music as something of a smoke screen for an exploration of his own methods and aesthetic ambitions. Had he set up Andrews as a writer, or even a painter, he would have been able to give a much more convincing account of his creative processes. However, the role of music in the novel is important, because it allows Dos Passos to connect with a depth of emotional response to events that is neither rational, nor verbal, nor concerned with political dogma. Although Andrews does at times respond to events and to physical desire with the sudden apprehension of melody, it is the underlying rhythm of military life, the strange jazz patterns that he improvises on the piano when playing for the "Y" man, that seem most alive. He also finds that he cannot shake off the crass but catchy tunes which his fellow soldiers sing. His intended classical masterpiece, "The Queen of Sheba," which he has planned and crafted for months, is abandoned as stilted and vacuous, like his contrived romance with Genevieve. It is his symphony, "The Soul and Body of John Brown," a curious identification with another soldier, but also another rebel individualist, which really catches his imagination in the closing chapters, and also highlights through its title the dualism between internal and external experience that is such a marked element of Andrews's character.

Andrews's music is thus the source of his redemption, the means by which he recovers his individuality, but also by which he comes to terms with his identity as a soldier and as an American—indeed, Brown as an anti-establishment yet patriotic icon conjures a powerful and disruptive brand of nationality.[65] In writing down the rhythms and refrains that have been confusedly churning through him throughout his time in the army, Andrews not only constructs his music but also rebuilds himself. The John Brown symphony, however, is also the source of his downfall; by lingering to write it, he allows the force of the law to catch up with him—though the dignity with which he accepts this fate at the end of the novel suggests that his art, rather than his military service, has brought him to maturity. He has composed himself, in more ways than one. No one, however, will hear Andrews's music. After his arrest, the final image in the book is of the sheets of music, for which Andrews has given up the chance of escape, blowing silently off the table as he is led away to life imprisonment. Like Keats's "unheard" melodies, this lost symphony represents an unattainable ideal of creativity, which, like Andrews himself, is yet another victim of the stupidity of war.[66] However, the aesthetic merit of his work is cast into doubt by his ironic discovery that he has all along simply been re-writing the tune of the marching song "John Brown's body lies a-mouldering in the grave." Masterpiece or derivative jingle, like the end-lessly reflecting mirrors of Versailles, like the novel *Three Soldiers,* or like the war itself, in the end Andrews's symphony is unknowable and repre-sents only whatever the individual reader supplies.

Both *Three Soldiers* and *A Son at the Front* draw a complicated com-parison between the figure of the soldier and that of the artist—and in both books these figures must come to an uneasy compromise, whether as father and son, as in Wharton's novel, or as two facets of Andrews's per-sonality, as in Dos Passos. The violence, anxiety, and bureaucracy of war are stifling for art in all its forms, halting the brush, silencing the music, or evaporating the words that might give it outlet; and the artist in wartime appears as a vulnerable figure, one who watches when he should act, or who hesitates when he should run. Nevertheless, for both Wharton and Dos Passos, the act of creation is a powerful one that provides a necessary corrective to the destruction of war. In both novels one can sense a memo-rializing instinct at work, but something more subtle is also taking place here. By focusing attention on the artist, visual or musical, at the close of these texts, both novelists identify the artist figure, not the soldier, as the representative consciousness for the future. As must have been obvious by late 1918, for better or worse, the soldier's work was now done, and the urgent cultural question was no longer how "civilization" could be defended from the military threats that assailed it from outside, but how it could ever reshape itself, having turned out to be so fatally flawed on the inside. The fact that both Campton and Andrews are engaged in artistic projects that look unlikely to succeed does not offer an optimistic view of the po-tential for regenerating the cultural landscape in the wake of war. How-ever, that very fallibility suggests something more interesting than a glib renewal of the aesthetic values of the past. Neither Campton nor Andrews has triumphed over the war; each is, in his own way, defeated by it and must give up what he treasures most. Nevertheless, each remains deter-mined to create, even out of a failure and sense of futility. Civilization, as James and Wharton envisaged it in 1914, had proved inadequate against violence; the institutions and tastes of the prewar years could not hold out against barbarism and inhumanity—but they could, in the end, come to a compromise. Both Campton and Andrews demonstrate that by absorbing the motifs of war and by continuing to work in the conditions that it imposed, some sort of synthesis was possible, in which the loss of trusty old meanings became a starting point from which other kinds of significance could be developed. The late war novels of Wharton and Dos Passos suggested that by this compromise, culture could certainly survive into the postwar world, but it would never be the same again.

Aftermath

ALL THIS, OF COURSE, WAS JUST the start. From 1919 onward, as the military and political events of the war drew to a close, the process of reflecting on the cost and the significance of those events could begin in earnest. The trouble for many writers was that most paying readers were reluctant to engage with this process. Burlingame notes:

> With the signing of the peace, the curtain came down. The American people as a whole wanted to forget, wanted "normalcy," prosperity and automobiles, and its attitude was reflected by the book-buying public. Editors shook their heads as manuscripts by soldiers bursting with their experiences poured into their offices. To publish these books, thrilling and fascinating as many of them were, would have been a waste of time, money and paper. . . . When the curtain rose again, the glory had departed. War reappeared as unadulterated hell. The panoply was drab, the bugles played in discord. High words about making the world safe for democracy were lost in the mud; the temper of all who wrote now of the war was one of disillusion.[1]

Much of this disillusion was political. Wilson's failure to persuade Senate to ratify the Treaty of Versailles or to join the League of Nations undermined many of the stated objectives of America's intervention in 1917. The Republicans in Senate had been willing to accept the treaty with reservations; however, Wilson refused to accommodate these, claiming that they

236

would require him to renegotiate. In the political stalemate that followed, the Republican Warren Harding won the presidential election of 1920, and concluded separate peace treaties with Germany, Austria, and Hungary. The Treaty of Versailles, with its punishing reparation payments against Germany, is often blamed for the advent of the Second World War, but had the treaty been upheld and enforced by all the Allies as agreed, it would have had a much better chance of preventing another major war in Western Europe.[2] However, readers also experienced more personal misgivings about how the war had been conducted and the emotions which it had aroused. Writing in 1923, the popular writer of sea stories William McFee (1881-1966) acknowledged a distaste for reading accounts of the war which recalled the militarist atmosphere of those years. Books such as Arthur Guy Empey's *Over the Top* (1917), he wrote, inspired "a feeling of vague discomfort, as though one were suddenly confronted with some evidence of a by-gone private shame." McFee found himself troubled by the lofty ideology that had been superimposed on the contingencies of wartime, or as he phrased it by the "tendency to confuse the bickerings and sharp animosities of a furious military conflict with the eternal struggle of the human spirit against its austere environment of physical perils and the malignities of our common life." It was tempting, he felt, to imagine that in the last five years society had "outgrown the crudities of those days," but this judgment, he realized, was probably "hasty."[3] As the previous chapter suggests, McFee was not the only reader struggling to form a coherent response to the literature of the war. The divided opinions of reviewers over Wharton's and Dos Passos's novels demonstrated a disagreement, not only about the quality of those books, but also about the interpretation of the events which they described and the underlying criteria for evaluating the worth of literature. This period immediately following the war was clearly a time of reappraisal and adjustment, and the repeated accusations of "propaganda" in reviews of the period reveal not just a political backlash against pro-Allied sympathies, but also a bad conscience about the ways in which literature had been commandeered as a vehicle of governmental policy in 1917-18.

So it must have been with something like a sigh of relief that the critical communities on both sides of the Atlantic turned to the latest literary theories of the 1920s, which appeared to distance the practice of literature from the muddy waters of international and social politics. This new sensibility, formally challenging and less constrained by proprieties, would foster what we know as "modernism," but as I noted in the opening pages of this book, "modernism" is not easy to know. The term is usually associated with a self-conscious rejection of the past and/or a self-reflexive focus on issues of form and expression rather than social content or context—criteria which, if rigorously applied exclude all but a tiny fraction of the literary output of the 1920s and 1930s in both America and Europe. Indeed, the fact that the term modernism emerged in the late 1960s and early 1970s, suggests that the concept was really constructed as a means of mapping (or constructing) the origins of certain strands of nihilist, theoretical and poststructuralist thought coming to the fore at *that* time. If this is so, then "modernism" is predicated on an arrogantly progressive model of literary judgment, which validates certain elements of style because they appear to be more "forward-looking," whereas what is really happening is simply the approval of texts which conform to prevailing tastes and criteria, instead of a genuine willingness to engage with and learn from the voices of the past. This is the root of my distrust of the term. As I hope preceding chapters have shown, the experience of war in many different arenas between 1914 and 1918, did create opportunities for testing out new and daring effects and forms in literature. The impact of these was significant, and fueled the proliferation of what would much better be known as *interwar aestheticism,* or some other phrase that reflects the curiosity in certain literary circles about the questions which the war had raised about the process of expression. However, the most thorny of these questions about the literature of the war and its aftermath was not how it was constructed, how it varied from that of previous (and future) decades, or even what to call it, but rather—what was it *for?*

As T. S. Eliot, spokesman for the new wave of literary experimentation, would later say, "each generation, like each individual, brings to the contemplation of art its own categories of appreciation, makes its own de-

mands upon art, and has its own uses for art."⁴ One of the growing demands of the reading generation of the 1920s and 1930s does seem to have
been a distancing of artistic criteria from moral agendas and party politics, almost certainly as a backlash against the official appropriation of art
and literature during the war. However, as Michael Levenson notes, this
trait has at times led to the "modernist" writers being caricatured as "those
who sought perfection of the work at the expense of social engagement,
who curled inside the 'autonomy' of art, safe from the historical instability
towards which they remained cool, indifferent, fastidious."⁵ One need
only think about Pound's *Jefferson and/or Mussolini* or Picasso's *Guer-
nica,* says Levenson, to realize that even the most self-conscious artists of
the interwar years were also profoundly political. Likewise, Gandal's
work shows that even Fitzgerald's *Great Gatsby* or Faulkner's *Sound and
the Fury,* so often seen to be about style, turn out on inspection to be about
race, class, and gender. One should also consider Woolf's feminist opinions, John Steinbeck's class consciousness, La Motte's activism against
the opium trade, and Dos Passos's suspicion of capitalism: the list goes on.
Clearly in the years following the First World War, concerns with social
injustice, the path of history, or the documentation of the everyday, regularly went hand in hand with an interest in experimental forms and
problems of artistic creativity—though this has often been pitched as an
unbridgeable dichotomy.

One of the difficulties that American war writing has had in finding
a place in the literary canon (as designed by critical scholars) has been
negotiating just this perception that any text concerned with the weighty
subject matter of war, almost by definition, cannot be sufficiently focused on the question of its own form to be of real aesthetic value. To
many readers, however, the aesthetic value of war writing is not its first
responsibility—its job is to tell the truth, to bear witness, to commemo-
rate. The vast majority of people nowadays who encounter texts from the
First World War do so via poetry performed at Armistice or Memorial Day
ceremonies, through school lessons, or in television or radio documenta-
ries, in which such works are regularly presented as historical record—
often very powerfully so. This is an old and instinctive use of literature,

and I cannot bring myself to say that it is wrong or naive. It is important that we know what happened on the frontlines and in the hospitals, prisons and army camps of the First World War, and the words of those who were there still have the power to call us to witness—although it can be disheartening to see certain forms of militarist rhetoric glibly repeated in some of our rituals of memory. As McFee noted, we do not easily outgrow the "crudities" of the past, even though we like to think that we do. Nevertheless, texts from the First World War retain the ability to move all kinds of readers and listeners, young and old, intellectual and unschooled. Thus, throughout the last century, war writing has found itself in a curious double bind. It has been seen to speak the truth in an age where truth telling has not been seen as the proper business of literature. Or to put this another way, it has been charged with recording reality in a century which has put "reality" in quotation marks.[6] It is no surprise, therefore, that war writing sits a little uneasily within the current literary canon. These days, the reading of war books with a critical eye requires compromise, or at least a willingness to look past certain theoretical criteria, especially the criterion of political detachment—though in an age such as our own, characterized by incoherence, superficiality, and intolerance, one has to ask again if detaching from politics is really a literary virtue. Surely, the writer should have something to offer? Surely, despite everything, words still matter?

Of course. Words matter because they have the power to shape the ways in which we think about ourselves and other people. In "The Body of an American," the concluding section of *1919*, written over a decade after the war, Dos Passos considers the process of selecting one corpse from the many unidentified dead of the American Expeditionary Force to lie in the Memorial Amphitheater at the Arlington National Cemetery, Virginia. "How did they pick John Doe?" he asks, and how did they "make sure he aint a guinea or a kike"? As Dos Passos suggests, such questions of national and racial identity fall apart in the face of the simple fact of death: "how can you tell a guy's a hundredpercent when all you've got's a gunnysack full of bones, bronze buttons stamped with the screaming eagle and a pair of roll puttees."[7] Here is a man for whom words have deteriorated, a man without a name, without a "dirty, easy label," whose identity tag lies at the bottom of the Marne. Robbed of life and speech, the Unknown Soldier can no longer choose his own words or shape his own identity—he has himself become a sign, a potent symbol of the war, and a symbol of America itself. The difficulty, as Dos Passos shows, is to work out the meaning which that symbol will convey. The identity of the single, broken, and putrifying body in the tomb gathers its power from its unknowability—meaning must be given to it, and this meaning is created through words. Thus in "The Body of an American," Dos Passos layers the official rhetoric of the burial ceremony, words which affirm the "*indisputable justice of his country's cause,*" with the language of newspaper reportage, and with the multiple interpretations which can be projected on to the decayed body. Born everywhere from Brooklyn to Portland, the Unknown Soldier was also "busboy harveststiff hogcaller boyscout champeen corn-shucker of Western Kansas bellhop at the United States Hotel at Saratoga Springs office boy callboy fruiter telephone lineman longshoreman lumberjack plumber's helper, worked for an exterminating company in Union City, filled pipes in an opium joint in Trenton, N.J."[8] In 1914, Henry James had characterized Civil War America as a "body rent with a thousand wounds." Here, Dos Passos repeats the trope of the single, shattered soldier as a representative for the nation. Like those words which James feared would flake away into uselessness, the body of the Unknown Soldier has deteriorated to "scraps of dried viscera and skin bundled in khaki." Nevertheless, it still retains the power to communicate—indeed it is *because* of its deterioration, because its identity and meaning has become insecure and variable that this body has acquired the ability to speak so powerfully, conveying a myriad of different meanings, depending on one's perspective. In its marble memorial, this body is both the record of a brave fight to sustain the values of a civilized society, and a bitter mockery of the greed and incompetence which sent so many men to needless deaths.

This flexibility of meaning in the aftermath of war does not just apply to the symbol of the body, but also to gesture and perhaps most of all to words. "Woodrow Wilson brought a bouquet of poppies," Dos Passos tells us—but we are not told whether to interpret this as an act of poignant,

Notes

Introduction

1. Borden, *Forbidden Zone*, 175.
2. P. Faulkner, *Modernism*, x.
3. Friedman, "Definitional Excursions," 30.
4. *New York Times*, 11 May 1915, 1.
5. *New York Times*, 3 April 1917, 1.
6. Harries and Harries, *Last Days of Innocence*, 32.
7. There are several versions of Martin Luther's unrepentant speech to the Diet of Worms in 1521, but his final words are usually translated as: "Here I stand. I can do no other. God help me." For a discussion of the various sources, see Gritsch, *Martin—God's Court Jester*, 41 and 231.
8. Dewey, 'What America Will Fight For,' *New Republic*, 68.
9. Bourne, *War and the Intellectuals*, 3.
10. Van Wienen, *Partisans and Poets*, 6.
11. See for example: Owen Wister, *Pentecost of Calamity;* Sherwood Anderson, *Marching Men;* Sinclair Lewis, *Jimmie Higgins;* and Dorothy Canfield, *Home Fires in France.*
12. Moffett, *Conquest of America*, 106–13 and 175–85.
13. Stein, *Alice B. Toklas*, 200.
14. La Motte, *Backwash of War*, vii.
15. Kennedy, *Over Here*, 60.
16. La Motte, *Backwash of War*, v.
17. Whalan, *American Culture*, 159–61.
18. Lasswell, *Propaganda Technique*, 221.
19. Harries and Harries, *Last Days of Innocence*, 49.
20. Keene, *Doughboys*, ix. See also Harries and Harries, *Last Days of Innocence*, 5 and 451.
21. Whalan, *American Culture*, 153.
22. Ibid., 4.
23. Cobb, *Cobb of "The World,"* 270.
24. *New York Times*, 3 April 1917, 1.
25. Roosevelt, foreword to *One Hundred Per Cent American*, vii.
26. Consider for example Henry May's seminal study *The End of American Innocence: A Study of the First Years of Our Own Time, 1912–1917.* Alan Price's

book about Wharton's wartime activities, *The End of the Age of Innocence: Edith Wharton and the First World War* and Meirion and Susie Harries's historical reappraisal of American attitudes to the war, *The Last Days of Innocence.*

27. Keith, *Rich Man's War, Poor Man's Fight.*

28. Harries and Harries, *Last Days of Innocence,* 7.

29. Reynolds, *Hemingway's First War,* 60–61.

30. Hemingway, *Farewell to Arms,* 165.

31. For a discussion of this question, see Buitenhuis, *Great War of Words,* 61.

32. Cooperman, *World War I and the American Novel,* viii.

33. Sherry, *Language of Modernism,* 7. For a reading of British war literature which *does* demonstrate this process, see Tate, *Modernism, History, and the First World War.*

34. Eliot, *Selected Poems,* 55. Eliot writes to his mother in November 1915 of having met Maurice for the first time: "It seems very strange that a boy of nineteen should have such experiences—often twelve hours alone in his 'dug-out' in the trenches, and at night, when he cannot sleep, occupying himself by shooting rats with a revolver. What he tells about rats and vermin is incredible— Northern France is swarming and the rats are as big as cats." *Letters,* 1:132.

35. Fussell, *Great War and Modern Memory,* 23.

36. For an overview of American war texts see Quinn, " First World War," 175–84.

37. See for example Dennis Brown, *The Modernist Self in Twentieth-Century English Literature: A Study in Self Fragmentation;* Jane Goldman, *Modernism, 1910–1945: Image to Apocalypse*; and Vincent Sherry, *The Great War and the Language of Modernism.*

38. Fussell, *Great War and Modern Memory,* 320.

39. See for example Jennifer Haytock, *At Home, at War: Domesticity and World War I in American Literature;* and Mark Whalan, *The Great War and the Culture of the New Negro.*

40. See for example Christine Hallett, *Containing Trauma: Nursing Work in the First World War.*

Chapter One. 1914—Civilization

1. Charles Eliot Norton to Chauncey Wright, 5 December 1869, in *Letters of Charles Eliot Norton,* 1:371.

2. Eliot, *Poetry and Criticism,* 15.

3. James to Wharton, 6 August 1914, in Powers, ed., *Henry James and Edith Wharton,* 289.

4. Eliot's reaction against Arnold's view of culture was evident as early as 1915 when he wrote to Ezra Pound on the subject of higher education that "the function of the university is not to turn out Culcher and Civic Pageants" and that "literature has rights of its own which extend beyond Uplift and Recreation." T. S. Eliot to Ezra Pound, 15 April 1915, *Letters*, 1:104.

5. Eliot, *Poetry and Criticism*, 151. Ralph Waldo Emerson: "The American Scholar," (1837); repr. in *Collected Works*, 1:52–70, 53.

6. In his use of *barbaric* Eliot borrows an established term from the field of cultural anthropology, in which evolving societies were often classified as "savage," "barbaric," or "civilized." Douglas Dowd summarizes the use of these terms by Thorstein Veblen and others: "A savage society is one dependent on hunting and gathering, a barbarian society had developed a settled agriculture with domesticated plants and animals and village life (among other things), and a civilized society is one characterized by a more complicated technology combined with relatively great specialization, writing, urbanization, and so on." Dowd, *Thorstein Veblen*, 8.

7. See, for example, Lankester, *Degeneration;* and Wells, *Time Machine*.

8. Veblen, *Theory of the Leisure Class*, 68 and 100.

9. James to A. C. Benson, 1 October 1896, *Letters to Benson and Monod*, 35.

10. In 1914, H. G. Wells wrote "This is already the vastest war in history. It is not a war of nations, but of mankind. It is a war to exorcise a world-madness and end an age." Wells, *War That Will End War*, 9.

11. Devlin, *Too Proud to Fight*, 135.

12. Wharton to Gaillard Lapsley, 23 December 1914, quoted in Price, *End of the Age of Innocence*, 35.

13. Moffett, introduction to *Conquest of America*, x.

14. For a fuller discussion of James's relationship to his father's religious ideas see Hutchison, *Seeing and Believing*, and Taylor, *Henry James and the Father Question*. Wharton's intellectual mentor, Egerton Winthrop, encouraged her to read widely in contemporary scientific and sociological thought, including works by Herbert Spencer, Thomas Huxley, and James Frazer. Lee, *Edith Wharton*, 69–71.

15. Dos Passos, *Mr Wilson's War*, 101 and 102.

16. Lubbock, *Portrait of Edith Wharton*, 158.

17. Wharton, *Son at the Front*, 193.

18. James to Wharton, 19 August 1914, in *Letters*, ed. Lubbock, 2:406.

19. James to Howard Sturgis, 4 August 1914, ibid., 398.

20. James to Rhoda Broughton, 10 August 1914, ibid., 403.

21. On 9 November 1914, James wrote to Wharton, "It's impossible to 'locate anything in our time.' Our time has been *this* time for the last 50 years, & if it was ignorantly & fatuously so the only light in which to show it is now the light of that tragic delusion. And that's too awful a subject. It all makes Walter Scott, him only, readable again." Powers, ed., *Henry James and Edith Wharton,* 316.

22. James to William James Junior, 31 August 1914, in James, *Letters,* ed. Lubbock, 2:410.

23. May, *End of American Innocence,* 30–32.

24. James, *Hawthorne,* 55.

25. Ibid., 56.

26. Arnold argues that America has material comfort and urban organization, but is not "interesting" because there is a lack of the "elevated and the beautiful." Arnold, "Civilization in the United States," in *Complete Prose,* 10:357 and 358. For a further discussion of James's relationship to Arnold, see Lustig, "James, Arnold, 'Culture' and 'Modernity.' "

27. James, *Parisian Sketches,* 41.

28. James, "France" in Stephens, *Book of France,* 1–8, 1. This book was one of the fund-raising ventures instigated by the French Parliamentary Committee's Fund for the Relief of the Invaded Departments. The book was a bilingual project; Stephens collated contributions from French writers and thinkers such as Maurice Barrés, André Gide, Anatole France, and Pierre Loti, and then asked prominent British figures, mostly members of the committee, to provide translations. The only original pieces in English were a poem by Rudyard Kipling entitled "France," and James's short essay of the same title. James's piece was first delivered as "Remarks at the Meeting of the Committee held on June 9, 1915," and was published as the prologue to the collection. See also Chapter Three.

29. Ibid., 5.

30. James to Wharton, 21 September 1914, in *Letters,* ed. Lubbock, 2:420 and 421. The shelling of Rheims Cathedral became a potent symbol of the German commanders' alleged disregard for history and culture in the American imagination. Richard Harding Davis published a vivid eyewitness account in *Scribner's Magazine* in January 1915: "The cathedral had been one of the most magnificent examples of early Gothic architecture. . . . We picked our way among the broken arms, hands, wings, halos of statues that for hundreds of years, to the glory of God, had faced the elements; our feet trod upon bits of glass more beautiful than jewels." Richard Harding Davis, "Rheims during the Bombardment," *Scribner's Magazine* 57 (1915), 70–76; 74.

31. James to Wharton, 17 October 1914, in Powers, *Henry James and Edith Wharton*, 310.
32. Wharton, *Fighting France*, 5.
33. James to Wharton, 3 September 1914 and 23 September, in Powers, *Henry James and Edith Wharton*, 299 and 304.
34. Greenslet, *Under the Bridge*, 135.
35. Wharton to Sara Norton, 27 September 1914, *Letters*, 338.
36. Wharton, *Backward Glance*, 349.
37. Lubbock, *Portrait of Edith Wharton*, 101. Benstock, *No Gifts from Chance*, 307.
38. Lee, *Edith Wharton*, 465.
39. Benstock, *No Gifts from Chance*, 307.
40. Price, *End of the Age of Innocence*, 34.
41. Ibid., xv.
42. "Mrs Wharton Asks for Funds to Aid Refugees," *New York Sun*, 18 January 1915, 2. Wharton, *Backward Glance*, 349.
43. Wharton to Mary Berenson, 20 December 1914, in *Letters*, 344.
44. Wharton to Mary Berenson, 12 January 1915, ibid., 346.
45. Hansen, *Gentlemen Volunteers*, 22.
46. The Morgan-Harjes unit was the first of the American ambulance units, and began operations in early October 1914. It was organized by Herman Harjes, senior partner of the Morgan-Harjes bank in Paris, and his wife. For an account of the founding of the unit see Hansen, *Gentlemen Volunteers*, 8-12.
47. Dos Passos, "Introduction, 1968," in *One Man's Initiation*, 25.
48. James, *Within the Rim*, 58.
49. Brooke, *Letters from America*, 180.
50. James to Wharton, 1 September 1914, in Powers, *Henry James and Edith Wharton*, 297.
51. James, *Autobiography*, 415.
52. For a summary of the critical debate about the nature of James's "obscure hurt," see Rawlings, *Henry James and the Abuse of the Past*, 167-68. For Hemingway's part in the controversy see Reynolds, *Hemingway's First War*, 17-18.
53. James, *Autobiography*, 415.
54. See for example: Rosenzweig, "Ghost of Henry James"; Hall, "Obscure Hurt"; Graham, *Henry James's Thwarted Love;* and McWhirter, "Restaging the Hurt."
55. Tintner, *Twentieth-Century World of Henry James*, 225.
56. Otten, *Superficial Reading*, 31.

57. James, "The Art of Fiction" (1884); repr. in *Literary Criticism,* 1:42-65, 53.

58. In the 1940s, Paul Rosenzweig interpreted James's participation in the First World War as a psychological replaying of, and an introverted compensation for, sitting out the Civil War. Likewise, Pamela Thurschwell describes James's desire to establish an overlap between his own body and that of the nation during the Civil War as willfully interiorized, "a relationship of simultaneous shameful and self-aggrandising identification," which is then repeated in his later prose and war writings. "That Imperial Stomach," 169.

59. James, *Within the Rim,* 12.

60. Ibid., 13 and 14.

61. Hyde, *Henry James at Home,* 138.

62. James to Rhoda Broughton, 1 October 1914, in *Letters,* ed. Lubbock, 2:423.

63. James, to Thomas Sargeant Perry, 25 October 1914, ibid., 433.

64. James, *Within the Rim,* 46.

65. James to Henry James Junior, 30 October 1914, in *Letters,* ed. Lubbock, 2:438.

66. James, *Within the Rim,* 99.

67. James, *Autobiography,* 68.

68. Tintner, *Twentieth Century World of Henry James,* 230.

69. Das, *Touch and Intimacy,* 123.

70. Devlin, *Too Proud to Fight,* 136-37.

71. James to Perry, 27 March 1915, in *Letters,* ed. Lubbock, 2:477.

72. Quoted in Edel, *Henry James,* 699.

73. James to Henry James Junior, 30 October 1914, in *Letters,* ed. Lubbock, 2:436, 437.

74. James to Elizabeth (Lily) Norton, 25 January 1915, ibid., 459.

75. For a discussion of James's relationship with the world of politics and current affairs, see Walker, introduction to *Henry James on Culture,* vii-xliv.

76. James to Mrs Alfred Sutro, 8 August 1914, in *Letters,* ed. Lubbock, 2:402.

77. Quoted in Burlingame, *Of Making Many Books,* 314.

78. Ibid., 315.

79. Hansen, *Gentlemen Volunteers,* 28.

80. James, *Within the Rim,* 68.

81. "American Volunteer Ambulance Corps."

82. James, *Within the Rim,* 72.

83. James, *Letters,* ed. Lubbock, 2:393.

84. Van Wienen, *Partisans and Poets,* 22.

85. Norton, *Roads,* 66.

86. Ibid., 69.

87. Weiss, "Grace Fallow Norton Notes," 2.

88. Donohue, "Aunt Grace Talking," 5.

89. Weiss, "Grace Fallow Norton Notes," 2.

90. Norton to Thomas Bird Mosher, 5 February 1911. Thomas Bird Mosher Papers, bMS Am 1096 (1137).

91. H.M.B., "Little Singer," *New York Times*, 5 May 1912, B.R. 273.

92. Amy Lowell, "Why We Should Read Poetry," 8.

93. This marriage later became of public interest when Rodman spoke out against regulations which obliged female teachers in public schools to quit employment on marrying. "Aided Mrs Edgell, Married Herself: Supposed Miss Rodman, Wadleigh High School Teacher, Admits She Is Mrs Fremery," *New York Times,* 19 March 1913, 8.

94. "Art Students' League Raided by Comstock," *New York Times,* 3 August 1906, 1.

95. Norton, *Sister of the Wind,* 40.

96. Norton to Greenslet, 23 May 1914, Houghton Mifflin Company Papers, bMS Am 1925 (1324).

97. Norton to Mosher, 26 December 1913, Thomas Bird Mosher Papers, bMs Am 1096 (1139).

98. Norton, *Roads,* 70–71.

99. For a study of the French cult of the bayonet in the Napoleonic era see Lynn, *Bayonets of the Republic.*

100. Théodore Botrel, "Rosalie," quoted in Sweeney, *Singing Our Way to Victory,* 122.

101. For a fuller analysis of this genre of erotic war songs, see Sweeney, *Singing Our Way to Victory,* 121–28.

102. Norton, *Roads,* 78.

103. Price, *End of the Age of Innocence,* 15.

104. Eliot found his German hosts "extremely hospitable and warmhearted," and returned to England "persuaded of the rightness of the German cause," until he found that the English papers were "making exact contradictions of the German." T. S. Eliot to Charlotte Eliot, 23 August 1914, *Letters,* 1:58. Six months later, Eliot would rationalize his impressions of German kindness rather differently in a letter to Isabella Stewart Gardner: "The Germans have that hospitality and cordiality which characterises the less civilised peoples." 4 April 1915, ibid., 101.

105. Nash, *Life of Herbert Hoover,* 367. See also Hoover, *Memoirs,* 1:141–48.

106. Norton, *Roads,* 85.

Chapter Two. 1915—Volunteers

1. James to Richard Norton, 19 September 1914, James Papers, *bMS Am* 1094.1 (183).
2. On House's failure to negotiate peace talks in 1915, see Devlin, *Too Proud to Fight*, 252–82.
3. For a fuller account of the IWW's reaction to the early stages of the war, see Foner, *History of the Labor Movement in the United States.*
4. Mark Van Wienen notes that even though the IWW opposed the war, ironically, it profited both economically and politically from the conflict because the high demand for both farm and factory labor gave the union a stronger bargaining position: "It is one of the sharpest ironies of U.S. wartime politics that the IWW, dogmatically opposed to capitalist wars, should have prospered from what was effectively a wartime economy in the United States between 1914 and 1916." Van Wienen, *Partisans and Poets*, 86.
5. Dos Passos, *Mr Wilson's War*, 150–51. See also Van Wienen, *Rendezvous with Death*, 80–82.
6. For a fuller analysis of the cultural and political impact of Du Bois during and after the war see Mark Whalan, *The Great War and the Culture of the New Negro.*
7. Bourne, "American Use for German Ideals" (1915); repr. in *War and the Intellectuals*, 48–52, 50 and 51.
8. For the publication and reception of "I Didn't Raise My Boy to Be a Soldier," see Van Wienen, *Partisans and Poets*, 39–72.
9. Van Wienen, *Rendezvous with Death*, 102 and 90–92.
10. For a survey of British wartime censorship and the impact of the Bryce Report, see Haste, *Keep the Home Fires Burning.* See also Buitenhuis, *Great War of Words*, 21–36.
11. Roosevelt, *Mr Roosevelt Speaks Out*, 5.
12. Ibid., 14.
13. Roosevelt interpreted the doctrine as a policy rather than a law, and one which allowed for American intervention overseas to take action in a policing role against "weak and delinquent" governments. Roosevelt, *Autobiography*, 520. See also Nathan Miller, *Theodore Roosevelt*, 390–96.
14. Roosevelt, *Mr Roosevelt Speaks Out*, 16.
15. *New York Times*, 11 May 1915, 1.
16. For examples of Eliot's ambivalence about the war see his letters to Eleanor Hinkley, 8 September 1914 and 21 March 1915, *Letters*, 1:61–62 and 98–100.

17. Quoted in Carpenter, *Serious Character,* 255. Pound, "Hugh Selwyn Mauberley," 122. For an account of Pound's war years in London, see Carpenter, *Serious Character,* 256–337.

18. Pound, *Literary Essays,* 296. In 1929, Pound added a footnote to this comment: "I should probably be incapable of writing this paragraph now. But that is how things looked in 1918 and I see no reason to pretend that I saw them otherwise."

19. H.D. fictionalized her wartime experiences in *Bid Me to Live: A Madrigal* (1960).

20. Mellow, *Charmed Circle,* 218–26.

21. James to Charles Eliot Norton, 4 February 1872, *Complete Letters,* 2:396.

22. Wharton, *Backward Glance,* 361

23. Ibid., 352.

24. Lubbock, *Portrait of Edith Wharton,* 11.

25. Wharton's friendship with Berry was a source of controversy for her contemporaries and remains so for her biographers. There appears to have been a romance between them in the 1880s, and they became intimate again in Paris in the years just before the war, and after the collapse of Wharton's marriage. They saw each other almost daily, and traveled together in Europe and North Africa. After her death in 1937, Wharton was buried near Berry in the Cimetière des Gonards in Versailles. It is not clear whether this was a physical relationship, though it was clearly a powerful factor in Wharton's emotional and intellectual life. For a fuller assessment of this friendship see Lubbock, *Portrait of Edith Wharton,* 47–48.

26. Wharton to James, 28 February 1915, *Letters,* 348–50.

27. James to Wharton, 5 March 1915, in Powers, *Henry James and Edith Wharton,* 326.

28. Wharton to James, 11 March 1915, *Letters,* 351.

29. Ibid., 352.

30. James to Alice James, 20 February 1915, *Letters,* ed. Lubbock, 2:466. For the history of James's volatile relationship with Roosevelt see Philip Horne, "Henry James and 'the Forces of Violence,'" 237–47.

31. Quoted in Price, *End of the Age of Innocence,* 15.

32. Wharton, *Backward Glance,* 352.

33. Ibid.

34. Wharton, *Fighting France,* xii.

35. Reus and Lauber, "In a Literary No Man's Land," 207.

36. Wharton, *Fighting France,* 57.

37. Ibid., 51.

38. Archibald, "The New Conditions in War," 347–58; 348. Archibald also spent time with the Austrian army in the Carpathian Mountains: "Fighting in the Carpathians," 453–66.

39. Wharton, *Fighting France*, 62.

40. Ibid., 63.

41. Abel Faivre, "Dans les Ruines," 1. See also Dwight, *Edith Wharton*, 195.

42. Lee, *Edith Wharton*, 485.

43. "At a French Pallisade," *Scribner's Magazine*, 58 (1915), 435.

44. Quoted in Lewis, *Edith Wharton*, 378.

45. Wharton, *Fighting France*, 81.

46. Reus and Lauber, "In a Literary No Man's Land," 210.

47. Dean, *Woolson and Wharton*, 77.

48. Julie Olin-Ammentorp remarks that Wharton's war writings do not adhere to "the basic attitudes and styles that most readers since World War I have come to expect in writings relating to that war." Olin-Ammentorp, *Edith Wharton's Writings from the Great War*, 7.

49. Wharton, *Fighting France*, 80, 82, and 83.

50. Ibid., 83.

51. Ibid., 65.

52. Anderson, *Imagined Communities*, 6–7.

53. Wharton, *Fighting France*, 108.

54. Chomsky and Herman. *Manufacturing Consent*.

55. Wharton to Bernard Berenson, 13 February 1917. Quoted in Price, *End of the Age of Innocence*, 148. Wharton is often portrayed as credulous of atrocity stories, a view supported by her early war letters. She wrote to Sara Norton on 27 September 1914, "As to the horrors and outrages, I'm afraid they are all too often true.—Lady Gladstone, head of the Belgian refugee committee in London, told a friend of mine she had seen a Belgian woman with her ears cut off. And of course the deliberate slaughter of 'hostages' in defenceless towns is proved over and over again." Wharton, *Letters*, 340. However, Wharton, like many others, came to a more balanced position on this issue during the course of the war. For a fuller discussion of the proliferation of atrocity stories see Buitenhuis, *Great War of Words*, 25–28.

56. Quoted in Lee, *Edith Wharton*, 486.

57. Price, *End of the Age of Innocence*, 50.

58. Alexander Powell, "On the British Battle Line," 466.

59. Wharton, *Fighting France*, 75.

60. Stein, *Alice B. Toklas*, 185.

61. Lewis was staying with Borden and her husband, along with the writer and editor Ford Madox Hueffer (later Ford) and his wife Violet Hunt, at a country-house in Berwickshire when the war broke out. Lewis's memoir describes "a very attractive American of the name of Mrs Turner . . . The attractive freshness of the New World, and of a classless community, cut her out in that bogus Eighteenth Century Mayfair décor, as a vivid silhouette." Lewis, *Blasting and Bombardiering*, 60. Lewis would later satirize Borden as Mrs Wellesley-Crooks in *The Roaring Queen* (1973). See Egremont, *Under Two Flags*, 17.

62. Borden, *Journey Down a Blind Alley*, 8.

63. Ibid., 9.

64. Conway, *Woman of Two Wars*, 42.

65. Anne Powell, *Women in the War Zone*, 4.

66. Conway, *Woman of Two Wars*, 47.

67. Borden, *Forbidden Zone*, 1.

68. Published under her married name, Mary Borden-Turner, three poems "Where Is Jehovah," "The Song of the Mud," and "The Hill" appeared with the heading "At the Somme" in the *English Review*. This issue also included "The Regiment" and the long poem "Unidentified." The *English Review* was established and originally edited by Ford Madox Hueffer in 1908.

69. The Defence of the Realm Act, passed in August 1914, made it an offense to publish information that might "be directly or indirectly useful to the enemy" or that was "likely to cause disaffection." As Sanders and Taylor point out, the act was not primarily designed to control public opinion, but this swiftly became one of its consequences, as publishers were increasingly reluctant to risk prosecution under its terms. Sanders and Taylor, *British Propaganda*, 9. See also Haste, *Keep the Home Fires Burning*, 30–31.

70. For example, "Enfant de Malheur" is clearly based on an incident described in a letter to Edward Spears while Borden's unit was stationed by the Chemin des Dames. "Night before last I was on night duty and assisted at such a pitiful death—the death of quite an ordinary lad of 20—not very brave—not very fine—He was quite conscious to the very end and he was afraid. He could not bear to be left alone. At twelve he whispered—'Je ne vois plus clair—Je ne vous voir preigne plus. Allez cherche le prêtre, mais soyez la vite revenue.' I ran for Guerin our Abbé in Salle IV, and then I stood by and watched that priest do a wonderful thing. He put all his strength, all his faith, all his tenderness at the disposal of that boy—and he reached across the chasm and got to him—Guerin by the force of his own will, changed for that

wretched terrified child, the character & quality of death. It was as if he quite simply, lifted him up and carried him across the river." Borden to Spears, 25 May 1917, Mary Borden (Lady Spears) Papers, SPRS 11/1/1.

71. Potter, *Boys in Khaki, Girls in Print,* 91.

72. For a discussion of allusions to American nineteenth-century texts in *The Forbidden Zone,* see Hutchison "Theatre of Pain."

73. Hallett, "Personal Writings of First World War Nurses," 321. See also Das, *Touch and Intimacy,* 189.

74. Borden, *Forbidden Zone,* 2.

75. Wharton, *Fighting France,* 65 and 83.

76. Borden, *Forbidden Zone,* 9 and 12.

77. Hawthorne describes how in moonlight "the floor of our familiar room has become a neutral territory, somewhere between the real world and fairy-land, where the Actual and the Imaginary may meet, and each imbue itself with something of the other." Hawthorne, *Scarlet Letter,* 28.

78. Borden, *Forbidden Zone,* 51 and 55.

79. Ibid., 55.

80. In book Six of the *Aeneid,* Aeneas travels to the underworld to visit his father and meets these same figures at the threshold of the Underworld:

> See! At the very porch and entrance way to Orcus
> Grief and ever-haunting Anxiety make their bed:
> Here dwell pallid Diseases, here morose Old Age,
> With Fear, ill-prompting Hunger, and squalid Indigence,
> Shapes horrible to look at, Death and Agony
> Sleep, too which is the cousin of Death; and Guilty Joys,
> And there, against the threshold, War, the bringer of Death:
> Here are the iron cells of the Furies, and lunatic Strife
> Whose viperine hair is caught up with a headband soaked in blood.

Virgil, *Aeneid,* 125. I am indebted to one of my dissertation students Mairi Powolny Brunning, for sharing her work on Borden's classical allusions.

81. Borden, *Forbidden Zone,* 62.

82. Ibid., 53.

83. Nosheen Khan, one of the first modern-day critics to reassess Borden's writing, points out that "Unidentified," (1917) portrays a world in which "There is no centre to hold it down," a phrase which Khan sees as prefiguring W. B. Yeats's similar phrase "the centre cannot hold" in his poem "The Second Coming" (1920). Khan, "Mary Borden's 'Unidentified.'"

84. Margaret Higonnet, *Nurses at the Front,* xx.

85. For discussions of Borden's portrayal of nurses see Das, "Impotence of Sympathy"; Freedman, "Mary Borden's Forbidden Zone"; Kaplan, "Deformities of the Great War"; and Krob, "Commentary on 'Rosa,'" 710–11.

86. Freedman, "Mary Borden's Forbidden Zone," 121.

87. Borden, *Forbidden Zone*, 60.

88. Borden, *Technique of Marriage*, 125. Borden's own mother considered this book so immoral in its attitudes to divorce and contraception that she bought as many copies as she could and burned them, urging her friends to do the same. Conway, *Woman of Two Wars*, 160.

89. Borden, *Technique of Marriage*, 127.

90. Jenny Gould writes that "when war broke out, the only military sphere in which women were accepted was their traditional role of caring for the sick and wounded," while the idea of them taking part in battle was generally seen as "disturbing and offensive." Jenny Gould, "Women's Military Services in First World War Britain," 116, 117.

91. Borden, *Forbidden Zone*, 117.

92. Ibid., 105.

93. Tylee, *Great War and Women's Consciousness*, 47–74.

94. Angela K. Smith notes, for example, the similarities between Borden and La Motte's work and that of the French military surgeon George Duhamel, who also utilizes techniques of detachment, discontinuity, and irony in *The New Book of Martyrs* (1918). Smith, *Second Battlefield*, 82–85.

95. James to Grace Norton, 1 January 1915, *Letters*, ed. Lubbock, 2:449.

96. Hansen, *Gentlemen Volunteers*, 28.

97. Buitenhuis, *Great War of Words*, 18.

98. See, for example, Henrietta Stackpole in *The Portrait of a Lady* (1881), George Flack in *The Reverberator* (1888), and the narrator of *The Aspern Papers* (1888).

99. Matthew Rubery, "Unspoken Intimacy," 355.

100. Lockwood and Eyre, *Sham*, 2, 11–12.

101. Lockwood, "Section in Alsace Reconquise," 21–50. After the war, Lockwood studied at Oxford as a Rhodes scholar, then returned to New York, where during the early 1920s, he taught journalism at Columbia University. His signature has been identified among those of the many writers and artists who signed the Greenwich Village Bookshop door, including Sherwood Anderson, John Dos Passos, Theodore Dreiser, Nicholas Vachel Lindsey, and Edwin Arlington Robinson. The door is now archived at Harry Ransom Center at the University of Texas, Austin. Lockwood later took up a career in law and was a partner in the firm Davisson, McCarty, and Lockwood from

1932. He also went on to be a director and then president of the Brewster
Aeronautical Corporation. He remained a trustee of the American Field
Ambulance Service Fellowship Fund until his death in 1951. "T. P. Lock-
wood, 59, Aviation Leader," *New York Times,* 1 April 1951, 92.

102. Bosanquet, *Henry James at Work,* 80.

103. I am grateful to Katie Sommer of the Center for Henry James Studies, Creighton University, Omaha, Nebraska, for help in verifying this information.

104. In a letter to Norton's aunt, Elizabeth (Lily) Norton, James apologizes that
his pamphlet about the corps, published in December, was only "a helpless
and empty thing." He went on, "You can't say things unless you have been
out there to learn them, and *if* you have been out there to learn them you can
say them less than ever. With all but utterly nothing to go upon I had to
make my remarks practically *of* nothing, and that the effect of them can only
be nil on a subscribing public which wants constant and particular news."
The letter goes on to imply that Elizabeth Norton has told James of the possibility of the corps being wound up through lack of funds: "What seems
clear, at all events, is that there *is* no devisable means for keeping the enterprise in touch with American sympathy, and I sadly note therefore what you
tell me of the inevitable and not distant end." James to Elizabeth (Lily) Norton, 25 January 1915, *Letters,* ed. Lubbock, 2:458.

105. Anesko, *Monopolising the Master,* 7. See also Horne, *Henry James and Revision,* 1–19.

106. James had used this phrase before in a letter to Lilla Perry. He described the
kaiser's invasion of Belgium as "the most fatuously arrogant 'Because I
choose to, damn you!' in all recorded history. James to Lilla Perry, 22 September 1914, *Letters,* ed. Lubbock, 2:422.

107. Lockwood, "Henry James's First Interview," 3.

108. Ibid., 4.

109. T. S. Eliot, "The Hollow Men," (1925); repr. in *Selected Poems,* 77.

110. "Within the Rim" was commissioned by Elizabeth Asquith, later the writer
Elizabeth Bibesco, daughter of H. H. Asquith, the British prime minister,
for a fund-raising album, which was never completed. It was published
posthumously in the *Fortnightly Review* in August 1917 and in *Harper's
Magazine* in December 1917.

111. "The Long Wards" was originally intended for the *New York Tribune,* but it
exceeded its word limit and was passed to Wharton instead for inclusion in
The Book of the Homeless. "Refugees in England" appeared in the *Boston Sunday Herald Supplement* and the *New York Times* on 17 October 1915, and was
reprinted posthumously as "Refugees in Chelsea," in the *Times Literary Sup-*

plement on 23 March 1916. *The Question of the Mind* was reprinted in *The New York Sun* and the *Philadelphia Ledger* magazine section on 1 August 1915. After James's death in 1916, "Within the Rim," "Refugees in Chelsea," "The American Volunteer Motor-Ambulance Corps in France," "France," and "The Long Wards" were collected by Percy Lubbock as *Within the Rim and Other Essays, 1914–1915*. Subsequent references are to Lubbock's collected edition.

112. In this extract James praises Britain for her "perfectly magnificent moral position, the proudest to my mind of her history." Honey and Muirhead, *Sixty American Opinions*, 92; Buitenhuis, *Great War of Words*, 57.

113. Quoted in Haste, *Keep the Home Fires Burning*, 27.

114. Central Committee for National Patriotic Organisations, Records, BNLW/4/9. As the war progressed, especially after conscription cancelled the need to persuade men to enlist, many of the committee's political activities were subsumed into those of the War Propaganda Bureau, and it became increasingly focused on publishing self-help pamphlets, such as those on gardening and running small businesses.

115. T. S. Eliot's British wife, Vivienne Haigh-Wood, was refused wartime employment in the British Civil Service on the grounds that she was married to a citizen of a neutral nation. Ackroyd, *T. S. Eliot*, 83.

116. James, *Within the Rim*, 30.

117. Edward Dicey, "Mr Gladstone and Our Empire," 297.

118. Walker, *Henry James on Culture*, xxvii.

119. James, *American Scene*, 89.

120. James, *Within the Rim*, 16.

121. Ibid., 20.

122. Ibid., 21

123. Ibid., 31.

124. See Collini, *English Pasts: Essays in History and Culture;* Grainger, *Patriotisms;* and Mandler, *English National Character.*

125. James, *Within the Rim*, 111

126. Ibid., 109.

127. Ibid., 113.

128. Ibid., 118, 119.

129. Wells, *Boon*, 108.

130. Ibid., 106.

131. James to Wells, 10 July 1915, *Letters*, ed. Lubbock, 2:508.

132. James to Gosse, 25 June 1915, ibid., 498.

133. James to Henry James Junior, 20 July 1915, ibid., 509.

134. "Mr Henry James: Adoption of British Nationality," *Times,* 28 July 1915, 5.
135. James to Gosse, 25 June 1915, *Letters,* ed. Lubbock, 2:498.
136. Ezra Pound, *Literary Essays,* 297.
137. James to Edward Marsh, 24 April 1915, *Letters,* ed. Lubbock, 2:485.
138. In a letter to Hugh Dalton, Brooke laments that he has only one evening free: "All other times I am dining with E. Gosse or H. James, or S. Olivier, and others of my contemporaries. How horrible it is to be bachelor." Meeting up with James is also mentioned in a note to Lady Eileen Wellesley in August. Brooke to Dalton, 5 July 1914, *Letters of Rupert Brooke,* 597 and 610.
139. *New Numbers,* 164–69. Although dated 1914, this issue was delayed until January 1915, and was the final publication of the journal.
140. James to Marsh, 6 June 1915, *Letters,* ed. Lubbock, 2:489.
141. For the full story of Marsh's relationship with the Brooke family, see Hassall, *Edward Marsh.*
142. For an account of the genesis of James's introduction to *Letters from America* and his assessment of Brooke as a poet, see Hutchison, "Art of Living Inward," 132–43.
143. James, introduction to Brooke, *Letters from America,* ix.
144. Ibid., xii and xiii.
145. Ibid., xx, xxii and xxiv.
146. Ibid., xiv.
147. Winston Churchill, "Rupert Brooke," *Times,* 26 April 1916, 5.
148. James, introduction to Brooke, *Letters From America,* xxv.
149. Percy Lubbock, unsigned review of *Letters from America,* by Rupert Brooke, *Times Literary Supplement,* 9 March 1915, 114.
150. For an account of Percy Lubbock's role in shaping James's literary legacy, see Anesko, *Monopolizing the Master,* 46–108.

Chapter Three. 1916—Books

1. Greenslet, *Under the Bridge,* 135–37.
2. Ibid., 137. For a broader survey of the impact of the war on American publishing see Tebbel, *Book Publishing in the United States,* 79–102.
3. Greenslet, *Under the Bridge,* 137.
4. Genthe, *American War Narratives,* 100.
5. Tebbel, *Book Publishing in the United States,* 86–87.
6. Greenslet, *Under the Bridge,* 163.
7. Bourne, *War and the Intellectuals,* 5.

8. Ibid., 10.

9. James to Wharton, 19 July 1915, in Powers, *Henry James and Edith Wharton,* 345.

10. Edith Wharton, "Belgium," in Kipling, *King Albert's Book,* 165.

11. Honey and Muirhead, *Sixty American Opinions,* v.

12. James to Wharton, 19 July 1915, in Powers, *Henry James and Edith Wharton,* 346.

13. Yeats later retitled his poem "On Being Asked for a War Poem," in his collection *The Wild Swans at Coole* (1919).

14. James invited Kipling to contribute to *The Book of the Homeless,* but he declined.

15. Kipling, *King Alfred's Book,* 5.

16. Wharton, *Book of the Homeless,* xxiv and xxv.

17. Scribner to Wharton, 30 August 1915, in Price, *End of the Age of Innocence,* 65.

18. Wharton, *Book of the Homeless,* x.

19. Wharton to Corinne Roosevelt Robinson, 11 June 1919, in *Letters,* 422.

20. See for example Roosevelt, *Great Adventure,* 1–8.

21. Madison, *Publishing in America,* 90–91. See also Burlingame, *Of Making Many Books,* 167–68.

22. For a fuller history of James's New York Edition, see McWhirter, *Henry James's New York Edition.*

23. Wharton, *Backward Glance,* 52.

24. Lee, *Edith Wharton,* 147 and 155.

25. For a description of the editorial processes involved in the creation of this volume, see Price, "The Making of *The Book of the Homeless,*" 5–21.

26. James to Wharton, 21 and 27 August 1915, in Powers, *Henry James and Edith Wharton,* 351–54.

27. Scribner to Grant, 10 August 1915, and Scribner to Wharton, 30 August 1915, in Price, *End of the Age of Innocence,* 70, 71.

28. Lee, *Edith Wharton,* 496.

29. Scribner to Wharton, 27 January 1916, in Price, *End of the Age of Innocence,* 70.

30. Price, *End of the Age of Innocence,* 77.

31. Ibid., 78.

32. *New York Times,* 30 January 1916, 21.

33. "Mayor Assents to Lusitania Meeting," *New York Times,* 12 May 1916, 4.

34. Norton to Greenslet, 15 May 1915, Houghton Mifflin Company Papers, bMS Am 1925 (1324).

35. Norton to Greenslet, 9 April 1916, ibid.

36. For a full list of the members and patrons of the American Rights Committee see American Rights Committee, "*Lusitania* Memorial Meeting: Order of Events" 19 May 1916.

37. Norton to Greenslet, 19 April 1916, Houghton Mifflin Company Papers, bMS Am 1925 (1324).

38. Greenslet to Norton, 11 April 1916, ibid.

39. Greenslet to Norton, 21 April 1916, ibid.

40. Greenslet to Norton, 26 April 1916, ibid.

41. Norton to Greenslet, 30 April 1916, ibid.

42. First included in 1914, this song was still part of the song book in the 1960s. Industrial Workers of the World, *Little Red Song Book*, 33.

43. Quoted in Van Wienen, *Partisans and Poets*, 77.

44. Van Wienen, *Partisans and Poets*, 77.

45. Dos Passos, *U.S.A.,* 718.

46. Norton, *What Is Your Legion?* 2.

47. Ibid., 21.

48. Ibid., 27.

49. Ibid., 5.

50. Ibid., 24.

51. Ibid., 13.

52. Norton, *What Is Your Legion?* 38.

53. Bunyan, *Pilgrim's Progress,* 169-77.

54. Norton, *What Is Your Legion?* 28.

55. 'Urge Retribution for the *Lusitania,*' *New York Times,* 20 May 1916, 1.

56. La Motte, *Backwash of War,* 22.

57. Stein, *Alice B. Toklas,* 184.

58. La Motte, "American Nurse in Paris," 333.

59. Ibid., 335.

60. Ibid., 336.

61. Ibid., 333.

62. Although it was her middle name, Edith Newbold Jones, was not a Newbold by descent. Her mother's sister Mary Rhinelander was married to Thomas Newbold, though a direct link to La Motte's relatives has thus far proved elusive. For Wharton's family tree see Lee, *Edith Wharton,* 763.

63. Ellen La Motte Collection, JHNHC, Collection LamE.

64. La Motte, *Tuberculosis Nurse.*

65. Review of "The Tuberculosis Nurse: Her Functions and Qualifications," *British Medical Journal,* 2, no. 2901 (5 August, 1916): 181. For a fuller discus-

sion of La Motte's methods for treating tuberculosis, and of her place in nursing history see Sugiyama, "Ellen N. La Motte," 132.

66. La Motte, "Hotel-Dieu of Paris," 225–40, and "Modern Italian Hospital,"
933–38.

67. La Motte to DuPont, 22 January 1919, DuPont Papers, Folder 1546.

68. Stein, *Alice B. Toklas*, 185.

69. La Motte, "Under Shell-Fire at Dunkirk," 692.

70. Ibid., 694.

71. Wharton, *Fighting France*, 75.

72. La Motte, "Under Shell-Fire at Dunkirk," 696.

73. Ibid., 698.

74. Ibid., 700.

75. Ironically, it was no great work of literature that repeated in Sassoon's mind
under bombardment, but an incomplete advertisement slogan for fountain
pens: "They come as a boon and a blessing to men, / The Something, the Owl
and the Waverley Pen." Sassoon, *Memoirs of an Infantry Officer*, 50. The missing "Something" was "Pickwick."

76. Roberts, "Preface: How it Happened," vii.

77. Borden, *Forbidden Zone*, 8.

78. There are archive materials relating to La Motte in the Gertrude Stein Col-
lection, Beinecke Library, Yale University; the Alfred I. DuPont Papers, James
Graham Leyburn Library, Washington and Lee University; and the Crane and
Lillie Family Papers, Chicago History Museum, Research Center.

79. La Motte, "Joy Ride," 481.

80. Claire Tylee treats Borden and La Motte together with May Cannan and Katherine Mansfield in a chapter entitled "The Magic of Adventure: The Western Front
and Women's Tales About the War," in *The Great War and Women's Consciousness*. Angela K. Smith groups them together with Enid Bagnold in "Accidental
Modernisms: Hospital Stories of the First World War" in *The Second Battlefield*.

81. Higonnet, "Cubist Vision in Nursing Accounts."

82. Warner, *My Beloved Poilus*, 46.

83. Ibid., 100.

84. Genthe, *American War Narratives*, 106 and 157.

85. Potter, *Boys in Khaki, Girls in Print;* Goldman, ed. *Women and World War I;*
Higonnet et al. *Behind the Lines*.

86. La Motte, *Backwash of War*, 15.

87. Higonnet, *Nurses at the Front*, xvii.

88. La Motte, *Backwash of War*, 112.

89. Hallett, *Containing Trauma,* 16.

90. La Motte, *Backwash of War,* 106.

91. Ibid., 167.

92. Ibid., 31.

93. Ibid., 94 and 97.

94. Ibid., 167.

95. Ibid., 109.

96. Borden (Lady Spears) Papers, Notes and Papers Relating to Mobile Ambulance, 1916–17, SPRS 11/2/1.

97. La Motte's war souvenirs were clearly delivered to DuPont on her return to the United States. At the end of the war, she wrote to him about a charitable venture run by a friend of hers, a Mrs McConihe: "She has got some big scheme on hand now, for the end of this month, and wants to have an exhibition of war trophies in connection with it—I told her you had a lot, and if she writes to you about it, you will know where she got the news!" La Motte to DuPont, 4 December 1918, DuPont Papers, Folder 1546.

98. La Motte, *Backwash of War,* v.

99. In the years after the First World War, La Motte regularly published articles and stories in prestigious journals, including the *Atlantic Monthly, Century Magazine, Harper's Magazine,* and the *Nation.* Her books, fictional and nonfictional, concerning the opium trade included: *Civilization: Tales of the Orient* (1919), *Peking Dust* (1919), *The Opium Monopoly* (1920), *The Ethics of Opium* (1924), and *Snuffs and Butters* (1925).

100. DuPont wrote: "While I am perfectly willing to take the responsibility so far as you as an individual are concerned, I could not do so with Mrs. Chadbourne, for I do not know her. Undoubtedly, before such passports could be issued a very careful investigation would be made by the Secret Service Department, with a view to establishing so far as possible the unquestioned loyalty of both you and Mrs. Chadbourne to the United States, and if peradventure it should come to the ears of the State Department that either Mrs. Chadbourne or yourself had voiced a position of absolute neutrality, you may be sure that no passports would be issued, but on the contrary you would be immediately placed under surveillance, if nothing worse. As you have perhaps discovered, the feeling in this country is running pretty high on the question of loyalty and is going to take on even more drastic and determined features before this war is over." DuPont to La Motte, 8 February 1918, DuPont Papers, Folder 1546.

101. *Liberator* 1, no. 2, April 1918: 42.

102. La Motte, *Backwash of War,* vi.

103. La Motte to DuPont, 1 August 1918, DuPont Papers, Folder 1546.

104. Review of *Backwash of War, New Republic* (7 November 1934), 374.

Chapter Four. 1917—Perspectives

1. Gregory, *Origins of American Intervention*, 43; Dos Passos, *Mr Wilson's War*, 189. See also Stevenson, *War and International Politics*, 66-67.

2. Seymour, *Papers of Colonel House*, 2: 417.

3. Lansing, *War Memoirs*, 228.

4. Devlin, *Too Proud to Fight*, 678.

5. Gregory, *Origins of American Intervention*, 126.

6. Lansing, *War Memoirs*, 234, 236.

7. *New York Times*, 3 April 1917, 1

8. Devlin, *Too Proud to Fight*, 671.

9. Harries and Harries, *Last Days of Innocence*, 73.

10. Dos Passos, *Mr Wilson's War*, 190.

11. Lloyd George, *War Memoirs*, 1106.

12. Borden *Forbidden Zone*, ix.

13. The 1917 manuscript of *The Forbidden Zone* is archived in the Mary Borden Collection, Howard Gottlieb Archival Research Center, Boston University.

14. Kazin, *On Native Grounds*, 345.

15. Cowley, *Exile's Return*, 38.

16. Borden, *Forbidden Zone*, 180.

17. Edward Spears to Leroy Lewis, 17 June 1918, Borden (Lady Spears) Papers, SPRS 11/2/1.

18. Conway, *Woman of Two Wars*, 72.

19. La Motte, *Backwash of War*, 45.

20. Borden, *Forbidden Zone*, 114.

21. Ibid., 117 and 120.

22. Ibid., 126.

23. Ibid., 135.

24. Borden to Spears, 11 September 1917, Borden (Lady Spears) Papers, SPRS 11/1/1.

25. See Hutchison, "Theatre of Pain," 226-27.

26. Stein, *Alice B. Toklas*, 185.

27. Mary Borden to Gertrude Stein, undated, Stein Papers, YCAL MSS76, 11/98/1888.

28. Higonnet, "Cubist Vision in Nursing Accounts," 160.

29. Borden, *Forbidden Zone*, 143.

30. Ibid., 145.

31. Carr, *John Dos Passos*, 40–45.

32. Dos Passos, "Against American Literature," 269–71.

33. Dos Passos, "Introduction, 1968," in *One Man's Initiation*, 5.

34. Dos Passos, *Travel Books and Other Writings*, 604.

35. Dos Passos, *Best Times*, 26.

36. Ibid., 44.

37. Carr, *Dos Passos*, 121 and 130. James and Wells, *America and the Great War*, 71. See also Boyer, "Gilded-Age Consensus."

38. Dos Passos, *Fourteenth Chronicle*, 73.

39. Dos Passos, *Best Times*, 42.

40. More, *Demon of the Absolute*, 63.

41. Dos Passos, *Fourteenth Chronicle*, 92.

42. Ibid., 93.

43. Ibid., 96.

44. Dos Passos, *Best Times*, 55.

45. See Hansen, *Gentlemen Volunteers*, 162–76.

46. *Abris:* dugout. Quoted in Dos Passos, "Introduction, 1968," in *One Man's Initiation*, 25.

47. Dos Passos, *Best Times*, 70.

48. Clark, *Dos Passos's Early Fiction*, 62.

49. Kazin, *On Native Grounds*, 343, 347, 342.

50. For a discussion of Dos Passos in relation to the pragmatism of William James, see Clark, *Dos Passos's Early Fiction*, 18–28.

51. Dos Passos, *One Man's Initiation*, 44.

52. Ibid., 125.

53. In *Nature* (1836) Emerson writes, "Standing on the bare ground,—my head bathed by the blithe air, and uplifted into infinite space,—all mean egotism vanishes. I become a transparent eye-ball. I am nothing. I see all." Emerson, *Collected Works*, 1:10.

54. Dos Passos, *One Man's Initiation*, 169, 174.

55. Plimpton, *Ernest Hemingway*, 67.

56. John Dos Passos, *Best Times*, 85.

57. Cummings to Rebecca Clarke Cummings, 7 April 1917 and 18 April 1917, *Selected Letters*, 15 and 16.

58. Kennedy, *Dreams in the Mirror*, 141–43.

59. Cummings, *Enormous Room*, 39.

60. The story of how Cummings's family worked to secure his release, eventually writing to President Woodrow Wilson for help in dealing with the

French authorities, is told in his father's introduction to the 1922 edition, reprinted in the 1978 edition, xxi–xxvi.

61. Quoted in George Firmage, afterword to Cummings, *Enormous Room*. 270.

62. Cummings, *Enormous Room*, 84.

63. Ibid., 17.

64. Ibid., 46.

65. Ibid., 122.

66. Ibid., 132.

67. Ibid., 38.

68. Ibid., 41 and 203.

69. For a fuller discussion of Cummings's handling of punctuation see Hutchison, "A Period in Limbo."

70. For the full textual history, see Firmage's afterword to *The Enormous Room*, 267–75.

71. Cummings, *Enormous Room*, 82.

72. Ibid., 132 and 196.

73. Cummings Papers, MS Am 1823.7 (7–20) and MS Am 1892.8 (1).

74. In the 1950s, Kingsley Widmer argued that Cummings's use of Bunyan's text was a literary device adopted in an attempt to "obscure the disorder," of his wartime experiences. In 1965, David E. Smith suggested it was evidence of a desire to reassert the "spiritual power and moral lessons" of *The Pilgrim's Progress*. More recently, Todd Martin has claimed the juxtaposition of texts produces an emblematic rendering of an existential journey through which Cummings's narrator is "introduced into the mysteries of what it is to be alive." Widmer, "Timeless Prose," 6; Smith, "*The Enormous Room* and *The Pilgrim's Progress*," 67; Martin, "Mysteries of Noyon," 125.

75. Gaull, "Language and Identity," 651.

76. For an overview of the development of speech-act theory from J. L. Austin to the present, see Miller, *Speech Acts in Literature*.

77. Wilde, preface to *Picture of Dorian Gray*, 22.

78. For a contextualized reading of Eliot's poetry against the backdrop of the First World War see Sherry, *Language of Modernism*, 191–225.

79. Dayton, "Wristers Etcetera," 116.

80. Bunyan, *Pilgrim's Progress*, 115–21.

81. Ibid., 168. For a fuller exploration of Cummings's use of "IS" see Martin, " 'IS' as an Action Verb," 80–83.

82. See Hansen, *Gentlemen Volunteers*, 157.

83. Cummings, *Enormous Room*, 242.

Chapter Five. 1918—Compromises

1. Hemingway, *Moveable Feast*, 18.
2. Dos Passos, "Introduction, 1968," in *One Man's Initiation*, 10.
3. James and Wells, *America and the Great War*, 34.
4. Whalan, *American Culture*, 174. Whalan also notes that the majority of African-American soldiers in France were assigned to labor battalions, to assuage fears in the white South about the mass combat training of black draftees.
5. For a discussion of this question see Stevenson, *1914–1918*, 440–43; and DeWeerd, *President Wilson*, 330–63.
6. Kennedy, *Dreams in the Mirror*, 175.
7. Tate, *Modernism History and the First World War*, 109. See also Minter, *William Faulkner*, 29–33; and Gandal, *Gun and the Pen*, 153–54.
8. Ackroyd, *T. S. Eliot*, 87.
9. Bruccoli, *Some Sort of Epic Grandeur*, 86.
10. Gandal, *Gun and the Pen*, 5.
11. Ibid., 36 and 37.
12. Hansen calculates that during his three weeks in Section 4 of the Red Cross Ambulance Corps at Schio, Hemingway drove an ambulance "only once or twice at the most." *Gentlemen Volunteers*, 160.
13. Arthur Mizener, "Gullivers of Dos Passos," 1951. Reprinted in Hook, ed., *Dos Passos: Critical Essays*, 162–70, 168.
14. Wharton, *Fighting France*, 68.
15. Wharton and Codman, *Decoration of Houses*, 2.
16. For a detailed account of Wharton's struggles with the American Red Cross, see Price, *End of the Age of Innocence*, 107–40.
17. Wharton, *Backward Glance*, 357.
18. Wharton, "Talk to American Soldiers" (1918); repr. in Olin-Ammentorp, *Wharton's Writings*, 261–72.
19. Cooperman, *World War I and the American Novel*, 42.
20. Ibid.
21. Wharton, *Marne*, 132.
22. Wharton to Bernard Berenson, 13 August 1918, in *Letters*, 409.
23. Wharton, "On Active Service—for R. S." (1918); repr. in Olin-Ammentorp, *Wharton's Writings*, 240.
24. Wharton, *Backward Glance*, 368.
25. Tuttleton, Lauer, and Murray, eds., *Wharton: Contemporary Reviews*, 344.
26. Olin-Ammentorp, *Wharton's Writings*, 149.

27. Wharton, *Son at the Front*, 104.

28. Ibid., 123.

29. Ibid., 32.

30. Ibid., 3.

31. Ibid., 193.

32. Ibid., 176.

33. Tuttleton, Lauer, and Murray, eds., *Wharton: Contemporary Reviews*, 341.

34. Wharton, "Talk to American Soldiers," in Olin-Ammentorp, *Wharton's Writings*, 262.

35. Tuttleton, Lauer, and Murray, eds., *Wharton: Contemporary Reviews*, 353.

36. Wharton, *Son at the Front*, 32.

37. Ibid., 202.

38. Ibid., 207.

39. Ibid., 71.

40. Ibid., 101.

41. Olin-Ammentorp, *Wharton's Writings*, 135-40.

42. For a survey of Wharton's use of the war in her postwar writings, see Olin-Ammentorp, *Wharton's Writings*, 154-211.

43. Fitzgerald, *Great Gatsby*, 106. For a reading of *The Great Gatsby* as a war novel see P. James, *New Death*, 63-118.

44. Dos Passos, *Best Times*, 71.

45. Tebbel, *Book Publishing in the United States*, 97.

46. Dos Passos, *Best Times*, 74.

47. Dos Passos, *Fourteenth Chronicle*, 236.

48. Ibid., 239.

49. Dos Passos, *Three Soldiers*, 193.

50. Ibid., 209.

51. Ibid., 339, 347.

52. Carr, *Dos Passos*, 131 and 160.

53. Clark, *Dos Passos's Early Fiction*, 79-82.

54. John Peale Bishop, "Review of *Three Soldiers*," (1921); repr. in Maine, *Dos Passos: The Critical Heritage*, 33-34; 33.

55. Norman Shannon Hall, "John Dos Passos Lies!" (1921); repr. in ibid., 47-51; 47, 48, and 50.

56. Harold Norman Denny, "Review of *Three Soldiers*," *New York Times*, 16 October 1921, section 3, 1.

57. Henry Seidel Canby, "Human Nature Under Fire," (1921); repr. in Maine, *Dos Passos: The Critical Heritage*, 37-42; 38, 40.

58. Coningsby Dawson, "Insulting the Army" (1921); repr. in Maine, *Dos Passos: The Critical Heritage*, 33–37; 37, 36.

59. Dos Passos, *Three Soldiers*, 68.

60. Dos Passos, *U.S.A.*, 564, 647.

61. For contrasting contemporary analyses of Dos Passos's politics see Granville Hicks, "The Politics of John Dos Passos," (1950), and T. K. Whipple, "Dos Passos and the U.S. A." (1938), both in Hook, *Dos Passos: Critical Essays*.

62. Blanch H. Gelfant, "John Dos Passos: The Synoptic Novel" (1954); repr. in Hook, *Dos Passos: Critical Essays*, 36–52.

63. Rosen, *John Dos Passos: Politics and the Writer*, 16, 20. Malcolm Cowley was first to use the term *Art Novel* with reference to *Three Soldiers*, in "The Poet and the World."

64. Richard Chase, "The Chronicles of John Dos Passos," (1961); repr. in Hook, *Dos Passos: Critical Essays*, 171–80; 173.

65. For a consideration of John Brown's cultural legacy, see Reynolds, *John Brown*, 480–506.

66. John Keats, "Ode on A Grecian Urn," in *John Keats*, 344.

Aftermath

1. Burlingame, *Of Making Many Books*, 320.

2. For an account of the 1919 Peace Conference and Wilson's subsequent political troubles see Stevenson, *1914–1918*, 503–33. See also Bailey, *Woodrow Wilson and the Lost Peace*.

3. William McFee, introduction to Larrouy, *Odyssey of a Torpedoed Transport*, vii.

4. Eliot, *Poetry and Criticism*, 109.

5. Levenson, *Modernism*, 7.

6. In the afterword to *Lolita*, Nabokov styles reality as "one of the few words which mean nothing without quotes." Nabokov, *Lolita*, 312.

7. Dos Passos, *U.S.A.*, 756.

8. Ibid., 757.

Bibliography

Ackroyd, Peter. *T. S. Eliot*. London: Abacus, 1984.

Aldrich, Mildred. *A Hilltop on the Marne*. Boston: Houghton Mifflin, 1915.

American Rights Committee. "*Lusitania* Memorial Meeting: Order of Events." 19 May 1916.

"The American Volunteer Ambulance Corps." *British Medical Journal* 2, no. 2817 (26 December 1914): 1111.

Anderson, Benedict. *Imagined Communities: Reflections on the Origin and Spread of Nationalism*. London: Verso, 1991.

Anderson, Sherwood. *Marching Men*. New York: John Lane, 1917.

Anesko, Michael. *Monopolising the Master: Henry James and the Politics of Modern Literary Scholarship*. Stanford, CA: Stanford University Press, 2012.

Archibald, James F. J. "Fighting in the Carpathians: As Seen with the Austrian Army." *Scribner's Magazine* 57 (1915): 453–66.

———. "The New Conditions in War: As Seen from the German Side." *Scribner's Magazine* 57 (1915): 347–58.

Arnold, Matthew, *The Complete Prose Works of Matthew Arnold*. Edited by R. H. Super. 11 vols. Ann Arbor: University of Michigan Press, 1977.

"At a French Pallisade." *Scribner's Magazine* 58 (1915), 435. Photo reproduced from a copy at the Special Collections Centre, University of Aberdeen.

Bailey, Thomas. *Woodrow Wilson and the Lost Peace*. Chicago: Quadrangle, 1944.

Barbusse, Henri, *Under Fire*. 1916. Translated by Fitzwater Wray. New York: Dutton, 1918.

Benstock, Shari. *No Gifts from Chance: A Biography of Edith Wharton*. Austin: University of Texas Press, 1994.

Bercovitch, Sacvan, ed. *The Cambridge History of American Literature*. 8 vols. Cambridge: Cambridge University Press, 1994–2005.

Borden, Mary. *The Forbidden Zone*. London: Heinemann, 1929.

———. *Jericho Sands*. London: Heinemann 1925.

———. *Journey Down a Blind Alley*. London: Hutchinson, 1946.

———. *Sarah Gay*. London: Heinemann, 1931.

———. *The Technique of Marriage*. London, Heinemann, 1933.

Borden, Mary (Lady Spears). Collection. Howard Gotleib Archival Research Center, Boston University.

———. Papers. Churchill College Archives, University of Cambridge.

Borden-Turner, Mary. "At the Somme." *English Review* (August 1917): 97–102.

———. "The Regiment." *English Review* (August 1917): 341–51.

———. "Unidentified." *English Review* (August 1917): 482–87.

Bosanquet, Theodora. *Henry James at Work.* Edited by Lyall H. Powers. Ann Arbor: University of Michigan Press, 2006.

Bourne, Randolph. *War and the Intellectuals: Collected Essays, 1915–19.* Edited by Carl Resek. New York: Harper, 1964.

Boyd, Thomas. *Through the Wheat.* New York: Scribner's, 1923.

Boyer, Paul S. "Gilded-Age Consensus, Repressive Campaigns, and Gradual Liberalization: The Shifting Rhythms of Book Censorship." In *A History of the Book in America, Vol 4: Print in Motion: The Expansion of Publishing and Reading in the United States, 1880–1940,* by Carl F. Kaestle and Janice A. Radway, 276–98. Chapel Hill: University of North Carolina Press, 2009.

Brooke, Rupert. *Collected Poems.* Edited with a memoir by Edward Marsh. London: Sidgwick and Jackson, 1918.

———. *Letters from America.* With an introduction by Henry James. London: Sidgwick and Jackson, 1916.

———. *The Letters of Rupert Brooke.* Edited by Sir Geoffrey Keynes. London: Faber, 1968.

———. Poems. *New Numbers: A Quarterly Publication of the Poems of Rupert Brooke, John Drinkwater, Wilfred Wilson Gibson, Lascelles Abercrombie* 1, no. 4 (1914), 164–69.

Brown, Dennis. *The Modernist Self in Twentieth-Century English Literature: A Study in Self-Fragmentation.* London: Macmillan, 1989.

Bruccoli, Matthew J. *Some Sort of Epic Grandeur: The Life of F. Scott Fitzgerald.* London: Hodder and Stoughton, 1981.

Buitenhuis, Peter. *The Great War of Words: Literature as Propaganda, 1914–1918 and After.* London: Batsford, 1989.

Bunyan, John. *The Pilgrim's Progress.* 1678. Reprint, Edinburgh: Nelson, 1903.

Burlingame, Roger. *Of Making Many Books: A Hundred Years of Reading, Writing, and Publishing, 1846–1946.* New York: Scribner's, 1946.

Canfield, Dorothy. *Home Fires in France.* New York: Henry Holt, 1918.

Carpenter, Humphrey. *A Serious Character: The Life of Ezra Pound.* London: Faber, 1988.

Carr, Virginia Spencer. *John Dos Passos: A Life.* 1984. Reprint, Evanston, IL: Northwestern University Press, 2004.

Cather, Willa. *One of Ours.* New York: Alfred A. Knopf, 1922.

Central Committee for National Patriotic Organisations. Records. Lincolnshire Archives, Lincoln, England.

Chomsky, Noam, and Edward Herman. *Manufacturing Consent: The Political Economy of the Mass Media.* London: Vintage Books, 1994.

Clark, Michael. *Dos Passos's Early Fiction, 1912–1938.* Selinsgrove, PA: Susquehanna University Press, 1987.

Cobb, Frank Irving. *Cobb of "The World": A Leader in Liberalism.* Edited by John L Heaton. New York: Dutton, 1924.

Collini, Stefan. *English Pasts: Essays in History and Culture.* Oxford: Oxford University Press, 1999.

Conway, Jane. *A Woman of Two Wars: The Life of Mary Borden.* London: Munday, 2010.

Cooperman, Stanley. *World War I and the American Novel.* Baltimore: Johns Hopkins University Press, 1967.

Cowley, Malcolm. *Exile's Return.* 1951. Reprint, London: Penguin Books, 1986.

———. "The Poet and the World." *New Republic* (27 April 1932), 303–4.

Crane and Lillie Family Papers. Chicago History Museum, Research Center, Chicago.

Crane, Stephen. *The Red Badge of Courage.* 1895. Reprint, Oxford: Oxford University Press, 1995.

Cummings, E. E. *The Enormous Room.* Afterword by George Firmage. 1922. Reprint, New York: Liveright, 1978.

———. Papers. Houghton Library, Harvard University, Cambridge, MA.

———. *Selected Letters of E. E. Cummings.* Edited by F. W. Dupee and George Stade. London: Andre Deutsch, 1972.

Cummings, E. E., S. Foster Damon, et al. *Eight Harvard Poets.* New York: Laurence J. Gomme, 1917.

Das, Santanu. "'The Impotence of Sympathy': Touch and Trauma in the Memoirs of the First World War Nurses." *Textual Practice* 19, no. 2 (2005): 239–62.

———. *Touch and Intimacy in First World War Literature.* Cambridge: Cambridge University Press, 2005.

Davis, Richard Harding. "Rheims during the Bombardment." *Scribner's Magazine* 57 (1915), 70–76.

Dawson, Coningsby. *The Glory of the Trenches.* New York: John Lane, 1918.

Dayton, Tim. "'Wristers Etcetera': Cummings, the Great War, and Discursive Struggle." *Spring* 17 (Fall 2010): 116–39.

Dean, Sharon. *Constance Fenimore Woolson and Edith Wharton: Perspectives on Landscape and Art.* Knoxville: University of Tennessee Press, 2002.

Devlin, Patrick. *Too Proud to Fight: Woodrow Wilson's Neutrality.* London: Oxford University Press, 1974.

DeWeerd, Harvey, A. *President Wilson Fights His War: World War I and the American Intervention.* London: Macmillan, 1968.

Dewey, John. "What America Will Fight For." *New Republic* (18 August 1917), 68–69.

Dicey, Edward. "Mr Gladstone and Our Empire." *Nineteenth Century* 2 (1877): 292–308.

Donohue, Berta Schmidt. "Aunt Grace Talking." Family memoir, ca. 1940. Private collection.

Doolittle, Hilda (H.D.). *Bid Me to Live: A Madrigal.* New York: Grove Press, 1960.

———. *Sea Garden.* London: Constable, 1916.

Dos Passos, John. "Against American Literature." *New Republic* (14 October 1916), 269–71.

———. *The Best Times: An Informal Memoir.* London: Andre Deutsch, 1966.

———. *The Fourteenth Chronicle: Letters and Diaries of John Dos Passos.* Edited by Townsend Ludington. London: Andre Deutsch, 1974.

———. *Manhattan Transfer.* New York: Harper, 1925.

———. *Mr Wilson's War.* New York: Doubleday, 1962.

———. *One Man's Initiation: 1917.* 1920. Reprinted with author's introduction, Ithaca, NY: Cornell University Press, 1969.

———. *Three Soldiers.* New York: Doran, 1921.

———. *Travel Books and Other Writings, 1916–1941.* New York: Library of America, 2003.

———. *U.S.A.* 1930–36. Reprint, New York: Library of America, 1996.

Dowd, Douglas. *Thorstein Veblen.* 1964. Reprint, New Brunswick, NJ: Transaction, 2000.

DuPont, Alfred I. Papers. James Graham Leyburn Library, Washington and Lee University, Lexington, VA.

Dwight, Eleanor. *Edith Wharton: An Extraordinary Life.* New York: Abrams, 1994.

Edel, Leon. *Henry James: A Life.* New York: Harper and Row, 1985.

Egremont, Max. *Under Two Flags: The Life of Major General Sir Edward Spears.* London: Weidenfeld and Nicolson, 1997.

Eliot, T. S. *The Letters of T. S. Eliot.* 3 vols. London: Faber, 2009.

———. *Selected Poems.* London: Faber, 1954.

———. *The Use of Poetry and the Use of Criticism.* 1933. Reprint, London: Faber, 1964.

Emerson, Ralph Waldo. *The Collected Works of Ralph Waldo Emerson.* 5 vols. Cambridge, MA: Harvard University Press, 1971.

Faivre, Abel. "Dans les Ruines." *Le Rire Rouge* 27 (22 May 1915): 1.

Faulkner, Peter. *Modernism*. 1977. Reprint, London: Methuen, 1991.

Faulkner, William. *The Sound and the Fury*. New York: Jonathan Cape and Harrison Smith, 1929.

Fell, Alison, and Christine Hallett, eds. *First World War Nursing: New Perspectives*. London: Routledge, 2013.

Fitzgerald, F. Scott. *The Great Gatsby*. 1926. Reprint, London: Penguin Books, 1990.

Foner, Philip S. *History of the Labor Movement in the United States*. Vol. 4, *The Industrial Workers of the World*. 1965. Reprint, New York: International Publishers, 1997.

Freedman, Ariela. "Mary Borden's Forbidden Zone: Women's Writing From No-Man's Land." *Modernism/Modernity* 9, no. 1 (2002): 109–24.

Friedman, Susan Stanford. "Definitional Excursions: The Meanings of *Modern/Modernity/Modernism*." In *Disciplining Modernism*, edited by Pamela Caughie, 11–32. London: Palgrave, 2009.

Fussell, Paul. *The Great War and Modern Memory*. 1975. Reprint, Oxford: Oxford University Press, 2000.

Gandal, Keith. *The Pen and the Gun*. New York: Oxford University Press, 2010.

Gaull, Marilyn. "Language and Identity: A Study of E. E. Cummings' *The Enormous Room*." *American Quarterly* 19, no. 4 (1967): 645–62.

Genthe, Charles. *American War Narratives, 1917–1918: A Study and Bibliography*. New York: David Lewis, 1969.

Goldman, Dorothy, ed. *Women and World War I: The Written Response*. London: Macmillan, 1993.

Goldman, Jane. *Modernism, 1910–1945: Image to Apocalypse*. New York: Palgrave, 2004.

Gould, Jenny. "Women's Military Services in First World War Britain." In *Behind the Lines: Gender and the Two World Wars*, edited by Margaret Higonnet et al., 114–25. New Haven, CT: Yale University Press, 1987.

Graham, Wendy. *Henry James's Thwarted Love*. Stanford, CA: Stanford University Press, 1999.

Grainger, J. H. *Patriotisms: Britain, 1900–1939*. London: Routledge, 1986.

Graves, Robert. *Goodbye to All That*. London: Jonathan Cape, 1929.

Greenslet, Ferris. *Under the Bridge*. Boston: Houghton Mifflin, 1943.

Gregory, Ross. *The Origins of American Intervention in the First World War*. New York: W. W. Norton, 1971.

Gritsch, Eric W. *Martin—God's Court Jester: Luther in Retrospect*. Philadelphia: Fortress Press, 1983.

Hall, Richard. "An Obscure Hurt: The Sexuality of Henry James." *New Republic* (28 April 1979), 25–31; (5 May 1979), 25–29.

Hallett, Christine. *Containing Trauma: Nursing Work in the First World War.* Manchester: Manchester University Press, 2009.

———. "The Personal Writings of First World War Nurses: A Study of the Interplay of Authorial Intention and Scholarly Interpretation." *Nursing Inquiry* 14 (2007): 320–29.

Hansen, Arlen J. *Gentlemen Volunteers: The Story of the American Ambulance Drivers in the Great War.* New York, Arcade, 1996.

Harries, Meirion, and Susie Harries. *The Last Days of Innocence: America at War, 1917–1918.* New York: Random House, 1997.

Hassall, Christopher. *Edward Marsh: A Biography.* London: Longmans, 1959.

Haste, Cate. *Keep the Home Fires Burning: Propaganda in the First World War.* London: Allen Lane, 1977.

Hawthorne, Nathaniel. *The Scarlet Letter.* 1850. Reprint, New York: W. W. Norton, 1988.

Haytock, Jennifer. *At Home, at War: Domesticity and World War I in American Literature.* Columbus: Ohio State University Press, 2003.

H.D. *See* Doolittle, Hilda.

Hemingway, Ernest. *A Farewell to Arms.* 1929. Reprint, London: Arrow, 1994.

———. *A Moveable Feast.* 1936. Reprint, London: Arrow, 2004.

———. *The Sun Also Rises.* New York: Scribner's, 1926.

———. Personal Papers, John F. Kennedy Presidential Library, University of Massachusetts, Boston.

Higonnet, Margaret. "Cubist Vision in Nursing Accounts." In *First World War Nursing: New Perspectives,* edited by Alison Fell and Christine Hallett, 156–72. London: Routledge, 2013.

———. *Nurses at the Front: Writing the Wounds of the Great War.* Boston: Northeastern University Press, 2001.

Higonnet, Margaret, et al., eds. *Behind the Lines: Gender and the Two World Wars.* New Haven: Yale University Press, 1987.

Honey, Samuel Robertson, and James Fullerton Muirhead, eds. *Sixty American Opinions on the War.* London: Fisher Unwin, 1915.

Hook, Andrew, ed. *Dos Passos: A Collection of Critical Essays.* Englewood Cliffs, NJ: Prentice Hall, 1974.

Hoover, Herbert. *The Memoirs of Herbert Hoover.* 2 vols. New York: Macmillan 1951.

Horne, Philip. "Henry James and 'the Forces of Violence': On the Track of 'Big Game' in 'The Jolly Corner.'" *Henry James Review* 27 (2006): 237–47.

———. *Henry James and Revision.* Oxford: Clarendon Press, 1990.

Houghton Mifflin Company Papers. Houghton Library, Harvard University, Cambridge, MA.

Hutchison, Hazel. "The Art of Living Inward: Henry James on Rupert Brooke."
Henry James Review 29, no. 2 (2008): 132–43.
——. "A Period in Limbo: Placing People and Punctuation in E. E. Cummings's
The Enormous Room." In *War and Displacement,* edited by Sandra Bark-
hof and Angela K. Smith, 134–49. London: Routledge, 2014.
——. *Seeing and Believing: Henry James and the Spiritual World.* New York:
Palgrave, 2006.
——. "The Theatre of Pain: Observing Mary Borden in *The Forbidden Zone.*"
In *First World War Nursing: New Perspectives,* edited by Alison Fell and
Christine Hallett, 139–55. London: Routledge, 2013.
Hyde, H. Montgomery. *Henry James at Home.* London: Methuen, 1969.
Industrial Workers of the World. *Little Red Song Book.* Chicago: Industrial
Workers of the World, 1969.
James, D. Clayton, and Ann Sharp Wells. *America and the Great War, 1914–
1920.* Wheeling, IL: Harlan Davidson, 1998.
James, Henry. *The American Scene.* 1907. Reprint, London: Granville, 1987.
——. *The Aspern Papers.* London: Macmillan, 1888.
——. *Complete Letters, 1855–1872.* Edited by Greg Zacharias and Peter Walker.
2 vols. Lincoln: Nebraska University Press, 2007.
——. *Hawthorne.* 1879. Reprint, London: Macmillan, 1967.
——. *Letters to A. C. Benson and Auguste Monod.* Edited by E. F. Benson. Lon-
don: Elkin Mathews & Marrot, 1930.
——. *The Letters of Henry James.* Edited by Percy Lubbock. 2 vols. London:
Macmillan, 1920.
——. *Literary Criticism.* Edited by Leon Edel and Mark Wilson. 2 vols. New
York: Library of America, 1984.
——. *Notes of a Son and Brother.* 1914. Reprint in *Autobiography,* edited by Fred-
erick Dupee, 239–544. Princeton, NJ: Princeton University Press, 1983.
——. Papers. Houghton Library, Harvard University, Cambridge, MA.
——. *Parisian Sketches.* Edited by Leon Edel and Isle Dusoir Lind. London:
Rupert Hart Davis, 1958.
——. *The Portrait of a Lady.* London: Macmillan, 1881.
——. *The Question of the Mind.* London: Central Committee for National Patri-
otic Organisations, 1915.
——. *The Reverberator.* London: Macmillan 1888.
——. *Within the Rim and Other Essays, 1914–1915.* Edited by Percy Lubbock.
London: Collins, 1918.
James, Pearl. *The New Death: American Modernism and World War I.* Charlot-
tesville: University of Virginia Press, 2013.

Kaplan, Laurie. "Deformities of the Great War: The Narratives of Mary Borden and Helen Zenna Smith." *Women and Language* 27, no. 2 (2004): 35–43.

Kazin, Alfred. *On Native Grounds*. London: Jonathan Cape, 1943.

Keats, John. *John Keats: The Complete Poems*. Edited John Barnard. Harmondsworth: Penguin Books, 1978.

Keene, Jennifer D. *Doughboys: The Great War and the Remaking of America*. Baltimore: Johns Hopkins University Press, 2003.

Keith, Jeanette. *Rich Man's War, Poor Man's Fight: Race, Class, and Power in the Rural South During the First World War*. Chapel Hill: University of North Carolina Press, 2004.

Kennedy, David M. *Over Here: The First World War and American Society*. New York: Oxford University Press, 2004.

Kennedy Richard, *Dreams in the Mirror: A Biography of E. E. Cummings*. New York: Liveright, 1980.

Khan, Nosheen. "Mary Borden's 'Unidentified' and W. B. Yeats's 'The Second Coming.'" *American Notes and Queries* 4, no. 1 (1991): 20–21.

Kipling, Rudyard, ed. *King Albert's Book*. London: Hodder and Stoughton, 1914.

Krob, Melanie Gordon. "Commentary on 'Rosa.' *Academic Medicine: The Journal of the Association of American Medical Colleges* 77, no. 7 (2002): 710–11.

La Motte, Ellen Newbold. "An American Nurse in Paris." *Survey* 34 (10 July 1915): 333–36.

———. *The Backwash of War*. 1916. 2nd edition, New York: G. P. Putnam, 1934.

———. *Civilization: Tales of the Orient*. New York: George H. Doran, 1919.

———. Collection. Alan Mason Chesney Medical Archives, Johns Hopkins Medical Institutions, Baltimore.

———. *The Ethics of Opium*. New York: Century, 1924.

———. "The Hotel-Dieu of Paris: An Historical Sketch." *Medical Library and Historical Journal* 4, no. 3 (1906): 225–40.

———. "A Joy Ride." *Atlantic Monthly* (October 1916), 481–90.

———. "A Modern Italian Hospital." *American Journal of Nursing* 4, no. 12 (1904): 933–38.

———. *The Opium Monopoly*. New York: Macmillan, 1920.

———. *Peking Dust*. New York: Century, 1919.

———. *Snuffs and Butters*. New York: Century, 1925.

———. *The Tuberculosis Nurse: Her Functions and Her Qualifications; A Handbook for Practical Workers in the Tuberculosis Campaign*. New York: G. P. Putnam, 1915.

———. "Under Shell-Fire at Dunkirk." *Atlantic Monthly* (November 1916), 692–700.

Lankester, E. Ray. *Degeneration: A Chapter in Darwinisim*. London: Macmillan, 1880.

Lansing, Robert. *War Memoirs of Robert Lansing*. London: Rich and Cowan, 1935.

Larrouy, Maurice (Y.) *The Odyssey of a Torpedoed Transport*. Translated by Grace Fallow Norton. 1918. Reprinted with an introduction by William McFee. Boston: Houghton Mifflin, 1923.

Lasswell, Harold D. *Propaganda Technique in the World War*. New York: Alfred A. Knopf, 1927.

Lee, Hermione. *Edith Wharton*. New York: Alfred A. Knopf, 2007.

Levenson, Michael. *The Cambridge Companion to Modernism*. Cambridge: Cambridge University Press, 1999.

Lewis, R. W. B. *Edith Wharton: A Biography*. London: Constable, 1975.

Lewis, Sinclair. *Jimmie Higgins*. New York: Boni and Liveright, 1919.

Lewis, Wyndham. *Blasting and Bombardiering*. London: Eyre and Spottiswoode, 1937.

———. *The Roaring Queen*. London: Secker and Warburg, 1973.

Lippman, Walter. *Public Opinion*. London: Allen and Unwin, 1921.

Lloyd George, David. *War Memoirs of David Lloyd George*. London: Ivor, Nicholson and Watson, 1933–36.

Lockwood, Preston. "Henry James's First Interview." *New York Times Magazine* (21 March 1915), 3.

———. "The Section in Alsace Reconquise." In *Friends of France: The Field Service of the American Ambulance Described by Its Members,* 21–49. Boston: Houghton Mifflin, 1916.

Lockwood, Preston, and Lincoln Eyre. *Sham: A Playlet of Two Scenes*. Privately published. Printed in St. Louis: Sisson-Woollet, 1914.

Lowell, Amy. "Why We Should Read Poetry." 1914. Reprinted in *Poetry and Poets: Essays*, 3–9. Boston: Houghton Mifflin, 1930.

Lubbock, Percy, *Portrait of Edith Wharton*. London: Jonathan Cape, 1947.

———. "Rupert Brooke's Letters." Unsigned Review of *Letters from America,* by Rupert Brooke. *Times Literary Supplement* (9 March 1915), 114.

Ludington, Townsend. *John Dos Passos: A Twentieth Century Odyssey*. New York: Dutton, 1980.

Lustig, Tim. "James, Arnold, 'Culture' and 'Modernity'; or, A Tale of Two Dachshunds." *Cambridge Quarterly* 37, no. 1 (2008): 164–93.

Lynn, John. *The Bayonets of the Republic: Motivation and Tactics in the Army of Revolutionary France, 1791–94*. Boulder, CO: Westview Press, 1996.

Madison, Charles A. *Publishing in America*. New York: McGraw-Hill, 1966.

Maine, Barry. *Dos Passos: The Critical Heritage*. London: Routledge, 1988.

Mandler, Peter. *The English National Character: The History of an Idea from Edmund Burke to Tony Blair*. New Haven: Yale University Press, 2006.

March, William. *Company K*. New York: Smith and Haas, 1933.

Martin, Todd. " 'The Mysteries of Noyon': Emblem and Meaning in *The Enormous Room*." *Spring* 6 (Fall 2000): 125–31.

———. "ɪs' as an Action Verb: Cummings and the Act of Being." *Spring* 17 (Fall 2010): 80–83.

May, Henry. *The End of American Innocence: A Study of the First Years of Our Own Time, 1912–1917*. 1960. Reprint, New York: Columbia University Press, 1992.

McWhirter, David, ed. *Henry James's New York Edition: The Construction of Authorship*. Stanford, CA: Stanford University Press, 1995.

———. "Restaging the Hurt: Henry James and the Artist as Masochist." *Texas Studies in Literature and Language* 33 (1991): 464–91.

Mellow, James R. *Charmed Circle: Gertrude Stein and Company*. London: Phaidon Press, 1974.

Melville, Herman. *Moby Dick*. New York: Harper, 1851.

Meyers, Jeffrey. *Edmund Wilson: A Biography*. Boston: Houghton Mifflin, 1995.

Miller, J. Hillis. *Speech Acts in Literature*. Stanford, CA: Stanford University Press, 2001.

Miller, Nathan. *Theodore Roosevelt: A Life*. New York: William Morrow, 1992.

Minter, David. *William Faulkner: His Life and Work*. Baltimore: Johns Hopkins University Press, 1980.

Moffett, Cleveland Langston. *The Conquest of America: A Romance of Disaster and Victory*. New York: Doran, 1916. Reprint, n.p.: Dodo Press, 2008.

More, Paul Elmer. *The Demon of the Absolute*. Princeton, NJ: Princeton University Press, 1928.

Mosher, Thomas Bird. Papers. Houghton Library, Harvard University, Cambridge, MA.

Nabokov, Vladimir. *Lolita*. 1955. Reprint, London: Penguin Books, 1995.

Nash, G. H. *The Life of Herbert Hoover*. Vol. 2, *The Humanitarian, 1914–1917*. New York: W. W. Norton, 1988.

Neill, Edward D. *History of Rice County*. Minneapolis: Minnesota Historical Society, 1882.

Norton, Charles Eliot. *Letters of Charles Eliot Norton*. Edited by Sara Norton. 2 vols. Boston: Houghton Mifflin, 1913.

Norton, Grace (Fallow). "The Princess and the Echo." *Abbot Courant* (January 1894): 15–17.

———. *Roads*. Boston: Houghton Mifflin, 1916.

———. *The Sister of the Wind*. Boston: Houghton Mifflin, 1914.

———. *What Is Your Legion?* Boston: Houghton Mifflin, 1916.

Norton, Richard. Papers. Houghton Library, Harvard University, Cambridge, MA.

Olin-Ammentorp, Julie. *Edith Wharton's Writings from the Great War*. Gainesville: University Press of Florida, 2004.

Otten, Thomas. *A Superficial Reading of Henry James: Preoccupations with the Material World*. Columbus: Ohio State University Press, 2006.

Plimpton, George. "Ernest Hemingway: The Art of Fiction." *Paris Review* 5 (1958): 60–89.

Potter, Jane. *Boys in Khaki, Girls in Print: Women's Literary Responses to the Great War, 1914–1918*. Oxford: Oxford University Press, 2005.

Pound, Ezra. "Hugh Selwyn Mauberley." 1920. Reprinted in *Ezra Pound's Mauberley*, edited by John J. Espey. London: Faber, 1955.

———. *Jefferson and/or Mussolini*. 1935. Reprint, New York: Liveright, 1970.

———. *Literary Essays of Ezra Pound*. Edited with an introduction by T. S. Eliot. London: Faber, 1954.

Powell, Alexander E. "On the British Battle Line." *Scribner's Magazine* 58 (1915): 465–69.

Powell, Anne. *Women in the War Zone: Hospital Service in the First World War*. Stroud, England: History Press, 2009.

Powers, Lyall H., ed. *Henry James and Edith Wharton: Letters, 1900–1915*. New York: Scribner's, 1990.

Price, Alan. *The End of the Age of Innocence: Edith Wharton and the First World War*. New York: St Martin's Press, 1996.

———. "The Making of Edith Wharton's *The Book of the Homeless*." Princeton University Library, *Chronicle* 47, no. 1 (Autumn 1985): 5–21.

Quinn, Patrick. *The Conning of America: The Great War and Popular American Literature*. Amsterdam: Rodopi, 2001.

———. "The First World War: American Writing." In *The Cambridge Companion to War Writing*, edited by Kate McLoughlin, 175–84. Cambridge: Cambridge University Press, 2009.

Rawlings, Peter. *Henry James and the Abuse of the Past*. Houndmills, England: Palgrave, 2005.

Remarque, Erich Maria. *All Quiet on the Western Front*. 1929. Translated by Brian Murdoch. London: Vintage Books, 1994.

Reus, Teresa Gómez, and Peter Lauber. "In a Literary No Man's Land. A Spatial Reading of Edith Wharton's *Fighting France*." In *Inside Out: Women Negotiating, Subverting, Appropriating Public and Private Space*, edited by

Teresa Gómez Reus and Aranzazu Usandizaga, 205–28. Amsterdam: Rodopi, 2008.

Review of *The Backwash of War*, by Ellen Newbold La Motte. *New Republic* (7 November 1934), 374.

Review of *The Tuberculosis Nurse: Her Functions and Qualifications*, by Ellen Newbold La Motte. *British Medical Journal* 2, no. 2901 (5 August 1916): 181.

Reynolds, David S. *John Brown, Abolitionist: The Man Who Killed Slavery, Sparked the Civil War, and Seeded Civil Rights*. New York: Vintage Books, 2006.

Reynolds, Michael. *Hemingway's First War: The Making of "A Farewell to Arms."* 1976. Reprint, London: Blackwell, 1987.

Roberts, F. J. "Preface: How it Happened." In *Wipers Times*, edited by F. J. Roberts, v–xxvii. London: Eveleigh, Nash and Grayson, 1930.

Roosevelt, Theodore. *An Autobiography*. New York: Macmillan, 1914.

———. Foreword to *One Hundred Per Cent American*, edited by Arnon L. Squiers, iv–vii. New York: Doran, 1918.

———. *The Great Adventure*. London: John Murray, 1919.

———. *Mr Roosevelt Speaks Out: His View of Britain's Case*. London: George Newnes, 1915.

Rosen, Robert, C. *John Dos Passos: Politics and the Writer*. Lincoln: University of Nebraska Press, 1981.

Rosenzweig, Saul. "The Ghost of Henry James." *Partisan Review* 11 (1944): 436–55.

Rubery, Matthew. "Unspoken Intimacy in Henry James's 'The Papers.' " *Nineteenth Century Literature* 61, no. 3 (2006): 343–67.

Sanders, Michael, and Philip M. Taylor. *British Propaganda during the First World War, 1914–18*. London: Macmillan, 1982.

Sassoon, Siegfried. *Memoirs of an Infantry Officer*. 1930. Reprint, London: Faber and Faber, 2000.

Seeger, Alan. *Poems*. New York: Scribners, 1917.

Seymour, Charles, ed. *The Intimate Papers of Colonel House*. 4 vols. London: Benn, 1926.

Sherry, Vincent. *The Great War and the Language of Modernism*. Oxford: Oxford University Press, 2003.

Smith, Angela K. *The Second Battlefield: Women, Modernism, and the First World War*. Manchester: Manchester University Press, 2000.

Smith, David E. "*The Enormous Room* and *The Pilgrim's Progress*." *Twentieth Century Literature* 11, no. 2 (1965): 67–77.

Stein, Gertrude. *The Autobiography of Alice B. Toklas.* 1933. Reprint, London: Penguin Books, 2001.

———. Papers. Beinecke Library, Yale University, New Haven.

Stephens, Winifred, ed. *The Book of France.* London: Macmillan, 1915.

Stevenson, David. *The First World War and International Politics.* Oxford: Oxford University Press, 1988.

———. *1914–1918: The History of the First World War.* London: Allen Lane, 2004.

Sugiyama, Keiko. "Ellen N. La Motte, 1873–1961: Gender and Race in Nursing." *Japanese Journal of American Studies* 17 (2006): 129–42.

Sweeney, Regina M. *Singing Our Way to Victory: French Cultural Politics and Music during the Great War.* Middletown, CT: Wesleyan University Press, 2001.

Tate, Trudi. *Modernism, History, and the First World War.* Manchester: Manchester University Press, 1998.

Taylor, Andrew. *Henry James and the Father Question.* Cambridge: Cambridge University Press, 2002.

Tebbel, John. *A History of Book Publishing in the United States.* Vol. 2, *The Expansion of an Industry, 1865–1919.* New York: Bowker, 1975.

Thomason, John W. *Fix Bayonets.* New York: Scribner's, 1925.

Thurschwell, Pamela. "'That Imperial Stomach Is No Seat for Ladies': Henry James, the First World War and the Politics of Identification." In *Modernist Sexualities,* edited by Hugh Stevens and Caroline Howlett, 167–83. Manchester: Manchester University Press, 2000.

Tintner, Adeline. *The Twentieth-Century World of Henry James.* Baton Rouge: Louisiana State University Press, 2000.

Tuttleton, James, Kristin O. Lauer, and Margaret P. Murray, eds. *Edith Wharton: The Contemporary Reviews.* Cambridge: Cambridge University Press, 1992.

Tylee, Claire. *The Great War and Women's Consciousness: Images of Militarism and Womanhood in Women's Writings, 1914–64.* Iowa City: University of Iowa Press, 1990.

Van Wienen, Mark. *Partisans and Poets: The Political Work of American Poetry in the Great War.* Cambridge: Cambridge University Press, 1997.

———. *Rendezvous with Death: American Poems of the Great War.* Urbana: University of Illinois Press, 2002.

Veblen, Thorstein. *The Theory of the Leisure Class.* 1899. Reprint, London: Allen and Unwin, 1925.

Virgil. *The Aeneid of Virgil.* Translated by C. Day Lewis. London: Hogarth Press, 1952.

Walker, Peter. *Henry James on Culture: Collected Essays on Politics and the American Social Scene.* Lincoln: University of Nebraska Press, 1999.

Warner, Agnes. *My Beloved Poilus*. St. John, New Brunswick: Barnes, 1917.

Weiss, Ellen. "Grace Fallow Norton Notes." Family memoir, 2004. Private collection.

Wells, H. G. *Boon*. London: Fisher Unwin, 1915.

———. *The Time Machine*. London: Heinemann, 1895.

———. *The War That Will End War*. London: Frank and Cecil Palmer, 1914.

Whalan, Mark. *American Culture in the 1910s*. Edinburgh: Edinburgh University Press, 2010.

———. *The Great War and the Culture of the New Negro*. Gainesville: University Press of Florida, 2008.

Wharton, Edith. *A Backward Glance*. New York: Appleton-Century, 1934.

———. *The Book of the Homeless*. New York: Scribner's, 1916.

———. *Fighting France: From Dunkerque to Belfort*. 1915. Reprinted with an introduction by Colm Toibin. London: Hesperus, 2010.

———. *French Ways and Their Meaning*. New York: Appleton, 1919.

———. *The Letters of Edith Wharton*. Edited by R. W. B. Lewis and Nancy Lewis. London: Simon and Schuster, 1988.

———. *The Marne*. New York: Appleton, 1918.

———. *The Mother's Recompense*. 1925. Reprint, New York: Scribner's, 1986.

———. *A Son at the Front*. 1923. Reprint, DeKalb: Northern Illinois University Press, 1995.

Wharton, Edith, and Ogden Codman. *The Decoration of Houses*. New York: Scribner's, 1902.

Widmer, K. "Timeless Prose." *American Literature* 4, no. 1 (1958): 3–7.

Wilde, Oscar. Preface to *The Picture of Dorian Gray*. 1891. Reprint, London: Penguin Books, 1987.

Wister, Owen. *The Pentecost of Calamity*. New York: Macmillan, 1915.

Yeats, W. B. *The Wild Swans at Coole*. London: Macmillan, 1919.

Index